·CONVERSATION·

Sage's *Series in Interpersonal Communication* is designed to capture the breadth and depth of knowledge emanating from scientific examinations of face-to-face interaction. As such, the volumes in this series address the cognitive and overt behavior manifested by communicators as they pursue various conversational outcomes. The application of research findings to specific types of interpersonal relationships (e.g., marital, managerial) is also an important dimension of this series.

SAGE SERIES IN INTERPERSONAL COMMUNICATION

Mark L. Knapp, Series Editor

·CONVERSATION·

How Talk Is Organized

Organized

Margaret L. McLAUGHLIN

Sage Series in Interpersonal Communication
Volume 3

 SAGE PUBLICATIONS Beverly Hills London New Delhi

For information address:

SAGE Publications, Inc.
275 South Beverly Drive
Beverly Hills, California 90212

1500896

SAGE Publications India Pvt. Ltd.
C-236 Defence Colony
New Delhi 110 024, India

SAGE Publications Ltd
28 Banner Street
London EC1Y 8QE, England

Printed in the United States of America

Library of Congress Cataloging in Publication Data

McLaughlin, Margaret L.
  Conversation: how talk is organized.

  (Sage series in interpersonal communication; vol. 3)
  Bibliography: p.
  Includes index.
  1. Conversation. 2. Speech acts (Linguistics)
I. Title. II. Series: Sage series in interpersonal communication; v. 3.
P95.45.M37   1984   401'.41   83-24596
ISBN 0-8039-2263-9
ISBN 0-8039-2264-7 (pbk.)

FIRST PRINTING

Contents

In memory of
James Edwin Savage

Series Editor's
Foreword

One of the goals of a book's foreword is to interest the reader in the book's content. For some books, this can be a formidable task; for this book, it should be sufficient to merely ask the reader to consider some of the topics discussed:

- The use of disclaimers to set the stage for offensive jokes;
- How the demands of politeness in conversation sometimes supercede the demands for clarity;
- How we go about the job of making conversational "repairs" following a faux pas or "failure" and how people will sometimes help us repair these conversational mistakes;
- When simultaneous talking occurs and how we respond to it;
- The variety of ways people request things of others (directly and indirectly) and how people reply to these requests (directly and indirectly);
- How the compliments we give seem to show very little variety in their syntactic and semantic structure;
- Ways we signal that a change of topic is imminent;
- How we label sections of talk ("That's really funny.") and forecast actions ("I have a question for you . . .");
- How we signal the exchange of speaking turns and how we tell others we're passing up the opportunity to take a turn;
- The rules we use in conversation and when we do and do not follow them;
- The extent to which our individual utterances are related to larger sequences and the overall structure of the conversation;
- The nature and role of stories in conversation;
- The sequences of acts followed in opening and closing a conversation; and
- Why people who are conversing for the first time will usually go to great lengths to overlook content which may lead to disruptions and arguments.

While there is something inherently fascinating about discovering the anatomy of behaviors we habitually (and sometimes unthinkingly) perform, the real significance of understanding the structure of conversations is its centrality for understanding human interaction in general. As McLaughlin goes about her task of reviewing what we know about how talk is organized, she is also forced to raise questions about the role of context, cognitive processes associated with intent and interpretation, the influence of co-occurring nonverbal signals, and issues associated with the meaning of communication competence. Thus, while the book is often concerned with what may seem to be microscopic elements in the stream of conversation, it is equally concerned with those processes which combine these elements into a coherent conversational whole.

Scholars from a wide variety of academic disciplines have been exploring the nature of conversations in recent years. The speed with which this body of literature has developed and the diversity of the sources of information have made it difficult for many interested professionals to keep abreast of the knowledge in this area. McLaughlin's integrative summary of the literature should serve those who seek updating on the study of conversations extremely well—regardless of one's field of study. As one of my colleagues who teaches a seminar in discourse analysis said when I gave him a prepublication copy of the McLaughlin manuscript, "It's head and shoulders above anything else currently on the market." Although the book was originally designed for professionals and graduate seminars, the style with which it is written may also make it suitable for some undergraduate classes. It is clearly a scholarly work, but it is organized and written to be read by a wide audience. The segments of actual conversations used as examples, the glossary of terms, and the summaries contribute much to the clarity of the volume.

In my opinion, *Conversation: How Talk is Organized* is a useful, timely, and important book. It brings together a wide variety of scientific materials, provides an assessment of what we know and don't know, and suggests guidelines for future research. While we have all been practitioners of conversation, this book should go far toward making us all students of conversation.

—Mark L. Knapp

Acknowledgments

My father, to whom this book is dedicated, was a prolific scholar and student of Elizabethan and Jacobean drama, who nonetheless did not write his first book until he was well into his sixties. When I asked him why he had waited so long to write a book, his reply was that up until then, he hadn't known enough to fill up that many pages. I would have been quite content to follow his example and postpone writing this book for quite a few more years, until I felt that I knew something; however, the editor of this series, Mark L. Knapp, and my husband and colleague, Michael Cody, convinced me that the time for a book on conversational organization was now. Now that the book is finished, I am glad that I listened to their advice. I will leave it up to the reader to judge, however, whether or not I should have waited for a while longer.

I would first like to acknowledge the contribution of a number of scholars, most of whom I have never met, who have had a profound influence on the ideas presented in this book. The structure of the chapter on conversational coherence was shaped in large part by ideas presented in a series of papers by Sue Foster and her colleague Sharon Sabsay. I am also heavily indebted to Jerry Hobbs for the treatments of conversational planning and local coherence relations presented in Chapter 2. The section on the functional organization of discourse was significantly influenced by the several works of W. J. Edmondson. I am indebted to Teun van Dijk for my understanding of global structures in conversational organization. Finally, no one who treads the terrain of "rules" can fail to be influenced by Susan Shimanoff's excellent survey and synthesis of that diffuse body of literature; Shimanoff's ideas feature prominently in Chapters 1 and 7.

A number of people have been so kind as to supply me with unpublished materials or to refer me to sources that I might have overlooked; they include Joan Cashion, Walter Fisher, Sue Foster, Sally Jackson, Mark Knapp, Allan Louden, Patricia Riley, Nancy Rosenstein, Michael Schneider, and Christopher Zahn. I am also indebted to Dayle Smith and Laree Kiely for their assistance with the library work. Special thanks are due to Keith Erickson, who has taught me everything there is to know about obtaining permissions, and to Robert Hopper for his encouraging comments. Al Goodyear of Sage Publications has been most helpful in steering me through some of the mechanics of the actual production of the book.

I am deeply indebted to Mark Knapp, who is as supportive an editor as one could hope to find, and whose suggestions were unfailingly helpful in alerting me to issues that I might have overlooked in early drafts of the manuscript.

My greatest debt is to Michael Cody, without whose help and encouragement I could not have written this book. His contributions were too numerous to mention them all, but they range from digging up copies of convention papers that I had given up for lost, to seeing to it that pets and children were fed, to dissuading me from writing overly vigorous rejoinders to positions with which I did not agree. The reader will also note the influence of his work on compliance-gaining strategies throughout the book. I would also like to thank the other members of my family for putting up with me through all of this, particularly my mother, Mary Savage, for always being there with a kind word when I needed it, and my son, Tommy McLaughlin, for all the uncomplaining hours he put in watching his sister Julia when he would rather have been watching football.

1

What Conversationalists Know: Rules, Maxims, and Other Lore

♦ Suppose that a social scientist had observed ♦ a pair of friends sitting on a park bench having a conversation; that is, our scientist had noted that the two seemed to be engaged in a relatively informal form of interaction in which the role of speaker shifted from one to the other at irregular intervals. Suppose further that the scientist approached the pair with the following: "Pardon me. I noticed that the two of you were having a conversation. As a scientist and a student of conversation, what I want to know is this: *How did you do that?*" Clearly the initial response to such a question would be utter befuddlement; the second would probably be "Do what?" Most of us regard conversation as *effortless*, as something anyone can do. To suggest to its unreflecting practitioners that it might be appropriately regarded as an *accomplishment* would be to create doubt as to the number of oars, so to speak, that one had in the water.

Despite the fact that most people take the ability to carry on a conversation for granted, closer inspection reveals that this informal and ubiquitous variety of social intercourse is a highly complex activity that requires of those who would engage in it the ability to apply a staggering amount of knowledge: not only what we might call *world knowledge* (that groceries cost money, that parents love their children, that dogs bite, etc.), but also more specific knowledge bases, such as the rules of grammar, syntax, etiquette, and so on, as well as specifically conversational rules such as "When someone has replied to your summons, disclose the reason for the summons," and "Before saying good-bye to a telephone caller, reach agreement that all topical talk is completed." What is fascinating about conversation is that the ordinary person rarely reflects upon the vastness of the knowledge store that is required to carry it on. He can retrieve rules and cite them when necessary, as he might do if he were interrupted, or if the relevance of a partner's utterance were in question. For the most part, the kinds of rules and maxims by which a person abides in carrying on a conversation, and that govern the way in which two parties coordinate their actions to achieve a conversation, lie below the surface of awareness and are "dredged up" only in their breach; their honoring is unremarkable. It is to be dredging up of these conversational rules and maxims that the energies of the present effort are directed.

Students of conversation in the field of communication and its related disciplines have given increased attention in recent years to the notion that conversation is a highly organized activity whose structure may best be understood by recourse to the notion of *rule* (Ervin-Tripp, 1972; Labov, 1972; Toulmin, 1974; Nofsinger, 1975; Pearce, 1976; Labov & Fanshel, 1977; Vucinich, 1977; Cronen & Davis, 1978; Sacks, Schegloff, & Jefferson, 1978; Jacobs & Jackson, 1979; Planalp & Tracy, 1980; Shimanoff, 1980; Sigman, 1980; McLaughlin & Cody, 1982). The current status of rule as a scientific construct for the study of conversation is due in part to a growing disenchantment with the ability of causal explanations, in the Humean sense, to account for regularities in social interaction, in part to the excesses of logical positivism, and to the notable failure of social science generally to discover incontrovertible laws of human behavior (Waismann, 1951; Taylor, 1964; Aune, 1967; O'Keefe, 1975; Phillips, 1981).

Although it is not our purpose here to revive debate between the proponents of action theory and those of the covering-law approach (Berger, 1977; Felia, 1977; Hawes, 1977; Miller & Berger, 1978), it might be useful to at least lay out some of the underpinnings of the rule-theoretic point of view. Harré and Secord (1972, p. 168) argue that law-like accounts of social interaction are in order only in those contexts in which the individual as a behaver can be shown to be merely a "passive recipient" of some effect, such that no intermediate construct need be invoked to account for the behavioral display. While Harré and Secord give lip service to the notion of causal explanations as useful in some situations, and reason-giving accounts in others, it is clearly their conviction that any observed deviation from a social-behavioral law is an argument in favor of human choice, and that the correct paradigm for the study of human social behavior is the view of man as a self-aware actor, who uses rules as criteria for the production of appropriate situated action (1973, pp. 150-151).

Harré and Secord assert that the simple cataloging of antecedents to behavior does not constitute explanation; that it is more proper to say that for social interaction, an observed antecedent provides a *reason* for the behavior, in the sense that the particular antecedent is covered by some rule of broad application which prescribes what is appropriate to do, or how things are done, given the general class of circumstances of which the antecedent is a member. Alternatively, one might explain the temporal priority of an antecedent A to a consequent C by finding that there is a rule such that in order for A to be achieved, C must be done (1972, p. 130).

Whille Harré and Secord and others have made persuasive arguments in favor of adopting a rule-following paradigm, the action theory approach is subject to criticism on a number of grounds. First, rules theorists have, for the most part, contented themselves with simple descriptions of communicative phenomena, neglecting the larger scientific aims of explanation and prediction. Few rules scholars have addressed themselves to the issues of how rules are adopted, why they have force, and how choices are made among competing rules (Berger, 1977). Even fewer advocates of the rules approach have attempted to account for deviation from rule-prescriptions in the same spirit that more traditional empiricists have tried to deal with unexplained variation. Finally, little attention has been directed to examining the relationship of rules to potential law-governed generative mechanisms. (For example, turn-taking behavior has been widely treated as rule-governed, yet speakers' behaviors with respect to floor switches are probably constrained by their information-processing capabilities.) Such inquiries are beyond the scope of this volume, which takes as its purpose the cataloging and evaluation of the accomplishments of the rules perspective with respect to the study of conversation, and those accomplishments have not for the most part advanced much beyond the level of surface descriptions. Despite the relative infancy of the field, the impenetrable and often imitative prose of some of its proponents, and the "caricatures," as Green and Cappella have put it (1982), of logical empiricism with which conversational analysts have fended off the opposition, the achievements of the rules perspective are real, and its vitality abundant.

CONVERSATIONAL RULES

Definitions of Rule

What does it mean to say that conversational activity is governed by rules? What is a rule? Let us first sample some definitions. Harré proposes that a rule is "what one does" to maintain face in civil society (1979, p. 53), and that sets of rules are the source of the unfolding structure of social episodes (1979, p. 273). (By "what one does" is meant what one ought to do, not necessarily that which is statistically normative.) Rules are, according to Harré, "performed, mandatory templates of the structure of action-sequences" (1979, pp. 131-132). Other rules theorists have proposed that rules constitute prescriptions for correct or appropriate action. Ganz defines rules as "utterances or inscriptions of the nature of critiques which specify the necessary procedures for satisfactorily carrying out an activity" (1971, p. 97). Similarly, Shimanoff (1980, p. 57) proposes that a rule is a "followable prescription" that states what sort of activity is "obligated, preferred, or prohibited" in particular contexts. While most theorists seem to agree that rules prescribe the behavior necessary to constitute a social act or to carry out an action sequence, none implies that rules prescribe *particular* behaviors, or reference idiosyncratic situations. Rules refer, of necessity, to areas of application more general than any specific context in which an actor might find herself, and consequently are best viewed as "guidance devices" or criteria for choice (Gottleib, 1968, p. 34); as "propositions" that "guide action" (Harré & Secord, 1972, p. 181). That is, actors know rules (and believe that others also know the same rules; Bach & Harnish, 1979, p. 94), and are able to recognize the appropriate contexts for their application.

While it is clearly the consensus that rules guide behavior, and in one way or another prescribe correct and appropriate contexted action, not all theorists agree on the extent to which rules are explicit in awareness. Ganz tells us that rules are "linguistic entities;" that they are "utterances" or "inscriptions" (1971, p. 47); evidently, that which has not been articulated cannot be a rule. Shimanoff, on the other hand, argues that much social behavior is generated by "implicit" rules (1980, p. 54), which is simply a way of saying that rules may be inferred from observation as well as explicitly taught— Toulmin's (1974) notion that rules are transmitted by a kind of "behavioral infection" (p. 209). The latter position, that rules need not be explicitly articulated, appears to have the greater merit; clearly, many behavioral routines that can be recovered analytically by the appropriate rule-set have been acquired through simple modeling processes. Rules are probably best conceived as propositions that model, at varying levels of awareness, our understandings of the situated evaluation of social behavior, and the ways in which social interaction should be constituted and carried out.

Form of Rule Statements

Rules theorists have also disagreed as to the form that rule-prescriptions take. Ganz claims that rules have no particular syntactic features (1971, p. 18). Von Wright proposes that rules "linguistically, are a very varied bunch" (1963, p. 102). Gottleib (1968, p. 40) points out that whatever the form in which they are inscribed or stored in memory, rules must be capable of being reformulated as statements that link situations to appropriate behavior in the following way: "in circumstances X, Y is required-permitted." Although some would take issue with the "permitted," arguing that rules circumscribe behavior much more narrowly, most theorists would agree that the canonical form of a rule-statement includes an "if-clause" referring to the circumstances in which the rule applies (the *protasis*), the behavior that the rule constrains (the *apodosis*), and an indication as to whether the behavior is required or prohibited (Gottleib, 1968, p. 43). Here are some rule formulations from, respectively, Harré and Secord (1972), Pearce (1976), and Shimanoff (1980), each of which conforms to this general format:

In order to achieve A (the act) do a_1 .... a_n (the actions) when S (the occasion or situation) occurs (Harré & Secord, 1972, pp. 182-183).

If we are enacting Episode₃ A, and he does Act B, then I am expected to or legitimately may do Act C (Pearce, 1976, p. 27).

If X, then Y is obligated (preferred or prohibited; Shimanoff, 1980, p. 76).

Further Characteristics of Rules

✘ We have already dealt with the notion that rules are prescriptive of correct behavior and that they may be implicit or explicit. Further characteristics of rules include the following:

(1) Rules can be followed; therefore, they can be broken. The now-classic distinction between a rule and a law is that the former can be broken and the latter cannot. This property of rule is referred to by Collett as the *condition of breach* (1977, p. 4). We cannot willfully choose, for example, to occupy two different points in space simultaneously, nor can we willfully choose to tumble from the earth (Ganz, 1971). Our motions are constrained by a set of laws in which the antecedent-consequent relationships are characterized by logical necessity. However, we can, and do, violate rules. We may, for example, interrupt another, neglect to return a greeting, refuse to answer a question, or fail to respond when summoned. While we may feel considerable pressure to follow a rule, a function of the extent to which the relation between context and prescribed behavior is strongly normative, nonetheless we may choose not to do so. Consequently, rules are about activities over which we have *control* (Shimanoff, 1980, p. 90). As a corollary, rules have less predictive power than laws (Ganz, 1971, p. 79), since we are not compelled or obliged to follow rules in the sense of necessity.

(2) Rules have no truth-value (Ganz, 1971, p. 24). Ganz contrasts rules, which are operative before they are obeyed, and regardless of whether or not they are obeyed, to descriptions, which are operative only if the behavior they characterize conforms to the

description (1971, p. 24). Consider the following example: it is a rule of polite usage that in informal dining the butter pat be removed to the butter plate with a fork. To use the knife for such an operation constitutes a gaffe. Stated formally as a rule, we have something like the following:

> When one wishes to present himself as a member of polite society, he should remove butter pats to the butter plate with his fork.

As a prescription of what ought to occur, the rule cannot be characterized as either true or false. Were we to rephrase the rule as a description, of, if you will, a normative statement, the issue of truth-value would pertain:

> People who wish to be regarded as members of polite society remove their butter pats to the butter plate with their forks.

Now we have a proposition that is susceptible of verification, and that, when put to the test, would probably be found to be wanting; similarly with such rules as "*Tuesday* should be pronounced [ˈtjuzde] as opposed to [ˈtuzde]," and "*harass* should be pronounced [ˈhærəs], as opposed to [həˈræs]," both of which are staples of etiquette books, yet neither of which is likely to constitute a statistical regularity when formulated as a description of what people actually do. Of course there are many rules that can be rewritten as descriptions and shown to be normative; for example, "When being introduced, one should extend one's hand in greeting." The point is that rules prescribe what (some people think) one ought to do, and consequently represent in the last analysis a value judgment, whereas descriptions or normative statements are propositions whose truth or falsity can be determined.

(3) Rules are conditional, but more general than the circumstances they cover. Given that individuals daily find themselves in a wide range of circumstances, some of which are novel, it is unlikely that the "fit" between the if-clause of a social rule and the current

circumstances in which guidance is required will ever be exact. The rules to which we subscribe are consensual social products, encapsulations of the prevailing wisdom about the proprieties of behavior in the recurring episodes of social life. Gottleib (1968) has argued that rules are necessarily generalizations, which "attempt to marshall the variety and richness of experience into manageable categories for the purpose of guiding decision" (p. 46). In this sense, rules are devised to have broad application—to be used over and over (Harré & Secord, 1972, p. 183). The central task for the rule user is to discover the nature of the relationship between the context in which guidance is required and the scope conditions of the many rules that might appear to apply (Gottleib, 1968, p. 44). Then too, since potentially applicable rules may prescribe complicated sequences of actions (Harré & Secord, 1972, p. 183), the rule user may have considerable work to do to carry out appropriately the *apodosis* of the rule. Furthermore, the context, as such, is not properly construed as a fixed tableau that serves as a backdrop for action; rather, the context is an emergent product of the developing interaction and is just as much *defined* by the interactants' rule use as it is a guide to them. Consequently, the rules that apply may well change over the course of the episode as further characteristics of the situation become apparent (Harré & Secord, 1972, p. 151). Turner has suggested that what interactants really expect of one another is behavior that can at least be *interpreted* as constrained by the rules pertinent to the occasion (Turner, 1962, p. 33). To balance all of these considerations requires what Cicourel (1973) has called an "interpretive competence," which we will have more to say later.

(4) Rules are "indeterminate and negotiable" (Wootton, 1975, p. 55). Collett has characterized rules as having the property of "alteration": rules can be canceled, changed, or replaced (1977, p. 4). Rules must be properly adopted; that is, persons must agree that a rule correctly specifies what constitutes a practice or appropriately contexted carrying-out of an action (Ganz, 1971, p. 99). However, rules remain in force only so long as they continue to serve the purposes of those whom they govern; that is, rules may be "unadopted" (Ganz, 1971, p. 104). Brittan has suggested that rules are always subject to "local" (interactionally managed) revising, so long as the revisions do not interfere with participants' sense of the structure of the episode (Brittan, 1973, p. 129). Morris and Hopper have dealt

with such local revisionism under the rubric of "remedial legisla-tion," in which parties to a misunderstanding negotiate, on-the-spot, new rules that, if followed, will structure subsequent interactions so as to obviate the need for repair (Morris & Hopper, 1980).

To summarize, rules have been described as propositions, which may or may not be explicitly available to consciousness, which model our understandings of what behaviors are prescribed or prohibited in certain contexts. Rules may be stored and retrieved in a variety of linguistic forms, but the canonical rule-statement is of the form, "If situation X occurs, do (do not do) Y." Rules may be followed or not, as the actor chooses; they are value-expressions whose truth cannot be determined. The behavior they prescribe is situation-bound. Rules are subject to alteration by consent of those whom they govern.

The Function of Rules:
Prediction, Interpretation, Evaluation

We have chosen to do without here a lengthy treatment of the functions of rules, since such an account may be found in Shimanoff (1980). It should be clear, however, that since rules serve to prescribe behavior, they also provide the basis for the prediction, interpreta-tion, and evaluation of behavior. We bring to social situations certain expectations about the rules that apply, and we ordinarily assume that those expectations are shared by others (Bach & Harnish, 1979, p. 105). Moreover, we locate ourselves in social episodes by comparing the action as it develops to the constitutive rules of social practice; and we coordinate our actions with those of others by presuming that their behaviors will conform to prescribed sequences. Thus, for example, when we initiate a summons sequence, we can anticipate that the person summoned will answer, and that she will anticipate that our next utterance will divulge the reason for the summons (Nofsinger, 1975). Similarly, we can anticipate that our telephone calls will terminate in a paired sequence of summarizations, well-wishings, and good-byes (Albert & Kessler, 1978).

We also employ rules to interpret *behavior*; that is, we make inferences along these lines: A is performing this-and-such a sequence of activities, in thus-and-such a context. Therefore, he must be doing this-and-so. We think in this context, for example, of how it is that persons recognize an indirect request, such as "Can you pass me the salt?" as a request as opposed to an inquiry about the hearer's capacity for salt passing (Labov & Fanshel, 1977). While some scholars have refused to acknowledge so-called interpretive rules (Shimanoff, 1980), or rules for hearing propositional utterances as particular speech acts, we find that interpretive rules may be easily transformed to behavioral prescriptions:

> If a speaker inquires about our ability to pass the salt, and it is patently obvious that we are able to do so, then treat the inquiry as a request for the salt.

In addition to facilitating the prediction and interpretation of behavior, rules are invoked to account for, explain, comment upon, and in general *evaluate* behavior. Ganz has described rules as "critiques" for behavior (1971, p. 54); rule-fulfilling behavior produces favorable evaluations, or at least provokes no notice, while behavior that fails to fulfill rules may result in unwanted notice, unfavorable regard, or even punishment. Rules are fitted by their propositional character to figure prominently in persons' versions of their own and others' behavior (Harré & Secord, 1972, p. 182); that is, rules make claims about what sorts of actions constitute an act or practice, or what sorts of actions are required to achieve some particular end, and may be invoked as *reasons* why the behaviors in question were undertaken (Harré & Secord, 1972, pp. 182-183). Rules may be used to condone omissions, as in the case of the customer who failed to tip her hairdresser because she took him, by his demeanor, to be the owner of the shop, and wished not to insult him. Rules may also be used to justify untoward acts, as in the recent case of the visit of the Queen of England to California, when the Deputy Mayor of a small city, operating under assumptions about the obligations of a gentleman, committed a minor act of *lèse majesté* by placing his hand on the small of Her Majesty's back to escort her in to lunch.

The Force of Rules

How is it that rules acquire force? Why do people follow rules if, as we have claimed before, rules can be broken? Rules theorists have offered several possibilities. First, Harré has suggested that following rules "falls in with a person's project" of presenting an acceptable social self and sustaining the face of others (Harré, 1979, p. 53). This has two implications. First, "seeing to it" (Ganz, 1971, p. 28) that one's behavior fulfills rules is a way of demonstrating one's commitment to the values and cumulative wisdom of the community; of making manifest that one may be relied upon not to disrupt the "social fabric" (Scott & Lyman, 1968). The underlying assumption one makes, of course, is that other people also know and value the rule (Collett, 1977), and can recognize that one's behavior is not only rule-fulfilling, or in conformity with the rule, but also that one is *making an effort* to abide by the rules. The second implication of Harré's proposal is that people assume that rules are critiques for behavior (Ganz, 1971); that they provide the basis for the evaluation of a person's activities. Bach and Harnish (1979, p. 105) assert that behavior that fails to fulfill rules attracts notice, and invites others to make attributions about its genesis; further, that most people regard compliance with or violation of rules as willful (1979, p. 95). Although many violations will go unremarked, or be charitably interpreted, the force of public opinion (Harré & Secord, 1972) combined with the fear of negative sanctions will often be sufficient to ensure compliance.

For certain kinds of rules, which some writers have referred to as "constitutive," force has to do with how social practices are recognized. According to Bach and Harnish (1979, p. 7), in making inferences about what others mean we operate under a presumption that whenever a speaker utters something, her intention is to *do* something in the utterance: to argue, complain, flatter, protest, and so forth. A speaker must adhere to certain rules that link utterances to the kinds of acts they perform (Harré & Secord, 1972). A speaker must also be aware of the way in which the meaning of a proposition shifts with context, or how it is contextualized by the episode in which it occurs. Furthermore, a speaker must be the "right" person to carry out the act if it is to have the intended force (Austin, 1962). A solicitous inquiry to a person of much higher status may be taken as an impertinence; similarly, only certain classes of persons are authorized to grant absolutions or admit one to manhood. In order to be taken seriously, and to be understood as we intend, it is necessary that we observe the conventions for performing particular kinds of acts through words, and that we demonstrate that we know how our utterances will count.

Typologies of Rule and Rule-Related Behaviors

Schemes for classifying *rules* seem to fall into two basic types: (1) those that distinguish rules that constitute an act from those which regulate a sequence of actions in a given context; and (2) those which classify rules according to their level of generality. Systems for classifying *rule-related behavior* (Shimanoff, 1980, pp. 177ff.) seem largely to be based upon the extent of the actor's knowledge of a rule, the degree of his conformity to it, and the extent to which the conformity is intentional. Let us first consider classifications of rules.

Constitutive versus regulative rules. Several theorists have distinguished between *constitutive* rules, those which prescribe the behaviors that are to count as particular acts, and *regulative* rules, which specify acts or sequences of acts that should be carried out in a specific situation. Pearce (1976) and Collett (1977) both make specific references to the terms constitutive and regulative. Pearce sees constitutive rules as "establishing acts/meanings which are required for the episode to be enacted," while regulative rules specify the set of permissible acts from which an actor may select (1976, p. 27). To Collett, constitutive rules are "essentially definitional," in that they indicate "what counts as what," while regulative rules tell us "what ought to be done" (1977, p. 6). Many theorists in trying to distinguish constitutive from regulative rules have fallen back on game analogies. Ganz, for example, distinguishes between rules which "determine whether or not players are playing" and those which specify correct procedures for action (1971, pp. 49-50). Gottleib proposes a similar distinction between *what it takes* for a ball to be "out," and *what happens given that* a ball is out (1968, p. 37). Satisfaction of the conditions for the former is the *operative fact*; the consequences of "outness" are the "resultant facts" (Gottleib, 1968, p. 37). Gottleib equates the operative fact with the protasis of a rule, and the resultant fact with the apodosis (1968, p. 37). Collett suggests that regulative rules depend on constitutive rules, in that we have to invoke constitutive rules to recognize the presence of the antecedent conditions and to perform the prescribed act correctly (1977), p. 6). For example, if we want to follow the regulative rule that questions should be followed by answers, we have to be able to recognize a question and we have to know how an answer is constituted. While some authors have dismissed the constitutive-regulative dichotomy (Shimanoff, 1980, pp. 84-85), it appears to have a limited amount of utility.

Rules and level of generality. Some who have written about rules have tried to classify them hierarchically on the basis of the extent of their coverage, or the degree to which they are subsumed by higher-order rules. Cicourel has distinguished between *surface rules*, or norms, and *interpretive procedures*, which are similar to deep structural grammatical rules in that they function as a "base structure" for "generating and comprehending behavioral displays" (Cicourel, 1973, p. 27). Ganz makes a not particularly compelling distinction between *rules*, which specify action, and *principles*, which supply the ideology or motivation for action (1971, p. 96). Harré categorizes rules as "etiquettes" or *first-order rules, principles* (the constitutive and strategic rules of rituals and games), which are described as "very weak universals," and *maxims*, which "control the style of action" generated by rules at the lowest levels (Harré 1974, pp. 161-165). Maxims are "dramaturgical" rules involved in self-presentation and image maintenance: for example, that one should not praise herself, but rather allow others to do it for her. Finally, Pearce and Conklin propose a rule hierarchy in which lower-level rules are embedded in or nested within higher-order ones (Pearce & Conklin, 1979). Identified are rules at four levels of generality: *information processing rules*, which tell us how to punctuate the stream of behavior into propositions; *rules of communication*, which relate propositions to the acts that they perform; *rules of sociation*, which contextualize the meaning of speech acts by the episode in which they occur, or lend internal structure to the sequences of acts that occur; and *rules of symbolic identification*, which relate episodes to archetypes, fundamental occurrences of social life such as courtship, barroom brawls, and the like (Pearce & Conklin, 1979, pp. 80-81).

Curiously, although each of the authors presents a rule hierarchy in which level of generality is the apparent criterion for ordering, none of the hierarchies seems to correspond to the others. Pearce and Conklin's taxonomy, unlike the rest, seems primarily to be concerned with constitutive rules. Ganz's "principles" seem to have less to do with the notion of *rule* than with alternative concepts such as *beliefs* or *motives*. Cicourel's deep structure rules are better construed as a set of procedures and assumptions, or an interpretive competency, for articulating surface rules with situated behavior displays so that the norms that pertain in a given context can be recognized (Wootton, 1975, p. 56). Harré fails to make clear how it is that the rules of etiquette are at a lower order of generality that the rules of rituals and games. Most attempts at classifying rules hierarchically have been either limited in scope, unconvincing, or injudicious in attributing varying levels of generality to rules and to things that-are-not-rules.

There are a number of real problems with trying to develop rule hierarchies. First, there does not appear as yet to be any real "theory" of situations to which such efforts can be linked, although there have been a number of attempts to uncover the underlying structure of the perception of situations (Frederiksen, 1972; Magnusson & Ekehammar, 1973; Price, 1974; Forgas, 1976; Wish, Deutsch and Kaplan, 1976; Cody & McLaughlin, 1980; Cantor, Mischel & Schwartz, 1982). If we do not have a reliable scheme for classifying contexts with respect to their generality, or archetypical quality, then we will encounter difficulty in trying to order classes of rules with respect to their breadth of application. Second, even if we could arrange rule-types into some sort of hierarchy, we would be faced with the problem that context is provided "bottom-up" as well as "top-down" (Hayes-Roth & Hayes-Roth, 1979; Hobbs & Evans, 1980); it is not just that we refer to the episode in which we find ourselves to make sense of and label propositional utterances, but also that the utterances define the episode as it unfolds. Thus, such an utterance as, "How about a cup of coffee?" we may choose to hear variously as an offer, a request, an invitation to sexual activity, or a hint to go home, depending upon whether we are in our own kitchen, a friend's kitchen, on our date's doorstep, or are lingering after a dinner party. More to the point, our choice of a "hearing" will also constitute a proffered definition of the episode to which the other party must respond, and that will contextualize subsequent acts. One further difficulty with existing hierarchies is that at the highest levels we may no longer be dealing with rules. So-called maxims, such as "be relevant," are not, strictly speaking, rules, in that they are not conditional but are assumed to apply unilaterally. In the final analysis, it seems that it might be more fruitful to try to center rules on the person, as opposed to the situation, particularly as we are operating not from a deterministic orientation in which the context compels, but rather from a choice perspective in which the actor uses his knowledge of context as a guide to appropriate behavior.

Classification of Rule-Related Behavior

Taxonomies of rule-realted behavior, notably those of Ganz (1971), Toulmin (1974), Collett (1977), and Shimanoff (1980), seem to be concerned with three dimensions: (1) whether or not the actor has knowledge of a rule; (2) whether or not the actor's behavior conforms to a rule; (3) whether or not the actor "sees to it" that his behavior conforms to a rule. In Figure 1.1, we have presented six kinds of rule-related behavior, generated from all possible triadic combinations of these three dimensions. Two of the combinations are "empty" in that one can't see to it that one's behavior conforms (or does not conform) to a rule that one does not know. We have used as an example the rule, "When addressing a superior, do not address him by his first name unless invited to do so" (Shimanoff, 1980, pp. 127-128). The categories are (1) *rule-following* behavior (Ganz, 1971; Shimanoff, 1980; called "Type D" by Collett, 1977, and "rule-applying" by Toulmin, 1974); (2) *rule-according* behavior (Ganz, 1971; called "Type D" by Collett, "rule-conforming" by Shimanoff, and "rule-following" by Toulmin; (3) *rule-fulfilling* behavior (Ganz; Shimanoff; called "Type B" by Collett and "rule-conforming" by Toulmin); (4) *rule-breaking* behavior (called "rule-violation" by Shimanoff and "Type C" by Collett); (5) *rule-violating* behavior (called "Type C" by Collett and "rule-error" behavior by Shimanoff); and (6) *rule-ignorant* behavior (called "Type A" by Collett). When an actor knows not to take the liberty of a first name with her superior, does not do it, and in fact makes a point of not doing it, we describe her behavior as *rule-following*. When the actor knows not to call his superior "Rudolph," does not do so, but this behavior is more or less automatic, we describe it as *rule-according*, in much the same sense as we would describe a speaker's not saying "ain't." When the actor uses the superior's title-plus-last-name, but doesn't know that he ought to by virtue of the other's superior status, we say that the actor's behavior is merely *rule-fulfilling*. Perhaps in such an instance the actor just has a preference for the more formal terms of address. When the actor makes a deliberate point of addressing her superior as "Harriet," knowing all the while that it just isn't done, we refer to her behavior as *rule-breaking*. When the actor knows that he ought to use title-plus-last-name, but unthinkingly blurts out the undue familiarity, we

| | Knows the Rule | | Does Not Know the Rule |
	Intentional	Unintentional	Intention Irrelevant
Behavior Conforms to the Rule	Rule-Following	Rule-According	Rule-Fulfilling
Behavior Does Not Conform to the Rule	Rule-Breaking	Rule-Violating	Rule-Ignorant

Figure 1.1 Taxonomy of Rule-Related Behavior

describe his behavior as *rule-violating*. Finally, when the actor addresses her superior by his first name, blithely unaware that it is inappropriate to do so, we refer to her behavior as *rule-ignorant*.

Not included in the taxonomy are Toulmin's (1974) category of *rule-checking* behavior (called "positive rule-reflective" behavior by Shimanoff, 1980), and Shimanoff's category of *rule-absent* behavior. In rule-checking, we evaluate the rule, making it an object of study. We monitor the effects of the rule as we follow it (Toulmin, 1974, p. 195). This category has been excluded from the taxonomy presented above because whether or not an actor observes the effects of her following a rule has no bearing on the actor's rule-knowledge, her intentions, or her conformity to the rule, nor does the monitoring affect the way in which her situated behavior is evaluated. One may call his superior "Mildred" in order to observe the result: however, the consequences of doing so are not going to be appreciably different as a result of the monitoring process, although they may be felt less severely by the offending actor. Following the rule may provide little information of interest to the actor-as-observer, anyhow, since most rule-fulfilling behavior will simply go unremarked.

We have also omitted Shimanoff's *rule-absent* behavior (1980, pp. 126-127), behavior that is neither controllable, situated, nor subject to evaluation, because it has no bearing on the underlying dimensions of our taxonomy.

MUTUAL BELIEFS, INTERPRETIVE PROCEDURES, AND MAXIMS

How is it that actors orient themselves to situations so that they know when a particular rule is operative? How are they able to recognize what Cicourel has called the "institutionalized features" of interaction? Are so-called surface rules a sufficient guide to the practices of conversation? Most scholars would argue that we *take for granted* (Hopper, 1980), and assume that others take for granted, many things.

Mutual Beliefs

Bach and Harnish (1979) have proposed the notion of *mutual contextual beliefs:* sets of propositions about the rules that apply to classes of persons and contexts that are mutually recognized by parties to an interaction to guide behavior and provide the basis for its evaluation. In addition to the mutual contextual beliefs that pertain to particular classes of events, there are also two more general beliefs, to which all subscribe, which serve as a guide for inference. The first, the *linguistic presumption*, is that when any member of a language community utters something in that language to another member, his hearer will be able to identify what was said, given an adequate vocabulary and background information (Bach & Harnish, 1979, p. 7). The *communicative presumption* is simply that whenever a speaker *says* (utters) something, she is doing so with the intent to *do* something: to agree, reassure, belittle, and so forth (Bach & Harnish, 1979, p. 7).

Interpretive Procedures

Several scholars have addressed themselves to the competencies and necessary background understandings we require in order to be guided by rules; in other words, what actors need to know, or must assume, in order to make sense of their experiences and behave in an appropriate manner.

Cicourel (1973) has treated at length a class of mechanisms for identifying the correspondences between features of settings and surface rules that he calls *interpretive procedures*. Interpretive procedures, which as Wootton (1975, p. 56) points out are general methods for determining the application of rules in particular settings, provide a sense of social structure of broad utility that allows us to generate and understand novel behavior. These interpretive procedures are such as to sustain us through a lifetime of social inter-action; they enable the actor to identify contexts, which then leads to the invocation of the appropriate surface rules. For example, in producing an appropriate response to the utterance "Don't you think it's cold in here?" the hearer has available to her a surface "rule for indirect requests" (Labov & Fanshel, 1977, p. 78c.), under which if a speaker inquires about the hearer's opinion of the need for an action (one of the *preconditions* of the successful performance of an action), the utterance may be interpreted as an indirect request for the action to be performed by the hearer, in this case closing the window. Wootton has suggested that these preconditions to which rules refer simply "model our competence" to recognize an utterance as doing something; they index the pertinent areas of knowledge we must consult in order to make sense of what we hear (1975, pp. 50-54). Not only would we have to consult our background knowledge about the need for the action (closing the window), but we would also have to make certain inquiries, implicit or otherwise, as to our own and the other's capability to perform the act, our own and the other's willingness to do so, and so on.

Cicourel has set forth the features of what he calls a "common scheme of reference" (1973, p. 34), a set of interpretive procedures and assumptions whose existence is presupposed by all parties. These include (1) an *assumed reciprocity of perspectives*, a taken-for-granted mutual orientation to the episode at hand (Cicourel, 1973, p. 34); (2) the assumption of *indexicality*, the mutual belief that words index larger systems of meaning, and that much is unstated and must be supplied by the hearer (1973, p. 35); (3) the *et cetera* procedure, which allows the hearer to suspend judgment on a lexical item whose meaning is unclear until such time as subsequent information arises to clarify it (p. 35); (4) the idea of *normal form typification*, which instructs the actor to categorize the particulars of an episode as to the normal forms of social life which they typify—Pearce has also talked about episodes as simply a repertoire of action patterns that parties to an encounter assume are common to both (1976, p. 21); and finally (5) the assumption that the other is *as we have always known him* (Schutz, 1964, p. 39)—that he has a set of "constitutive traits" (Schutz, 1964, p. 39), which remain the same from one encounter to the next.

Maxims

Related to Cicourel's notion of interpretive procedures are Grice's *cooperative principle* and *conversational maxims* (Grice, 1975, p. 45) that, although they appear to be rules or meta-rules as a function of their prescriptive form, are, given their nonconditional nature, best characterized as a set of assumptions, to which all subscribe, about the features of concerted social interaction. Grice has proposed that persons assume that these maxims are operative, and that any appearance to the contrary gives rise to inference (1975, p. 49). The *cooperative principle*, the ultimate maxim, is that one ought to make his contribution to conversation "such as is required, at the stage at which it occurs, by the accepted purpose or direction of the talk exchange" in which one is engaged (Grice, 1975, p. 45). Grice also proposes a set of maxims, which if adopted will result in a cooperative contribution. The first is the *Quantity* maxim, which in effect states that one's contribution ought to be neither more nor less informative than is required (Grice, 1975, pp. 45-46). The *Quality* maxim (1975, p. 46) requires that one state only that which one believes to be true, and for which there is sufficient evidence. The *Relevancy* maxim (Grice, 1975, p. 46) requires that a contribution be pertinent in context. Finally, the *Manner* maxim states that one ought to avoid obscure expressions, ambiguity, excessive verbosity, and disorganization (1975, pp. 46-47). Conversational behavior that appears to violate or blatantly flout the maxims ordinarily gives rise to speculation as to why the cooperative principle does not appear to be in force, and this state of affairs invites *conversational implicature*, broadly construed the engagement of a set of interpretive procedures designed to figure out just what the speaker is up to. For example, suppose that A and B are dining out and, as they linger over their coffee, A inquires of B: "How much are they paying you over there at Exxon?" to which B replies, "I believe I *will* order the chocolate mousse." In order to interpret B's utterance, A must go through a series of inferences based on assumptions about the principles and maxims to which B subscribes. For example: "B's remark violated the maxim of Relevance, yet I assume he's being cooperative. I'm sure that he heard me, and I'm sure that he knows how much he makes, and I'm sure that he knows that I don't know, and I doubt that he has to keep it a secret. Rather than lie about it, and violate the Quality maxim, he has chosen to flout the Relevance maxim and thereby deliberately refuse to advance the topic. Therefore, he must not want to talk about it. Therefore, what he is *doing* is telling me in a nice way that it's none of my business." Of course, much conversational implicature, as in the case of indirect requests ("Can you hand my my glasses?") is quite conventionalized, so that an inferred meaning is for all practical purposes a literal one. We will have more to say about conversational implicature in a subsequent chapter.

Bach and Harnish have proposed two additional presumptions that are components of the reciprocal perspective of communicators, and that give rise to inference if violated; they are the "politeness maxim" and the "morality maxim" (Bach & Harnish, 1979, p. 64). The politeness maxim holds that the speaker must not be offensive, vulgar, rude, and so on, while the morality maxim presupposes that the speaker does not repeat that which she sought not to, ask for privileged information, require the hearer to say or do something that she ought not, or do things for the hearer that the hearer has no interest in having done (1979, p. 64). Bach and Harnish also propose a "principle of charity" (1979, p. 68): "Other things being equal, construe the speaker's remarks so as to violate as few maxims as possible."

Finally, Edmondson (1981a) has proposed that conversation, at least in English, is further characterized by "hearer-supportive" maxims, such as "Support your hearer's costs and beliefs," and "Suppress your own costs and beliefs." Edmondson arrived at this conclusion after a dimensional analysis of English illocutionary verbs, lexical items that correspond to distinct speech actions such as promising, advising, acknowledging, and so forth.

Edmondson used a five-dimensional scheme to generate a matrix of illocutionary verbs: (1) whether or not an event or state of affairs *is/was*, or *will be* the case; (2) whether the actor involved in the event is speaker (S) or hearer (H); (3) whether *S (H)* is *responsible* or *not responsible* for the event; (4) whether the event in question had *desirable* or *undesirable* outcomes; and (5) whether the consequences of the event affected *S* or *H*. Edmondson found that the distribution of illocutionary verbs lends credence to the notion of H-supportive and S-suppresive maxims. Consider, for example, the case in which an event occurs that has undesirable consequences for H. There are illocutionary verbs (*sympathize, commiserate*) that denote that S does not hold H *responsible* for the unhappy event. There is an illocutionary verb (*apologize*) that means that S holds *herself* responsible for the event that had undesirable consequences for H. There does not, however, appear to be an illocutionary verb to fill the slot "S does not hold S responsible for an action which had negative outcomes for S," and the appropriate nouns ("self-pity" and so forth) have an unattractive connotation. Similarly, while there is an ample number of illocutionary verbs denoting that "S holds H responsible for an event that had desirable consequences for H" (*praise, congratulate*), the verbs that denote that "S holds himself responsible for an act which had positive outcomes for S" have rather an ad hoc quality ("self-congratulate," "self-praise,"; Edmondson, 1981, p. 495). On the basis of these and other evidences, Edmondson concludes that hearer-support, but not speaker-support, is lexicalized in English.

SUMMARY

Conversational behavior is seen to be governed by rules: propositions about the propriety of action in context. Conversational rules, which constrain but do not compel behavior, are best viewed as critiques or criteria for decision making in social situations. The force of rules derives from their use as the basis for the evaluation of behavior. Rule statements, which usually take the form "If in situation S, Y is required (prohibited)," are not to be taken as descriptions, but rather as prescriptions for what the social community regards as appropriate situated action. Further, rules are subject to revision both at the level of community and by local (interactionally managed) negotiating. Rules may be classified as constitutive or regulative. Rule-related behavior seems to vary along three dimensions: (1) the actor's knowledge of the rule; (2) the actor's conformity to the rule; and (3) the extent to which that conformity (or lack thereof) is intentional.

Surface rules, however, are an inadequate guide to social practice. (Should the reader be in doubt, she might do well to consult de Beaugrande, 1980, pp. 243-244, who lists among those things persumed to be known by parties to conversation (1) "typical and determinate concepts and relations in world knowledge," (2) "cultural and social attitudes," (3) "conventional scripts and goals," (4) traits of the current context, and (5) episodic knowledge of shared experiences.) To use rules effectively as guides for action, actors orient themselves to conversational situations through assumed mutual beliefs about the contexts in which they find themselves. Certain interpretive competencies are required to identify areas of correspondence between the features of contexts and the scope conditions of surface rules. Not only must the actor have a considerable store of background knowledge, but he must also be privy to and honor certain assumptions: that S and H have reciprocal perspectives; that the other's personhood is consistent; that both are cooperating; that one's own and the other's politeness and veracity may be taken for granted; and so forth. In subsequent chapters, we will examine in detail the operations of surface rules, interpretive competencies, and assumptions.

2

Conversational Coherence

◆ In this chapter, we will explore the manifes- ◆
tations and ramifications of the injunction to be relevant, at several
different levels of of conversational structure. Specifically, we will
examine coherence and cohension relations as they are displayed in
the conversational *text*, in *propositional* organization, and in
functional or *speech act* organization (Foster & Sabsay, 1982;
Sabsay & Foster, 1982). We will touch only lightly on cohesion
relations at they appear in text, as these relations are probably of
greater interest to text grammarians than to students of conversation.
In looking at propositional and functional structure, we will be
concerned with how *utterance-by-utterance* and *global* coherence
requirements both respond to and constrain the plans and goals of
actors. (By utterance-by-utterance level we refer to the organization
of conversation at the level of thought or propositional units
(independent or dependent clauses and their substitutes) rather than
turns or sentences. By global coherence we refer to the apparent unity
of discourse as a whole.

RELEVANCE, COHERENCE, AND COHESION

Foster and Sabsay (1982) have emphasized the importance to cooperative social interaction of the maxim of Relevance: in order to proceed in conversation, each party must assume that the other is trying to make relevant contributions. Just what is meant by a *relevant* contribution? Grice's original maxim of Relation ("be relevant") was, as the author put it, rather terse (1975, p. 46); he elaborated only to say that one's contributions ought to be "appropriate to immediate needs at each stage of the transaction" (1975, p. 47) Foster (1982) has proposed that there are two kinds of relevance relationships: (1) a strict contingency on the immediately preceding utterance; (2) a dependency of the utterances on the "global concern" of the discourse topic. Most scholars who have considered the question have treated relevance as a property of an utterance with respect to the discourse that precedes it. Werth (1981, p. 153), for example, defines relevance as "the appropriateness of an utterance meaning to the meaning of the previous utterance, together with the context in which they occur." Wilson and Sperber (1981) treat relevance as a relationship between the propositional content of an utterance and the immediately relevant set of propositions (uttered or implicit) to which the hearer has access in memory. Similarly, Keenan and Schieffelin (1976) see a large part of the work of achieving relevance as the formulation of conversational topics out of prior propositions in (or implicated by) the conversation-so-far.

While some authors (Tracy, 1982) have treated local (utterance-by-utterance) and global relevance as an either-or proposition, it seems that the class of pairs of adjacent utterances in conversations with purely local relevance of the second member of the pair to the first is rather limited—for example, the exchange might be restricted to a few utterances, as in a passing greeting, or it might constitute a cooperatively authorized "detour" from the conversational topic mandated by some environmental exigency:

B: So I told her that I wouldn't let her borrow it again because the last time she

A: (Oh, hi, Tony!

B: He's SO:OO good looking!

A: Yeah, but he's going with Lisa Bradley. Anyhow, so you told her . . .

It seems that the relevance of an utterance is largely a matter of its fitting in with the whole of some discourse context, such that its pertinence both to an immediately prior utterance and to the conversation-to-date is apparent. Thus, if A is recounting an incident in which her birthday gift to her mother was mailed out from the gift shop with the price tag still on it, and as a "unit" of the narrative refers to the clerk who took the order, a question by B—"Was she new?"—would be relevant locally by virtue of the coinciding entities "clerk" and "she" and globally relevant by reference to the overriding issue that "a mistake was made."

There does appear to be evidence (Vucinich, 1977; Tracy, 1982) that utterances may vary in *degree* of relevance. If, for instance, one's partner is telling a story that she hopes will illustrate the point that people take advantage of tourists in Mexico, and tells of an event in which she was overcharged for a taxi ride, a response by the hearer about taxi drivers' recklessness may appear to be a locally relevant utterance, what McLaughlin, Cody, Kane, and Robey (1981) term "tangential talk," but will probably be regarded as less relevant and competent than, say, a story about being overcharged at a hotel in Acapulco.

Keenan and Scheiffelin (1976) have pointed out that underlying the notion of relevance is the requirement that the speaker make his topic known. Making a (transparently) relevant utterance is one way to make the topic known; the speaker may, however, be required to resort to a number of devices to do so, including the provision of information adequate to identify discourse entities and form appropriate representations of the semantic and functional relationships between her utterances and previous ones. Providing the necessary information requires that the speaker make a proper estimate of the hearer's knowledge, so as to avoid condescension on the one hand and mystification on the other (Keenan & Schieffelin, 1976, p. 361).

One factor that clearly emerges from an examination of relevance is that having a notion of the topic of a conversation is critical to making a pertinent contribution. We shall explore the idea of topic in greater detail in a subsequent section.

What is the relationship between relevance and conversation *coherence*? Are these terms synonymous with each other? with the notion of conversational *cohesion*? It appears that the three terms are used somewhat differently. Generally, it would seem that relevance refers to the relationship of a single utterance to the preceding utterances (Hobbs, 1978), while coherence is a characteristic of a sequence of utterances taken as a unit or whole. While Werth (1981, p. 153) equates relevance and coherence in that the two terms have "coinciding implications," it would seem that coherence is a more global property of "relatedness" between sequentially produced utterances (Sabsay & Foster, 1982). Most scholars invoke the idea of an overriding proposition, *macroproposition* (van Dijk, 1980, 1981), or *primary presupposition* (Keenan & Schieffelin, 1976) to account for coherence. For instance, Ellis et al., (1983, p. 268) define coherence as "a correspondence or a congruity arising from some principle common to a sequence." Similarly, Sabsay and Foster (1982, p. 4) argue that an entire proposition must be presupposed if a discourse is to have coherence; that is, it is not sufficient that a sequence of utterances be "about" some entity, but must rather be about a *predication* of that entity. Hobbs (1978) proposes that discourse is coherent if it exhibits certain structural relationships among the utterances: that there is a finite set of coherence relations that "corresponds to coherent continuation moves" (Hobbs, 1979, p. 68) a speaker can undertake. These coherence relations (Elaboration, Specification, Generalization, and so forth; Hobbs, 1978) are about propositions expressed by adjacent utterances as they pertain to the theme of the discourse as a whole. Hobbs (1978, pp. 9-10) has pointed out that some authors treat coherence as the trace of an actor's plan, in which each utterance can be seen to be directed toward the attainment of some particular end. Hobbs rejects this view for the most part as being "too strong," for conversants often seem to talk past one another, and to be unaware of or oblivious to each other's goals.

Coherence differs from cohesion in that the latter seems to be used to describe the ways in which the different utterances in a sequence can appear to be about the same referents or objects. Cohesion generally refers to the presence of a set of devices that we can see explicitly in a text (anaphora, repetition and so on); as Edmondson put it, "those devices by means of which TEXTURE is evidenced" (1981b, p. 5). Coherence is equated with the *interpretability* of a discourse (Edmondson, 1981b, p. 5). Hobbs (1978) proposes that a coherent text necessarily has cohesion, but that a text with cohesion may not be coherent. That is, a string of utterances may each be related in a chain-like fashion, where cohesion (identity of referents) is present at the local level, but the coherence of the sequence as a unit is absent:

A: I saw a duck at the lake yesterday.
B: I like to swim in lakes.
A: I swam in a race last summer.

COHESION AT THE LEVEL OF THE TEXT

Edmondson (1981b, p. 4) has defined text as "a structured sequence of linguistic expressions forming a unitary whole." When we examine cohesion at the level of text we are not interested in going beyond the sentence-level units of meaning that are literally present (Foster & Sabsay, 1982, p. 7); hypothetical macropropositions, primary presuppositions, bridging propositions, or any other elements of the discourse implied but not present will not be invoked to account for connectedness. According to Halliday and Hasan (1976, p. 4), cohesion takes place when in order to interpret some entity in the text one has to refer to another, such that the former presupposes the latter. Thus in the following "she" presupposes "Judy," and the discourse is easy to process:

A: I like Judy.
B: Yeah, she's always friendly.

It will be noted that what is being presupposed is not a proposition but rather an isolated semantic element (Sabsay & Foster, 1982, p. 4). McLaughlin et al. (1981) noted that in the sequencing of stories, participants sometimes demonstrated the relevance of their stories to a partner's previous narrative by referring to some implicit or explicit proposition or "significance statement" (Ryave, 1978) that seemed to inform both stories, but often a subsequent story was made to appear relevant in sequence by text-level cohesion markers such as *embedded repetitions* or *marked repeats* ("speaking of hockey").

It is probably fair to say that the extent to which a person's utterance in respect to prior text is marked by cohesion devices reflects the state of the speaker's cognitive processes (or at least reflects the way his cognitive processes are judged). For example, Fine and Bartolucci (1981) proposed that the following basic categories of cohesion relations distinguish between thought-disordered and nonthought-disordered schizophrenics:

(1)   *substitution:* "I love the little kittens in the pet shop. I wish I could have *one*."
(2)   *ellipsis:* "I love the little kittens in the pet shop. I wish I could have the *brown*.
(3)   *reference:* "I love the little kittens in the pet shop. *They* look so cute.
(4)   *lexical:* "I love the little kittens in the pet shop. They're *Siamese*.

Similarly, Rochester and Martin (1977) hypothesized and found that the explicitness of reference (for example, exophoric versus endophoric) differentiated between thought-disordered and normal subjects.

Cohesion devices may also be said to affect the ease with with utterances are processed. For example, the cohesion device with which most readers will be familiar is *anaphoric reference*, in which the interpretation of a pronoun is dependent upon some other element in the text (Frederiksen, 1981). Frederiksen has shown, at least for written materials, that processing time is slowed when a lexical element is pronomialized in a subsequent utterance, as opposed to simply being repeated. Further, when there is a greater number of potential referents that coincide in number and gender with the pronoun, processing time is slowed. However, the speed of processing is not affected by introducing additional utterances between the one containing the entity referred to and the subsequent one containing the pronoun (Frederiksen, 1981, p. 340).

The reader who wishes to pursue further the issue of cohesion markers in text is urged to consult Halliday and Hasan (1976). We concur with Sabsay and Foster (1982), who conclude that while the textual markers of discourse both evidence and contribute to structure in discourse, they are not the most important sources of connectedness.

CONVERSATIONAL GOALS AND PLANS

Winograd (1977) has proposed that any utterance may be viewed as the culmination of a "design process," in which the actor uses whatever linguistic and conversational resources are available to her to produce a message aimed at realizing some *goal*; that is, some state of affairs in the hearer or in herself that the speaker hopes to achieve (Hobbs & Evans, 1980). Cohen and Perrault (1979, p. 184) see the planning process as searching for a sequence of actions such that the first is applicable in the actor's "current world model" and the last gives rise to a new world model "in which the goal is true." Similarly, Jackson and Jacobs (in press) argue that the organization of a sequence of utterances depends on how the utterances coincide with a "goal-oriented plan." Much of the work in making a relevant contribution has to do with deducing the goals of the speaker, responding to those which one is intended to recognize (Hobbs, 1979), and integrating those responses with one's own current plans and goals.

Competence in a hearer requires that one be aware of common goals in conversation. Winograd (1977, p. 69) suggests that these may include: (1) inducing the hearer to perform some action; (2) manipulating the hearer's inference processes; (3) conveying information about a known entity; (4) creating a new conceptual element to correspond to an entity already in H's knowledge store; and (5) directing the hearer's attention. In general, one might construct the goal of the speaker as increasing the correspondence between what S knows, wants, and believes, and what H knows, wants, and believes (Hobbs, 1978, p. 12). In order to do so, S is required to have a model of the hearer. That is, S must know what it is that H currently knows, wants, or believes, and what is in H's active memory (Winograd, 1977, p. 76). In this context, speech acts may be seen to be operating on S's model of the hearer (Cohen & Perrault, 1979). Hobbs and Agar (1981) argue that any list of a speaker's goals must include that of *maintaining local coherence*. Ordinarily the demands of local coherence will act as a constraint on speakers' goal-attainment, as evidenced by such common complaints (or excuses) as "I just couldn't find the right moment to bring it up," or "I just couldn't get it in." Then, too, speakers recognize the importance of strategic timing with respect to the achievement of *covert* goals: if one is to bring off successfully an action of dubious social standing, for example a *boast*, it is best that the act appear to be occasioned effortlessly by the preceding discourse; thus, the speaker must bide his time until an opportune moment arises. Hobbs and Agar (1981, p. 12) suggest that the requirements of local coherence pose not just an obstacle to goal-attainment, but may be also regarded as a conversational resource: "since local coherence typically reflects memory structure, it serves as a means for finding a next thing to say." One consequence of local coherence goals is that memory may be jogged, prompting a return or reprise of a topic previously closed.

In addition to local coherence goals, a speaker may have a larger goal of conversational maintenance. McLaughlin and Cody (1982, p. 299) found that lapses in conversation were sufficiently embarrassing that members of dyads so afflicted would often resort to "masking behaviors" such as coughing, whistling, and singing to cover the gap. A number of studies (Arkowitz, Lichtenstein,

McGovern, & Hines, 1975; Weimann, 1977; Biglan, Glaser, & Dow, 1980; Dow, Glaser, & Biglan, 1980) have demonstrated either that being credited with responsibility for a conversation lapse is associated with lowered competency ratings, or that those with poor social skills generally tend to have longer response latencies. In light of these gloomy findings, one can understand that the desire to sustain conversation may take precedence over any exogenous goals such as persuading H to grant a request. Thus, one might thrash about for something (anything!) to say in order to ward off an awkward silence, and the propositional content of whatever happens to "pop out" may well dictate, an an opportunistic fashion, what goals S will be able to meet in subsequent utterances.

In order to achieve a goal, one often constructs a *plan*. Hayes-Roth and Hayes-Roth (1979, p. 275) define planning as "the predetermination of a course of action aimed at achieving some goal." Similarly, Hobbs and Evans (1980) treat a plan as "some consciously constructed conceptualization of one or more sequences of actions aimed at achieving a goal." Ferrara (1980a) claims that the only way in which a sequence of speech acts can be understood is through a grasp of the connection among the goals that give rise to them. While Ferrara's claim may seem extreme, he is clearly correct in his argument that the status of a speech act in a plan is proportionate to its importance with respect to goal-attainment. Consequently, we can distinguish between *main* and *subordinate* acts on the basis of their prominence in the plan: "given a pair of goals and a contexts, I will take the one which can conceivably be aimed at, without presupposing any other, as the main goal; and those which are also intended . . . as subordinate goals" (Ferrara, 1980a, p. 247). Thus, a speaker may make a simple plan for a dinner date that involves a subordinate goal of determinining H's availability, which, if successfully met, and in the affirmative, will enable the main goal of requesting a date. The plan might be realized in a sequence like the following:

A: Are you free Friday night?
B: I think so.
A: How about dinner?
B: O.K.

In the event that the subordinate goal of checking out a precondition is met, but not in the affirmative, the plan may call for the main act to be jettisoned:

> **A:** Are you free Friday night?
> **B:** No, I'm afraid I'm tied up.
> **A:** Oh. O.K.

Alternatively, the actor may indulge in a bit of opportunistic planning:

> **A:** Are you free Friday night?
> **B:** Well, I have a class until ten.
> **A:** Good, we'll have a late supper.

Thus, while the plan may be "top-down" as originally conceived, it ordinarily will be sufficiently flexible to allow the exploitation of alternative opportunities should they arise (Hobbs & Agar, 1981, p. 5).

How may a "conversational plan" be characterized? Hobbs and Agar (1981, p. 4) treat a conversational plan as a cognitive representation of an actor's goals and the actions which she intends to undertake to achieve them: "it is in general a tree-like structure whose nonterminal nodes are goals and subgoals, i.e., logical representations of states to be brought about, and whose terminal nodes are actions" that the actor can perform to facilitate the attainment of those goals. It is appropriate to think of goals and subgoals as coincident with "topic" and "subtopic" (Hobbs & Agar, 1981, p. 4) when referring to the propositional structure of conversation and with "global action" and "subordinate action" in the context of its functional structure.

While one may have a global plan for a conventional exchange, say, to ask Dad for the use of the car in pursuit of the goal of obtaining the use of the car, the plan will probably not be complete beyond one or two of the nonterminal nodes. That is to say, goals may be achieved in increments, and planning itself may be incremental (Hobbs & Agar, 1981, p. 5; Hayes-Roth & Hayes-Roth, 1979, p. 305). It is unlikely than an actor would construct specific contingency plans in the event that, at the level of a subgoal (for example, determining if Dad is planning to use the car himself) the plan is thwarted. Cohen and Perrault (1979, p. 178) propose that we expect and desire others to recognize our plans, and to help us to meet our goals. Consequently, we depend to some extent on a conviction that a "way" or path to the goal will emerge from the interaction, given the cooperation of H, whom we expect to honor the spirit, if not the letter, of our plans.

Hobbs and Agar propose that in the midst of interaction, we conduct a "bidirectional search"; that is, we check locally to determine which of currently possible paths might suffice to reach our goals, as well as constructing possible action sequences top-down from the goal. Planning is only lightly constrained, and in fact, opportunistic planning is the exception rather than the rule (1981, p. 12). Hobbs and Agar provide an example of an "associative slide," when an actor's attention to an overriding plan wanders and he rambles in a merely locally coherent way through "adjacent chunks" in memory. Global goals may through the process of interaction lose their power to constrain, and ultimately be replaced by new goals.

Cohen and Perrault (1979) have proposed a set of "heuristic principles" that actors use in constructing plans. They are, at the time the plan is constructed, that (1) S should include in the plan only those actions whose effects are not yet applicable in the desired model of the world; (2) S may insert in the plan an action that achieves E if E is a goal; (3) S may add to the plan all the preconditions to achieving E that are not already true (the need for the action, the willingness or availability of H to perform the action, and so on)—in other words, determine which subordinate goals have to be met in order that the main or "top-level" goals may be met (Winograd, 1977, p. 69); (4) S may create a goal that she know the truth-value of some proposition; or (5) the value of some description, if such knowledge is needed in order to complete planning (in other words, the actor is not required to construct a whole plan prior to carrying it out); and (6) each party assumes that the other will plan in this way.

Ochs (1979, p. 55) has examined some of the characteristics of planned as opposed to unplanned discourse. A *planned discourse* is one that has been designed and given thought before it is expressed; an *unplanned discourse* "lacks forethought and preparation" (Ochs, 1979, p. 55). Ochs has discovered a number of features that characterize what she terms *relatively unplanned discourse*. First, speakers depend more upon the immediate context to supply connections between referents and predicates. For example, referents may be *deleted*, as in

A: Still tryin' to graduate?
B: Better believe it!

where the referent "you" is omitted in both utterances. There is also greater use of the *referent plus proposition* construction, in which the semantic relation between a referent and what is predicated of it is omitted:

A: Richard- he's in our lit class, he got an A.

Ochs (p. 75) noted that this construction was especially likely to occur when a speaker had competition for the floor. The noun phrase (NP) holds the floor until the S has had time to encode the appropriate predication.

Parties to relatively unplanned discourse are also more likely to leave it up to the hearer to puzzle out the nature of the relationship between propositions. Words like *because*, *therefore*, and so on are less likely to appear. Thus, in a discourse like

> **A:** I really feel down today. Roger brought home a bad
>   report card again.

it is up to H to infer the nature of the link between A's state of mind and Roger's report card: to supply the missing semantic connective *because* (or possibly *and*, if the context suggests that Roger's bad report card only *contributed* to a feeling that was already present). Planned conversations seem to have more subordinate or dependent clauses, indicating that the speaker put more effort into the task of encoding (Ochs, 1979, p. 67).

A third feature of relatively unplanned discourse reported by Ochs is a greater dependence on morphosyntactic structures characteristic of the early states of language acquisition. These features included (1) less frequent use of definite articles ("Mr. Jones, the neighbor across the street," as opposed to "this guy I know"); (2) greater use of the active as opposed to the passive voice; (3) more frequent use of the present ("so he says to her") as opposed to the past or future tenses ("so he said to her").

Finally, relatively unplanned discourse is frequently amended or improved upon as a function of afterthought; consequently, there tends to be a larger number of repetitions and substitutions of lexical items. One consequence of such on-the-spot revising is that utterances tend to be longer than they might be in planned discourse (Ochs, 1979, p. 72).

TOPICAL ORGANIZATION

Referent Approaches

One of the fundamental ways in which a conversation shows signs of structure is that it appears to be "about" something. There seem to be at least two relatively distinct views of what a topic is, of what it means for a discourse to be about something (Reinhart, 1981). The first we shall characterize as the *referent* approach, the second as the *propositional* approach. The referent approach is exemplified by the work of Schank (1977) and Clark and Haviland (1977). Schank argues for the notion that the topic of an utterance (called the "New Topic") is inferred from the intersection of two sets of elements: the "Reduced Old Topic," a subset of elements contained in the immediately previous turn, and the set of new elements introduced in the current turn. For example, suppose that A had said

A: I went to the Newport Harbor Museum yesterday to see the Munch exhibit.

and B had replied

B: I heard the museum was exhibiting Kokoschka next spring.

The Reduced Old Topic would be X = (museum, exhibit), the set of elements appearing in both utterances. (The elements [Munch, yesterday] are not contained in B's utterance. The New Topic equals the intersection of X = (museum, exhibit) and the set of new elements introduced by B (Kokoschka, spring). A Potential Topic for a subsequent utterance by A may be composed from the elements in the intersection of the sets Reduced Old Topic and New Topic. Thus, in this utterance-by-utterance view of topic, B may exploit pathways from any of the elements (museum, exhibit, Kokoschka, spring) as a Potential Topic for a subsequent turn.

As is apparent from Schank's work, the referent approach is characterized by a concern for determining the entity or entities to which an utterance *refers*. Strawson (1979) has suggested two criteria for such a determination: (1) the principle of *presumption of knowledge*—what knowledge does S presume that H already possesses? and (2) the *principle of relevance*—what operations is S trying to perform on H's presumed knowledge; that is, what is the entity about which S hopes to expand H's knowledge (Reinhart, 1981)? Reinhart characterizes the referent approach as the "topic-as-old information view": topic is a "property of the referents denoted by linguistic expressions in a given context" (1981, p. 61).

The most widely read proponents of the referent approach are Clark and Haviland (1977). Their work is particularly noteworthy for two concepts: the *maxim of antecedence* and the *given-new contract*. The latter is conceived as a tacit contract between S and H as to how old and new information should be ordered in sentences

(Clark & Haviland, 1977, p. 3). The maxim of antecedence, which is subsumed by Grice's maxim of manner, requires that the speaker minimize processing for the hearer by seeing to it that the given or old information in any utterance has a unique antecedent (Clark & Haviland, 1977, p. 4). Should A say "I saw Henry and Jayne at the Bistro last night" and should B have no unique antecedent in memory for Henry and Jayne, A has violated the maxim of antecedence, albeit perhaps inadvertently if he has simply overestimated H's knowledge.

Both S and H are presumed to share a knowledge base or information structure pertinent to the conversation, which consists of a set of hierarchically ordered propositions and equivalence relations, both explicit and implicit in the discourse. An H ordinarily relates an utterance to the relevant information structure by (1) distinguishing old from new information; (2) retrieving from memory the intended, unique antecedent for the old information; and (3) incorporating the new information into the knowledge base after it has been "attached" to the retrieved antecedent (Clark & Haviland, 1977). Hobbs (1979) has been critical of this three-step approach as being overly simplistic. Hobbs argues that the process by which given and new information are distinguished is left unspecified; further, that it is usually very difficult to specify a unique antecedent. Perhaps it is fair to say that one makes a good *guess* as to the antecedent of the given information, and trusts that subsequent developments in the conversation will affirm that the choice made was correct.

Clark and Haviland suggest that violations of the given-new contract may be the result of negligence, may result from a conscious intent to deceive, or may be the result of an explicit attempt to induce implicature. In the case of a negligent violation of the given-new contract, S either misjudges what H knows or doesn't know, or does not trouble to take H's knowledge into account. In a covert violation, H is a victim of the fact that S has deliberately induced him to construct in memory an antecedent for a given that in fact does not exist. Explicit violations are designed to manipulate or confuse H's inference processes. For example, in a joke, or pun, humor may arise from the fact that there are two equally plausible antecedents for the same "old" informaton, as in the joke, "Did you hear about the hockey match between the two leper colonies? There was a face-off in the corner."

When S violates the antecedence maxim, for whatever reason, H has recourse to several procedures (Clark & Haviland, 1977). For example, for explicit violations, H may make sense or get the point of an utterance by supplying a *bridging proposition*; that is, "form an *indirect* antecedent by building an inferential bridge from something he already knows" (Clark & Haviland, 1977, p. 6). For some utterances, the listener must *add* to memory, if only tentatively, a "new node" to stand as the unique antecedent. Given an utterance like "The man from Mars told me that . . ." H can adopt the *et cetera* position and hope that subsequent events will supply the missing antecedent: "The man from Mars told me that candy bars are going to go up to 50¢."

Propositional Approaches

Clark and Haviland and Schank are exemplars of the "local" approach to conversational coherence; a sort of chaining notion in which the topic changes with each successive utterance (Tracy, 1982). In contrast, advocates of the *propositional* approach view topic as being "about" a proposition, specifically a *macroproposition* or *global topic* (van Dijk, 1980, 1981; Foster & Subsay, 1982; Sabsay & Foster, 1982) that is the most parsimonious summary of the topic (Foster & Sabsay, 1982, p. 10). Conversational coherence is not just a matter of semantic links at the level of individual utterances; rather, coherence derives from an over-arching proposition, in light of which successive utterances are interpreted and constructed (van Dijk, 1981, p. 84). From the propositional perspective, a "topic" is about the relationship between "an argument and a proposition relevant to a context" (Reinhart, 1981, p. 61). Let us sample some definitions. Hobbs (1978, p. 8) defines topic as "the proposition about which some claim is being made or elicited." Keenan and Schieffelin (1976, p. 344), treat topic as the "primary presupposition" of an utterance; "the PROPOSITION (or propositions) about which the speaker is either providing or requesting new information" (p. 338). The point is that topic is not just about some entity, but rather that topic has to do with some *predication* with respect to one or more entities. Sabsay and Foster (1982) argue that this notion is supported by much research on recall of discourse.

The notion of a topical *macrostructure* (van Dijk, 1980, 1981) is that topic is a tree-like nexus of hierarchically ordered propositions, some of which correspond to actual utterances and some of which are implicit, having been furnished by the participants in the form of bridging propositions, presuppositions, additions, and the like. Each proposition in the macrostructure has a demonstrable relation not only to the macroproposition, but also to the immediately higher node (Foster & Sabsay, 1982, p. 17). A macrostructure is understood as a "global" representation of a conversation, with its "psychological correlate" a "cognitive schema which determines the planning, execution, understanding, storage, and reproduction of the discourse" (van Dijk, 1981, p. 188). The hypothesis of a macrostructure accounts for the ability of persons to provide summaries of and answer questions about a conversational event long after individual utterances have departed from memory (van Dijk, 1981, p. 210). In describing macrostructure, one might say that they are "built up" from individual utterances. Operating on utterances are a variety of *macrorules*, of which we will have more to say later, which "map sequences of propositions onto sequences of (macro)propositions" (van Dijk, 1981, p. 188).

Before we proceed further with the notion of how discourses are mapped onto macrostructures, we need to introduce the notion of a *context set* (Foster & Sabsay, 1982), to which we have in a fashion made reference before with the Clark and Haviland concept of an *information structure*. Karttunen and Peters (1979) also dealt with the notion of a context set under the rubric *common ground*. A context set is a stored tree of propositions (Foster & Sabsay, 1982, pp. 27-28) against which each new utterance is interpreted; a pool (Reinhart, 1981, p. 78) of the textual propositions and presuppositions "which we accept as true at this point." What is in the context set, of course, will probably not be the same for S and H, although they will behave as it were. Karttunen (1977, p. 150) treats context as a "set of logical forms" descriptive of the body of presuppositions to which the speaker assumes that he or she and other conversationalists jointly describe.

It is appropriate to view the context set as changing and evolving incrementally with each successive utterance: "when a participant says something, thereby advancing the conversation to a new point, the new set of common presumptions reflects the change from the preceding set in terms of adjunction, replacement, or excision of propositions" (Karttunen & Peters, 1979, pp. 13-14). Several authors have examined the notion of local incrementation of the context set. Werth (1981) asserts that it is a matter of negotiation between speaker and hearer. Both Gazdar (1979) and McCawly (1979) speak to the notion that the context set is subject to *temporary incrementation*; that is, that it is composed of *potential presuppositions* and propositions that are subject to excision should conversational developments render them inapplicable. As Werth put it, the incrementation process is rarely smooth, and the idea of a "pending file" is quite attractive (1981, p. 149).

Let us look more closely for a moment at the notion of presupposition. In addition to explicit propositions as they are contained in utterances, the context set also contains some subset of the propositional inferences supplied by the parties to facilitate the comprehension of each others' locutions. Crothers (1978) has suggested a few of the kinds of inferences (inferred propositions) that might be part of the context set for making sense of a discourse. We will mention two of them. First, *a priori presuppositions* are those that are temporally prior to a particular text, or the discourse it records; a priori presuppositions cannot be derived from any other presupposition internal to the actual body of utterances. In the following dialogue, a fragment of a conversation between a dyad in a laboratory setting where an audio recorder was plainly visible, an a priori presupposition of the explicit text is that "we are here for a research project;" further, that "two strangers are being forced to converse." (In subsequent text, examples from this laboratory-generated corpus will be marked with an asterisk.)

B: No-we not-we need to talk now.
        It's not relaxed in here.
A: (I know. Well . . .
B: Just tension. It's this thing runnin' here.

A priori presuppositions serve to provide a sense of episodic unity and mutual orientation.

Also pertinent to the context set are *a posteriori presuppositions* (Crothers, 1978, p. 60), which can be derived as consequents of propositions explicit in the text. These propositional inferences, also called *consequent presuppositions*, have the function of linking earlier parts of the explicit text to later parts (Crothers, 1978, p. 61). In the following excerpt, also from the laboratory study cited above, one of the consequent presuppositions of B's explicit utterances is "B doesn't have to go and do something," which leads A to tap into his world knowledge about options for women and propose a plausible alternative to "doing;"

B: Well but I mean there's no-this may sound real bad but*
        there's not as much pressure on- I mean like for guys you
        have to go and you know do somethin' you know, I mean . . .
A: Oh, so you're lookin' for a M.R.S. degree.

The presence of consequent presuppositions in the context set serves to facilitate the coherence of a conversation by virtue of exhibiting the connections among its several parts.

Ordering of propositions. The organization of propositions in a context set is hierarchically structured, such that an overriding proposition is at the uppermost node (Foster & Sabsay, 1982, p. 17). Cues as to the appropriate ordering of propositions, explicit and otherwise, in the set may be present in such features of the conversation as clause order, stress, intonation pattern, and so on. Clark and Haviland (1977, p. 11) propose that focal stress is associated with the new as opposed to the given information in a sentence. Werth (1981, p. 153) describes what he calls the "machinery of *emphasis-placement*," whereby "non-anaphoric items are focused, positively anaphoric items are reduced, and negatively anaphoric items are contrastive." Wilson and Sperber (1979) also emphasize the utility of focal stress in ordering the implications of a proposition.

Clause order also provides information as to the relative importance of an utterance within the context set. Van Dijk (1981, pp. 139-143) provides a set of principles governing the ordering of presupposed and new information: (1) if one fact causes another, then normally the causal fact is stated first (thus, "The sink is clogged. I'm calling the plumber." is more common than "I'm calling the plumber. The sink is clogged"); (2) if we observe that some fact p is temporally prior to some other fact q, we might conclude that the linear ordering implies that q is a consequence of p; (3) what the hearer already knows normally comes first; "the sequence of assertions must respect the structure of presupposition and information distribution" (van Dijk, 1981, p. 142); (4) all the needed "premises, backings, and warrants" must be supplied for each assertion (1981, p. 142).

Macrorules. Van Dijk (1980, 1981) has also provided a set of macrorules that may be understood as possible operations on the context set that result in a global structure: the rules "derive macro-structures from microstructures" (1980, p. 46). Macrorules reduce, abstract, and organize: they generally model which information in the discourse is important. Macrorules are described by van Dijk as inference procedures that link propositions in a text to propositions used to define its global concern (1980, p. 46). The most basic such procedure is that of *deletion-selection*. All propositions that are not presupposed by other propositions are excised; to turn it around, all propositions that are necessary for the interpretation of other propositions are retained. Thus, for example, one might delete trivial details of a description.

A second macrorule is *generalization* (van Dijk, 1980, p. 47): the procedure is to construct from several micropropositions a more general proposition, grouping the thematic participants and subsuming the predicates of the respective micropropositions in such a manner as to disregard the "variation between participants and their properties." This all of course assumes that there is a higher-order concept or concepts that organize the encounter. If not, such a rule cannot apply (van Dijk, 1980, p. 50). The procedure is constrained by the stipulation that the *least possible* generalization be made: that is, that we take only the immediately higher superset. Thus, for example, if propositions had been expressed about the clerical behaviors of Judy, Gail, and Maria, we might have "secretaries" as a thematic participant in the more general proposition, but not "women." There will usually be some "upper bound" to the generalization process (van Dijk, 1980, p. 49).

The *construction* macrorule stipulates that a proposition be formed that subsumes what the micropropositions denote as the *"normal components, conditions, or consequences"* of some global fact (van Dijk, 1980, p. 48). The macroproposition denotes a sequence of actions or subissues that, considered jointly, constitute the global act or issue denoted by the macroproposition. For example, a narrative in which such disparate actions as approaching a salesclerk, complaining that a purchase was defective, and receiving a refund are all represented in single propositional utterances (or even several sequences of utterances), can be constructed as a new proposition, with a new predicate, *returning* a purchase, which denotes the complex events of which the other propositions each represent a part. Van Dijk notes that only sequences that fit in with conventional schemas or scripts can be handled by such a rule; thus, if the narrative were to include a digressive microproposition about complimenting the sales clerk on her earrings, either a new macroproposition would have to be constructed or the microproposition deleted.

Local propositional coherence relations. What are some of the ways in which propositions as expressed in conversation can be seen to cohere on an utterance-by-utterance basis? That is, in terms of topic or the propositional structure of conversation, what are some of the demonstrably "relevant" ways in which S can continue speaking, or H can respond to an immediately prior utterance?

A: I saw Ted at the beach and
B: (Ted who?

Hobbs (1978, p. 10) has characterized local or utterance-by-utterance coherence relations as being like "conventionalized ways of being reminded of things." Hobbs proposes four classes of coherence relations: (1) *Strong Temporal Relations;* (2) *Evaluation;* (3) *Linkage Relations;* (4) *Expansion Relations.* Under the heading Strong Temporal Relations, Hobbs first examines the *occasion* relation. An occasion relation is said to hold between two utterances if the second proposes that there is a change the final outcome of which is implicit in the first utterance; for example:

A: My VCR is broken again.
B: Are you gonna have it repaired?

Similarly, an occasion relation pertains when implicit in the first utterance is a state which is the beginning state of the change asserted in the second (Hobbs, 1978, p. 14):

A: I think I'd like to get my hair cut.
B: Yeah, real short would be nice for the summer.

In an *enablement* relation (see also de Beaugrande, 1980) the state implied in the first proposition can be inferred to enable the state or event asserted in the second:

A: Dina said she'd watch Julia Sunday afternoon.
B: Good, then I can work on my book.

In a *causal* relation (called a "joining relation" by Reichman, 1978), a causal chain is asserted or may be inferred from a state implied in the first proposition to one implied in the second:

A: I drank too much last night.
B: No wonder you have a headache.

Hobbs's second category, *evaluation*, refers primarily to feedback utterances, in which there appears to be a relationship between the second utterance and some goal of the speaker implicit in the first utterance:

A: Could you loan me ten dollars?
B: Are you crazy? You still owe me twenty-five!

Linkage relations occur when it is necessary to ground or provide context for a first utterance: they grow out of a need to link new information to that which is old knowledge to the hearer (Hobbs, 1978, p. 18). Two types of linkage relations are identified: (1) *Background* linkage occurs when the second utterance provides information which is functional in the succeeding conversation:

(2) *Explanation* linkage occurs when that which is bizarre, rare, or different in the first utterance is connected in the second to the hearer's background knowledge:

A: Joanne walked right past me today in the gym
and didn't speak.
B: She probably wasn't wearing her glasses.

Finally, Hobbs proposes that utterance-by-utterance linkage is often a matter of *expansion* (1978, p. 21). Two propositions may display a *parallel* linkage, by which some predication may be inferred of entities in both propositions, both entities belonging to some "independently definable subclass:"

A: I've go a reaction paper due for Jones
next Thursday.
B: Mine's due on Tuesday.

Generalization linkages (see also Reichman, 1978) occur when the second proposition allows one to infer some predication of a superset (A), and the first the same predication of some member (a) of (A):

A: John left his underwear on the bathroom floor again
this morning.
B: All men are slobs.

Exemplification (called an "Illustrative Relation" by Reichman, 1978) linkages occur when the second proposition is a specific instance of the first:

A: The Dean never gives you an answer right away.
B: Yeah, he said he'd mull it over and get back to me.

Contrast is the negation of a *parallel* linkage, in that although thematic participants in two propositions belong to the same superset, the predication to be inferred from the first proposition cannot be inferred from the second (Hobbs, 1978, p. 24):

A: The people in my apartment building aren't very friendly.
B: Gee, my neighbors are really friendly.

Elaboration linkage occurs when the same proposition may be inferred from two adjacent utterances, but one of the "arguments" of the proposition is specified more completely in the second:

A: I feel so good since I started jogging.
B: Really feel like you're getting in shape?

De Beaugrande (1980) uses the expression "class inclusion links" for Expansion relations.

De Beaugrande (1980) has collected a set of so-called LINK-types for follow-up questions, which would appear to have implications for studying the relevance of continuations in general. Using the example of possible responses to a narrative, these include "Why did you do that? (*reason-of*); What happened then? (*proximity-in-time-to*)"; "What was your purpose in doing that? (*purpose-of*); When did that happen? (*time-of*); Where did that happen? (*location-of*)"; "How did you find out? (*apperception-of*)"; and so on (italics mine; de Beaugrande, 1980, p. 248). De Beaugrande suggested a "maxim" of sorts, though it appears to be more on the order of a continuation strategy: *"Select an active node of the discourse world and pursue from it a pathway whose linkage or goal node is problematic or variable"* (italics mine; 1980, p. 248). For example, one might inquire as to the reason for an unusual action.

Coherence relations among context spaces. Reichman (1978) has directed her attention to the coherence relations among structured units she calls "context spaces." A context space is a sequence of utterances that taken together constitute a unit or whole. Local utterance-by-utterance relationships depend upon whether or not the pair occupy the same context space, or if not upon the nature of the connections between the spaces to which they respectively belong. There appear to be two fundamental types of context spaces, according to Reichman. An *Issue* context space is concerned with some issue, the actors involved in it, when and for how long it was (is) an issue, and so on. An *Event* context space is concerned with some particular episode and the sequence of events that constituted it, along with actors, a time and place, a "point-of-view" expressed by the space, and so on. In the following fragment, for example, the Issue context space is from lines 5-6, and the Event space from lines 1-5:

```
1   A:   Gosh!*
2   B:   I thought he'd shoot himself. Sit down
3        and sort them.
4   A:   Were they numbered?
5   B:   Naa. In BA we have T.V. screens. No
6        cards to worry about.
```

The Issue space here corresponds to Ryave's (1978) notion of a "significance statement."

While much of conversational activity is not so easily parceled into Events and Issues, Reichman's categories of context space relationships are worth mentioning, because from them she develops some interesting rules for making appropriate continuations, which we shall explore shortly. Reichman's *Illustrative Relation* occurs between an Event context space and a prior Issue context space that the event exemplifies. A *Generalization Relation* occurs when an Event context space is followed by an Issue space in which the issue is a generalization of the Event. These two relations are like Hobbs' Expansions except that they apply to relationships between (potentially) longer stretches of discourse than single utterances. Similarly, Reichman's *Joining Relation* treats the Issue of a first context space as the cause of a second.

While illustration, generalization, and joining refer to kinds of semantic coherence, having to do with the nature of the propositions being expressed, others of Reichman's context space relationships have to do with the structural links between context spaces. In a *Restatement Relation*, the connection between Issue and Event is restated in order to close off the topic. In a *Return Relation*, S or H goes back to a former Issue or Event space following a digression. In an *Interruption Relation*, the connection between context spaces is that one is a digression from the other. In a *Total Shift Relation*, a succeeding context space introduces a topic completely unrelated to a former context space that has been exhausted (Reichman, 1978, p. 297). If S can be said in some sense to "know" some of these relations, she will know how to behave appropriately in the matter of topic management. In the next section, we discuss a set of rules that Reichman and other scholars have proposed for the proper interpretation, exploitation, and handling of issues related to topic.

Rules for Topic Management

To be guided by rules about topic management presupposes that an actor has an intuitive notion of topic and that he is sensitive to topic boundaries. What evidence is there that language users are competent at identifying topics and topic boundaries? Planalp and Tracy (1980) had 40 subjects view videotapes and read transcripts, and 20 subjects read transcripts only, of two 30-minute conversations. Subjects were asked to segment the transcripts into topics, using brackets to indicate where topic shifts occurred. Reliabilities for topic shifts were quite high: .926 for the first conversation and .919 for the second. Having viewed the videotape did not appear particularly to facilitate the placement of topic boundaries on the transcript. Verbal cues alone appeared to be sufficient to locate changes in topic. Along the same lines, Schwarz (1982) had native English speakers mark topic boundaries on a transcript of a doctor-patient interview. Subjects generally concurred as to the location of topic shifts, although naive language users were somewhat less adept at the task than linguists. In general, the evidence seems to indicate that language users recognize topic boundaries without difficulty.

Of particular interest to scholars are those cues that are available to the ordinary language user to detect topic shifts. Reichman (1978) has identified a number of linguistic features which correspond to context space transitions. First, there are certain *clue words* that mark that a shift is forthcoming. "Like" suggests that there is about to be a transition from an Issue context space to an Event space. "Incidentally" signals that a digression (the Interruption Relation) is about to occur. "So" suggests that a topic is being closed. "Anyway" signals that a digression is concluded and a former Issue or Event space will be subject to a Return (Reichman, 1978, pp. 307-309). Clue words may (1) signal that S is moving from one context space into another; (2) comment on the state of the immediately previous context space; or (3) hint at the context space that is to come.

A second class of topic shift cues consists of labeled markers such as "speaking of X" (called *marked repeats* by Jefferson, 1978). The category *disjunct* marker includes, "Oh, I forgot to tell you that X," "not to change the topic but . . .", "which reminds me," and so forth. These devices display S's sensitivity to conversational rules and concerns for easing H's processing task; given such a marker, H will not have to flounder about searching for an implicit proposition that will bridge the apparently unrelated context spaces. The "aboutness" of a topic may also be marked by the extent of pronomial reference to thematic participants (Reichman, 1978; van Dijk, 1981, p. 185). The *focus* or overall priority accorded to an entity in the discourse as a unit determines the way in which that element is referred to; those entities that are high priority or in high focus are usually pronomialized after the first reference, while names or descriptions are characteristically used to refer to entities of lesser importance (Reichman, 1978):

1 **A:**   What do you think about Khomeini?*
2 **B:**   He's pretty bad, but I guess
3 **A:**   (Why do you say
4   he's bad?

5	**B:**	Cause, well, he has a lot of influence on his
6		people you know and he just
7	**A:**	Well don't you think his interests and his
8		uh objective to reach what he's tryin' to
9		do are justified?
10	**B:**	What *is* he tryin' to do? What do you
11		think he's tryin' to do?
12	**A:**	He's tryin' to bring attention to what
13		went on in Iran.
14	**B:**	With the Shah and everything?
15	**A:**	Yeah, see the Shah—he left the country
16		because of the Shah.

Note that subsequent to the first reference to Khomeini in line 1, the pronouns *he* and *his* are consistently used. The Shah is a lesser character in the Issue space, and consequently is named, while Khomeini, who is still in high focus (that is, the passage is about some property of Khomeini), continues to be referred to as *he*.

Reichman also proposes that repetitions may be used to mark the return to an Issue or Event space following a digression. Such devices have been called "embedded repeats" by Jefferson (1978), and have been found by McLaughlin et al., (1981) to discriminate between males and females in terms of their frequency of use in marking relationships between stories in conversation.

Finally, Reichman notes that a tense shift may coincide with a transition from one context space to another. For example, a tense shift at line 9 is coincident with a transition from an Issue to an Event space:

1	**A:**	You know those cabbies, those cabbies*
2		over there- the cab drivers?
3	**B:**	OO:h?
4	**A:**	I don't know, they're just crazy. They're
5		always out hustling to take you. They'll
6		take you anywhere you want to go for a
7		dollar, you know=
		( )
8	**B:**	Yeah.
9	**A:**	=and once we said, well, we want to go
10		to the bar to this one- to this one cabby . . .
		(McLaughlin et al., 1981, p. 100)

(A tense shift is certainly not an infallible transition marker, however, since many storytellers, including A in the remainder of the episode above, move easily and unself-consciously back and forth between the past and present tenses even during narrative.)

Foster and Sabsay (1982), reporting on data collected by Schwarz (1982), list a number of markers of change in the direction of the conversation that readers of an interview transcript appeared to use to determine topic boundaries. All of the subjects commented on the presence of such *frames* (Sinclair & Coulthard, 1975) as "now," "alright," "well," and "right." (Experience suggests that frames like these are primarily encountered in situations in which one of the parties is given more or less exclusive control of the floor, as is the case for teachers in Sinclair and Coulthard's classroom situations or the questioner in an interview setting.) Foster and Sabsay (1982) go on to suggest that topic boundaries often appear to coincide with the boundaries of speech act sequences. For example, in the following dialogue a topic shift at line 11 takes up simultaneously with the first pair part of a question/answer sequence; working backward, it occurs immediately following B's partial "confession" in a protracted accusation-grant/denial sequence:

1	**A:**	Oh, so you're looking for an M.R.S.*
		degree.
2	**B:**	No, no, no, I'm not really.
3	**A:**	Yes you are.
4	**B:**	No I'm not.
5	**A:**	Ha ha. Yes you are.
6	**B:**	No, I'm not. But I'm gonna have more
7		time to-there's not as much pressure-
8		put it that way.
9	**A:**	That's uh- female chauvinism right there.
10	**B:**	I know. But too bad. I don't care.
11	**A:**	(Well, how
12		do you feel about ERA?

Finally, topic shift may be signaled by a cessation of reference to "thematic participants and their anaphors" (Foster & Sabsay, 1982, p. 11).

Assuming that there is a sufficiency of material available in an explicit sequence of utterances for ordinary language users to recognize topics and their boundaries, what rules for the management of topic can we propose? Interesting work along these lines has been done by Planalp and Tracy (1980) on topic shifts, and by Tracy (1982) and Reichman (1978) on topic continuation. Planalp and Tracy were concerned with the perceived competence of a speaker's choice of topic shift mechanism. They proposed a typology of change strategies based on three dimensions: (1) *contextual focus*—whether or not the topic to which S shifts can be understood by reference to the conversation itself, or whether it depends for its interpretation on information external to the conversation; (2) *accessibility of context*—whether information needed for processing is immediately accessible in memory, or must be retrieved; (3) *designation of context*—whether or not the source of context is explicitly cited by S. From 30-minute taped conversations, Planalp and Tracy drew samples of the eight types of topic shift generated from all possible combinations of the three dimensions, and had subjects rate each of 24 topic-change excerpts (three examples of each of the eight categories) against scales measuring speaker competence, ease of information integration, and speaker involvement and attentiveness. When all such judgments were combined into a single competence scale, it appeared that the most competent topic-switch type was an *immediate* shift, essentially without regard for whether the source of context was marked or not. That is, subjects preferred topic changes in which the new topic is relevant to the immediately prior topic.

Generally, Planalp and Tracy found that explicit marking of a topic change was judged about equally competent to implicit marking. Rated least competent were environmentally contexted shifts, in which the speaker grounded a new topic not in the conversation but in something going on external to the conversation—for example, a passing acquaintance or some aspect of the speaker's physiological state upon which he feels obliged to comment (Planalp & Tracy, 1980, p. 245). Planalp and Tracy concluded that the rule to be derived from their observations of judgments of topic change devices is that the *speaker should manage topics so as to meet the information-processing needs of the listener*. That is, it is important that the context for a topic change be *accessible* to the hearer; she should not have to undertake an exhaustive search, nor struggle to supply a bridging proposition as coherence is strained to its limits. The burden of relevancy is, in effect, on the shoulders of the speaker. One other rule suggested by the Planalp and Tracy study is that in switching topics, *conversation-centered topics should be selected as opposed to those suggested by the extra-conversational environment*. This preference for a conversationally contexted topic may have to do with hearer's processing capacities; just as likely, it derives from hearers' vanity and the "support-your-hearer" maxim.

Both Tracy (1982) and Reichman (1978) have been concerned with the notion of what types of topic continuations are most appropriate. Tracy hypothesized that given a fragment of conversation that contained both an Issue and an Event, most people would choose the

Issue as the topic of the passage. (This is consistent with the hypothesis of macrostructures.) Looking at the rated appropriateness of different continuation types, Tracy found that Issue-oriented continuations were rated as more appropriate than Event-oriented continuations when a preceding topic contained both an Issue and an Event. Consider the following discourse, which contains both kinds of context spaces, and the relative propriety of each of two possible continuations of the discourse:

1	**A:**	Everybody out here is so impressed
2		by money. Like this girl in my class
3		she said her roommate won't go out with
4		a guy unless she's checked out his
5		watch and his shoes.
6	**B₁:**	Did she say what kind of shoes they
7		have to have?
8	**B₂:**	I know. They always seem to be
9		competing with each other to see who
10		can wear the most designer labels
11		at the same time.

Although both B_1 and B_2 are locally coherent, B_1, by being an event-oriented continuation, seems somehow less responsive to the gist of A's utterance than B_2, which addresses itself to the issue raised in lines 1 and 2. Tracy found that when the conversational segments judged did *not* appear to be informed by an issue, event-oriented continuations were regarded as more appropriate. Tracy concluded (1982, p. 297) that "the rule is this: *A conversant should respond to the issue of his or her partner's talk*" (italics mine). This rule, which we could sum up as a ban on "tangential talk" (McLaughlin et al., 1981) requires that *in the presence of a context space in which an Event is exemplifying an Issue, to comment upon an element in the Event that is not a further instance of the Issue is inappropriate* (Reichman, 1978). Further, *any element in the Event space in an Illustrative Relation should be assigned a low focus level* (Reichman, 1978).

Reichman proposed a number of additional rules for managing topic and making appropriate continuations. For example, *if a context space has been interrupted by a digression, it is inappropriate to digress from the digression to introduce a new context space* (Reichman, 1978, p. 324). Thus, in the following segment, A and B

have an obligation to return to the topic from which they detoured at
line 6:

1	**B:**	When are you leaving for Dallas?
2	**A:**	I don't know. I wonder should I take
3		that flight that leaves from LAX Friday
4		at 8:15. That's the one John always
5		takes and he said
6	**B:**	(Who's John?
7	**A:**	My brother.
8	**B:**	Oh, yeah. How often does he go there?
9	**A:**	Three or four times a year when they
10		have the big shows.
11	**B:**	Uh huh.
12	**A:**	So anyhow that's the one I'll probably
		take.

FUNCTIONAL ORGANIZATION

In examining the functional organization of conversation, we are
interested in how *action* is organized in talk. Specifically, we're
concerned with the structure of the pragmatic aspects of language-in-
use; that is, with the appropriateness of language action in context.
Functional structure may be distinguished from propositional or
topical structure in that the former relates to the organization of
action as it is manifested in sequences of utterances, while the latter
refers to the organization of ideas. This boils down to a simple
distinction between what we are saying in an utterance (its propositional or locutionary aspect) and what we are doing in it—its status as
an *illocutionary* act. According to Austin (1962), to perform a
locutionary act is to utter "certain noises" (a "phonetic" act); to utter
certain "vocables or words" (a "phatic" act); and to use sentences
with an essentially specific sense and reference, or meaning (a
"rhetic" act; pp. 92-93). An illocutionary act, if successfully
performed, produces a particular effect on the hearer; to wit, it
produces *uptake* in the hearer of the speaker's *intention* in saying that
thus-and-so. Van Dijk (1980, p. 178) proposes that the salient
distinction between locution and illocution is that the former may be
accomplished when one is alone, while the latter requires an audience
and at least some rudimentary goal to alter the world model of the
hearer.

The Illocutionary Act

The same act may of course have both a locutionary and an illocutionary force. Illocutionary force goes beyond the notion that H recognizes an utterance as a sentence in a particular language with a definite sense and reference; the illocutionary force of an utterance lies in its recognizable intent. That is, illocutionary force is satisfied if H recognizes what S had in mind or intended to do in saying that X (Bach & Harnish, 1979). This does not necessarily mean, according to the classic notion of an illocutionary act, that some alteration of the hearer's world model is effected: "in the case of illocutionary acts we succeed in doing what we are trying to do by getting our audience to recognize what we are trying to do. But the effect on the hearer is not a belief or a response, it consists simply in the hearer understanding the utterance of the speaker" (Searle, 1969, p. 47). Thus, the illocutionary force of an act consists in the recognition of the speaker's purpose in uttering that X, and not in the effect that the utterance might have had on the hearer. The latter is called the "perlocutionary effect." An intended perlocutionary effect is equivalent to the goal the illocutionary act is designed to realize (Jackson & Jacobs, in press; Ferrara, 1980a).

Bach and Harnish (1979) have proposed a taxonomy of so-called *communicative illocutionary acts*. These are acts in which S not only expresses her intended-to-be-recognized attitude toward the propositional content of the utterance, but also her intent to have some effect on the hearer. For example, to apologize is not only to convey that one regrets doing an action, but also to induce the hearer to recognize that the speaker wants H to regard her as contrite. Whether or not H accepts the apology is another matter; what is important is that H treat it as an apology. Bach and Harnish have proposed that there are four basic categories of communicative illocutionary acts: *constatives*, *directives*, *commissives*, and *acknowledgments*. Constatives are acts that express the speaker's beliefs together with his intent that H adopt a similar belief (Bach & Harnish, 1979, p. 41). The constative class includes such acts as predicting, informing, suggesting, asserting, and describing. Directives express the stance of the speaker with respect to a potential action by H together with S's desire that his wish for the action be taken as a sufficient motive for H to perform it; directives include requests, questions, advice, prohibitions, and so forth. Commissives express S's willingness to perform some future action and his desire that H recognize that a commitment is being made. The commissive class includes such acts as promising and offering. Finally, acknowledgments is a diffuse category of acts expressing feelings toward the hearer or acts of the hearer, including such actions as apologizing, congratulating, thanking, accepting, and rejecting.

Speakers have the knowledge needed to perform illocutionary acts by virtue of constitutive rules that lay out what it is that makes up the act of requesting, apologizing, advising, and so on. Such definitions usually consist of a set of preconditions that must be met in order for the act to be performed successfully. For example, Searle (1969) has formulated a set of conditions under which an utterance by S can be said to count as a particular act; that is, for its performance to be "happy" or "felicitous" (Austin, 1962). Cohen and Perrault (1979) give an example of the happy performance of a request, using Searle's conditions. First, the input-output conditions have to be normal. S should be capable of speaking and H should be capable of hearing. Second, the propositional content of the utterance must predicate some future action of the hearer ("S will pass the salt). Third, certain preparatory conditions must be met, such as that H be capable of performing the action, and that the speaker believes that this is the case; further, that it is not obvious to the speaker that H will eventually perform the action without benefit of a request. Fourth, a request can only be performed happily if the speaker is *sincere*; if it is true that she wants H to perform the action. Finally, the *force condition* (Cohen & Perrault, 1979, p. 188) requires that the speaker not undertake the speech act unless he intends to communicate that he is indeed making a request. S must want H to recognize that S wants her to perform some action.

In classical speech act theory (Austin, 1962; Searle, 1969), much interest centered on explicit *performatives*: verbs in English that when uttered are said to count as the performance of some act, such as "I advise you to do A" or "I warn you not to do A." Searle's claim has been that for any speech act, there is some English sentence whose utterance is a realization of the act. Gazdar (1981, pp. 78-79) argues that there are numerous contexts in which "asserting, requesting, questioning and so on are possible acts" and "utterances of the corresponding performative sentences are not possible ways of achieving those acts." Edmondson (1981a, 1981b) rejects the performative analysis that one is actually *doing* in saying that X. He prefers what he calls a *descriptivist* position: that there are certain English verbs that describe what it is that S claims to be doing in an utterance. According to Edmondson conventional treatments of illocutionary force are defective because, for example, they overlook such cases as "I'll be there, and that's a promise," in which the illocutionary verb is being used as a description (1981b, p. 23) or "I won't get killed, darling, I promise," in which a problem is posed by the nonliteral usage of the illocutionary verb (1981b, p. 24). Edmondson's position is basically that the illocutionary force of a speech act is a function of its treatment by H in the discourse, not in terms of whether or not H does what S wants, but in terms of whether H recognizes the utterance as a request or promise, and so on. Further, there are some acts that have to be achieved cooperatively between S and H; it is not sufficient for their achievement that S just do them unilaterally.

Edmondson poses a number of serious challenges to the traditional speech act approach. First, Edmondson (1981b) argues that Searle's characterization of illocutionary acts is inadequate. To continue with our example of the performance of requests, the beliefs of S with respect to H's capacity for performing an action are not always transparent given only the discourse as a resource. What is or is not "obvious" to S about the intentions of H with respect to doing the action is usually not open for inspection either (Edmondson, 1981b, p. 21). Second, the sincerity condition is not particularly useful, since under the Gricean cooperative principle sincerity is taken for granted. Edmondson concludes that Searle's characterization refers not to conversational units but rather to "concepts evoked by a set of lexical items in English-illocutionary verbs" (1981b, p. 23).

Gazdar (1981) has been concerned with the relationship between utterances and the actions they are said to achieve; that is, with the problem of *speech act assignment*. How is it that we know what S is doing in saying that X? If there is some function that maps utterances onto acts, what are the properties of such a function? One thing that seems clear is that different speech acts can manifest the same illocutionary force; thus "I'll be home by six-thirty," "I'll have it to you first thing Monday morning," and "I'll never leave you" all have the illocutionary force of a promise even though they are distinct acts. Gazdar (1981, p. 69) concludes that any function that assigns speech acts to utterances is at best a partial function, since there will be some contexts for which the function will be undefined (for example, one cannot "happily" promise to do something yesterday).

A second problem with finding an assignment function is that while Heringer (1972) and Sadock (1979) argue that for each utterance (or sentence) there is only one associated illocutionary force, Gazdar finds such a claim to be false. Searle (1975) and others have claimed of so-called double-duty utterances that one of their meanings is literal, not that they have two associated illocutionary forces. Consider the utterance "Do you mind if I borrow your pencil?"; inasmuch as either a response of "No" or "Sure" could be heard as meaning that the pencil may be borrowed, it would appear that there are two distinct illocutions at work, one constituting a request, the other constituting an inquiry into one of the preconditions for carrying out the requested action.

A final problem with an assignment function, Gazdar concludes, is that very often the actual utterance "may not of itself determine the illocutionary force component of any of the speech acts assigned to it" (1981, p. 76).

Levinson's assessment of the utility of speech act theory in modeling conversational behaviors is equally unenthusiastic. His basic claim is that speech act theory yields neither a finite set of analytical categories nor a "small but powerful" set of interpretive procedures, but rather "a huge and *ad hoc* set of conventional rules" (1981, p. 106). Levinson, as well as Gazdar, rejects the notion that there is a "specifiable conventional procedure" for speech act assignment (1981, p. 98). Like Gazdar, Levinson argues that some utterances seem to realize more than one act at the same time. His example is "Would you like another drink?" which is simultaneously a question and an offer, as indicated by the most probable reply, "Yes, I would," part of which acknowledges the offer and part of which responds to the question. Of course, it could be argued that the way in which an offer is made in polite company is indirect, by inquiring about the preconditions of acceptance; consequently, such an utterance is heard as having the single illocutionary force of offering. However, not all such double-duty utterances work in this way, and the problem thus posed for the notion of an assignment function is a real one. Levinson argues that, at least in theory, the set of act-interpretations for some utterances is indefinitely large (1981, p. 100); he complains further that often the interpretation of what act has taken place must be inferred from the "slot" it occupies in a sequence.

A second problem with the idea of a speech act assignment function is that the motives of speakers in uttering something are often complex and unavailable to the observer (Levinson, 1981). Trying to specify an assignment function means grappling with the fact that for any utterance there is a limitless variety of projected intents that

Hearer might reasonably attribute to S. With respect to this problem, Edmondson argues for an ad hoc assignment procedure in which to determine what an utterance counts as, we examine how it is treated in the conversation; that is, examine the behavior to which it leads.

Levinson further argues that speech act models seem to be linked to the notion of "sentence," and that this is not always the appropriate unit at which to assign action or intention. Here Levinson seems to be attacking a straw man; his claim is that utterance units and act units are not independently identifiable. While this may be the case in the classical speech act framework, there are schemes available (for example, Stiles, 1978; Auld & White, 1956) for segmenting discourse into propositional units, without regard for the kinds of acts they might perform. Of course there are the troublesome questions of silences, which can't be unitized at the semantic level and yet clearly function as speech acts on some occasions, and the case of utterances such as "Yeah" and "Uh huh," whose status as a unit of the discourse (back-channel versus thought unit) seems to depend upon the function they fulfill (Levinson, 1981, pp. 102-103).

Levinson concludes that an assignment function whose domain and range are poorly specified will be difficult to determine; he concurs with Gazdar's (1978) assessment that the mapping onto speech acts must be from sentence-context pairs and not sentences (1981, p. 104). Similarly, Ferrara (1980b) argues that an illocutionary act cannot "count" or be performed happily if it does not display the proper relationship to other acts in the sequence. Van Dijk (1981, p. 218) proposes that all of the following are taken into account by a hearer in determining the illocutionary force of an utterance: the grammatical mood of the utterance, nonverbal correlates of the utterance, perceptions of the present situation; knowledge of the speaker, knowledge about the superstructure or form of the episode, the relevant propositions and presuppositions, rules and norms, and other knowledge of the world. If indeed all of the foregoing is brought to bear, the search for a fully specified speech act assignment function is probably fruitless. For the conversational analyst, the most reasonable approach to the problem of assigning function to utterances, at least for the time being, has been provided by Edmondson (1981b, p. 50): "with regard to the identification of interactional moves, I propose a 'hearer-knows-best' principle, such that H's interpretation of S's behavior may be said to determine what S's behavior counts as at that point in time in the conversation." Such a principle must be applied with sufficient flexibility to allow for H's "updating" of her interpretation as subsequent conversational developments warrant.

Conditional Relevance

The most important source of functional organization at the local or utterance-by-utterance level is the notion of *conditional relevance* (Schegloff, 1972, p. 76):

> When one utterance (A) is conditionally relevant on another (S), then the occurrence of S provides for the relevance of the occurrence of A. If A occurs, it occurs (i.e., is produced and heard) as "responsive" to S, i.e., in a serial or sequenced relation to it; and, if it does not occur, its non-occurrence is an event, i.e., it is not only non-occurring (as is each member of an indefinitely extendable list of possible occurrences), it is absent, or "officially" or "notably" absent.

Schegloff and Sacks (1973, p. 296) propose that utterances circumscribe for subsequent turns a pertinent, finite range of actions that they may perform. As Firth (1964, p. 94) puts it, "the moment a conversation is started whatever is said is a determining condition for what in any reasonable expectation may follow." This aspect of local organization is termed "sequential implicativeness" by Jefferson (1978); each utterance may be seen to have an *occasioning* aspect as well. The idea of local occasioning and sequential implicativeness may be seen to coincide on a functional level with Schank's (1977) notions of Potential Topic and Reduced Old Topic at a semantic level. Goffman (1971) proposes that the demand for conditional relevance is so great that virtually any proposition can be interpreted as an appropriate reply if it occurs at the relevant point.

Adjacency pair organization. The prototypical instance of the requirement for conditional relevance in conversation is the *adjacency pair* (Schegloff, 1977, pp. 84-85). Adjacency pairs consist of sequences that properly have the following features:

(1) Two utterance length,

(2) Adjacent positioning of component utterances,

(3) Different speakers producing each utterance,

(4) Relative ordering of parts (i.e., first pair parts precede second pair parts), and

(5) Discrimination relations (i.e., the pair type of which a first pair part is a member is relevant to the selection among second pair parts.

Owen (1981) describes adjacency pairs as the smallest functional unit; unlike Schegloff, Owen puts the conditional linkage at the level of action rather than utterance. Goffman (1976, p. 257) refers to the pairs as "couplets" or "minimal dialogue units" tied to interactional moves, moves being defined so broadly that a silence following a first pair part will be regarded as a "rejoiner in its own right." Van Dijk (1981, p. 276) speaks of a principle of conditional connection by virtue of which an antecedent act alters the pragmatic features of context so that appropriateness conditions are laid down for the performance of a subsequent act; such pairs of acts are called "action-reaction pairs."

The first pair part of an adjacency pair, as an illocutionary act, establishes an expectation that in a second pair part H will comply with the "conventional perlocutionary effect" of the previous utterance (Jacobs & Jackson, 1979) by providing an answer to a question, complying with a request, and so on. A number of different adjacency pairs have been identified, including *question-answer*; *summons-answer*; *greeting-greeting*; *compliment-accept/reject*; *closing-closing*; *request-grant/deny*; *apology-accept/refuse*; *threat-response*; *insult-response*; *challenge-response*; *accuse-deny/confess*; *assertion-assent/dissent*; and *boast-appreciate/deride* (Jacobs & Jackson, 1979; Benoit, 1980). While we will consider these pairs in some detail in a subsequent chapter, we present a few examples here. We leave behind us for the moment the issue of speech act assignment, hoping that in the examples below the function assignments are relatively unambiguous.

(1)		**A:**	Too many Mexicans in there.*
	accuse	**B:**	Oh. You're prejudiced
	deny	**A:**	No. Well, you know, they just kinda take over.

(2)	request	A:	Just tell me about yourself.*
	deny	B:	Well, that's not fair.
	offer	A:	You want me to tell you about myself?
	accept	B:	Yeah, if you want to.

(3)	question	B:	Oo- you don't go into surgery, do you?*
	answer	A:	Yeah. No. I don't do it every day.
	question	B:	But you do stuff in there- like hand 'em the stuff?
	answer	A:	Hand 'em stuff or fold stuff out of the way.
	question	B:	Skin? Ha ha ha.
	answer	A:	Organs, skin.

(4)	insult	A:	You can't raise a kid in a small town* and expect him to be intelligent.	
	response	B:	Oh, now, wait a minute, that's an insult to me!	accuse
		A:	No, no, no, that's not an insult to you.	deny

B's utterance in (4) is a good example of a double-duty utterance in that in its retrospective aspect it functions as a response to A's insult (B is a small-town girl, as A knows), and in its prospective aspects it functions as an accusation to which A responds with a denial.

Goffman (1976, p. 263) has proposed that the generative mechanism for adjacency pairs lies in the fundamental requirement of the communication system for the provision of feedback. Speakers need to know if they have been heard, and if the hearing has been correct. They have to fill in the gaps in their knowledge, and count on the cooperation of others to supply the needed information. Similarly, no individual is totally self-sufficient, and requests must be granted or at least acknowledged. When an apology or explanation is offered, S needs to receive feedback in order to know when to cease accounting, whether to make restitution, and so on (Goffman, 1976).

Critique of the adjacency pair concept. While much has been made of the adjacency pair as the sin qua non of the local organization of talk (Jackson and Jacobs, in press, refer to the adjacency pair as the "centerpiece" of the sequencing-rules approach), the concept is not without its detractors. Edmondson (1981b) argues that the original definition by Schegloff is faulty, in that the conditional links are between acts or *moves* rather than utterances. Further, it is not necessary for the first and second pair parts to be immediately adjacent; the definition ought to allow for expansion through insertion sequences, contingent queries (Garvey, 1977), and the like, as illustrated in the example below, in which the conditional relevance of B's second pair part to A's first is undiminished by the question-answer pair separating them:

question1	**A:**	Are you going to Brenda's party?
question2	**B:**	What time does it start?
answer2	**A:**	Not 'til nine.
answer1	**B:**	Yeah, I guess so.

Edmondson also complains that the definitional criteria are not sufficiently specific to determine if adjacent utterances do indeed constitute a pair (Edmondson, 1981b, p. 47). He further argues that for some types of adjacency pairs providing a second pair part that is not the conventional perlocutionary effect would evoke more negative comment than others; for example, it is more socially acceptable to refuse an offer than it is to refuse a greeting (Edmondson, 1981b, p. 47). Wells, MacLure and Montogmery (1981) propose that some utterances, like questions, are highly implicative, while others, like assertions, are only weakly so. Edmondson's final criticism of the adjacency pair framework is to chastise the ethnomethodologists who are its proponents for their "selective" approach to data; he argues that their data is chosen because it is highly analyzable in terms of their constructs.

Wells et al. (1981) find the utility of the adjacency pair to be doubtful for two reasons: (1) there are many structurally related utterance sequences that are not accounted for by the notion, and so the adjacency pair framework is not adequate to account for a complete text; (2) the description of adjacency pairs fails to discriminate between those acts that fall within the framework and those that do not. Like Edmondson, Wells et al. regard the units and relationships of the adjacency pair notion to be poorly defined. The issue of completeness has also been raised by Jackson and Jacobs (in press): they point out that the adjacency pair model cannot account for the absence of second pair parts unless it can be claimed that the "non-SPP" is actually in service of conditional relevance, as, for example, in checking out a precondition for the satisfaction of a second pair part.

A further point raised by Jackson and Jacobs is that the adjacency-pair framework is hard pressed to account for why some utterances get to initiate pairs, and others do not. Many illocutionary acts that are initiated seem to have very weak implications for subsequent acts. Goffman (1976, p. 290) suggests that the adjacency pair may not be a natural unit of conversation. Goffman proposes that a three-part unit on the order of *mentionable event, mention, comment on mention* might be more fundamental (1976, p. 290). It is certainly more flexible, but suffers even more severely than the adjacency pair notion from ill-definedness.

Levinson makes the case that the adjacency pair concept has been overemphasized; he claims that "the bulk of conversation is not constructed from adjacency pairs" (1981, p. 107). Levinson offers no data to support his claim, which appears to be at odds with Benoit's (1980) findings on adjacency pair production in children's discourse in a laboratory setting. Benoit reported that 53.72% of the interactional moves recorded contained complete or incomplete adjacency pairs. While work by Foster (1982) suggests that the ability to maintain coherence in speech act organization at the utterance-by-utterance level is a very early acquisition for children, and will later be supplemented by topic management skills, nonetheless, it would be wise to look further before accepting Levinson's claim.

Levinson further supports his judgment that adjacency pair organization is overemphasized by pointing out that constraints on response to first pair parts are often topical; that is, an answer must be *about* the proposition expressed in a question, a denial must be of the proposition expressed in an accusation and not some other proposition, and so on. Models of discourse structure based on speech act theory are therefore inadequate, in Levinson's view, because they ignore topical constraints.

While the argument that adjacency pairs constitute the primary source of structural coherence at the local level has been criticized from a number of angles, there nonetheless does appear to be support for the notion in studies of actual and reconstructed conversations. Benoit (1980) found that in naturalistic observations of interaction between pairs of children and between children and adults at a child development center, 57.05% of the interactional exchanges could be classified as adjacency pairs, with the most frequently occurring pairs being the *direct request for action-response* and the *direct request for information-response* pairs. Similar findings on the importance of adjacency pair organization in child discourse have been reported by Garvey and Hogan (1973; they call them "exchanges") and Foster (1982). McLaughlin and Cody (1982) hypothesized that if structural coherence were disrupted, as it would be given the presence of a long conversational lapse under conditions in which the silence would be experienced by interactants as awkward, that the parties would be most likely to resort to the initiation of a first pair part to reestablish structure. McLaughlin and Cody found that many of the behavior sequences following a conversational lapse contained an adjacency pair, usually a *question-answer* couplet.

Mixed evidence for adjacency-pair organization has been found in studies of subjects' abilities to reconstruct conversation. Clarke (1975) found that subjects were able to resequence a "scrambled" dialogue with greater than chance accuracy. The following pairs were resequenced with significant accuracy (Clarke, 1975, p. 377):

(1) **A:** What are you doing on Saturday night?
   B: Going to dinner, which is at seven o'clock
        and then doing a . . . singing in a
        concert.

(2) **A:** Going to dinner, which is at seven o'clock
        and then doing a . . . singing in a
        concert.
   B: (Oh, well . . .) Ah, and what time do you
        finish that, because there's a party which
        you're invited to!

(3) **A:** Ah, another party, I'm invited to Bill's
        party as well. Bill Taylor.
   B: (Mmm) Oh he didn't invite me.

(4) **A:** It's near the station.
   B: Oh Golly, Cherry Lane or something?

Analysis of these paired turns from Clarke's hypothetical conversation (1975, p. 336) suggests that adjacency pair organization was not particularly important in reconstructing the conversation. First, only one of the four sets of turn pairs is obviously an adjacency pair: the question-answer sequence (1). Inasmuch as the conversation of twenty lines contained three other question-answer pairs and a summons-answer sequence, significant recognition of only one adjacency pair is not very impressive. Second, the nature of the links between the three remaining pairs of turns that were significantly likely to be resequenced adjacently seem to be largely propositional in nature; specifically an occasion relation in (2), a contrast relation in (3), and an elaboration relation in (4). Clarke does not provide a confusions matrix, so it is not possible to determine if subjects' sequencing errors support the adjacency-pair framework.

Ellis, Hamilton, and Aho (1983) had 81 subjects attempt to resequence the following 20-turn conversation, for which the turns had each been written on an index card and the deck shuffled before presentation:

1 **A:** Ah, I know what I wanted to tell you.
2 **B:** What?
3 **A:** What are you doing Saturday night?
4 **B:** Going to dinner and then a show.
5 **A:** Well, what time to you get done because there is a party which you are invited to?
6 **B:** Another party, I got invited to Bill's party too.
7 **A:** Really, he didn't invite me.
8 **B:** I guess I shouldn't have said anything.
9 **A:** I talked to Bill the other day.
10 **B:** Well, I was going to after the show.
11 **A:** Maybe I wasn't invited because he knows I was already going to a party.
12 **B:** Mmm. I believe . . .
13 **A:**   It's Sara's party and it should be fun.
14 **B:** Yea, where's it at?
15 **A:** Somewhere over on MAC.
16 **B:** This side of Saginaw?
17 **A:** I am not sure. Pete's going to find out this afternoon.
18 **B:** Yea, well the thing is the show gets out pretty late and . . .
19 **A:**   I'll see Peter this afternoon and then let you know exactly where it is.
20 **B:** Well, we'll see. (Ellis, Hamilton, & Aho, 1983, p. 272)

Ellis et al. reported that subjects were significantly likely to pair turns 1 and 2, 3 and 4, 4 and 5, 6 and 7, and 7 and 8. Subjects were highly likely to recognize the initiation of a so-called demand ticket sequence (Nofsinger, 1975) in the first two turns (aborted because rather than "tell B what," A asked B a question); and to notice the question-answer adjacency pair in turns 3 and 4, which appears to have been initiated so that A could determine if the preconditions existed for the *offer* in line 5. However, we would be hard pressed to classify the significant pairings of turns 6 and 7 and 7 and 8 as adjacency pairs; here local coherence seems to be achieved more by virtue of propositional than functional links, such as the contrast relation between 6 and 7. The confusions data seem to provide a certain amount of clarification of the mixed findings. For example, the pair (14, 15) was not paired with sufficient frequency to reach significance, but the transition matrix indicates that a number of respondents paired turn 14, the question, "Yea, where's it at?," not with its proper answer "Somewhere over on MAC," but rather with another plausible answer, "I'm not sure. Pete's going to find out this afternoon." Similarly with the pair (16, 17): a number of respondents proposed turn 19 as the appropriate second pair part to the question "This side of Saginaw?" Ellis et al. suggest that these confusions resulted from the absence of lexical cohesion devices that would have made the adjacency of turns more obvious.

Stech (1975) was interested in determining the extent of sequential structure in interaction in such diverse settings as discussion groups, the classroom, and police inquiry desks. Stech found that in discussion groups, a not uncommon pattern was *question* or ask for information, *answer* or give information, followed by positive or negative *reactions*. This sequence would then lead to the initiation of a new question or problem statement. In classroom interaction, a common pattern was a *question* or *request*, an *answer* or *response*, followed by *acceptance* or *rejection*. Civilian calls to police complaint clerks were primarily sequenced in two ways: (1) the caller would make a *request* for assistance, the police clerk would ask pertinent *questions*, the caller would *answer* the questions, and the assistance would be *granted* or *denied*; (2) the caller would ask a *question*, the police clerk would provide an *answer*, and the caller would evaluate the answer. Although Stech did not specifically couch his analysis in the adjacency-pair framework, there is little doubt but that the sequences he uncovered provide support for the notion of pair-wise conditional relevance.

Alternatives and improvements to the adjacency-pair framework. Wells et al., (1981), as mentioned earlier, find the adjacency-pair framework unsatisfactory because of its lack of completeness and the inadequacy of its definitions. They propose instead that local coherence is achieved through the collaborative construction of *exchanges*, minimal units of conversation that consist in an *initiating move* and a *responding move*. Two basic exchange types are proposed: *solicit-give* and *give-acknowledge* (Wells et al., 1981, p. 74). Solicit-give encompasses such diverse exchanges as question-answer, request-grant/deny, offer-accept/decline, and so forth. Give-acknowledge covers exchanges like assert-agree/disagree, compliment-accept/reject, and the like. Exchanges are characterized by different degrees of *prospectiveness*: solicit utterances are highly prospective or implicative for subsequent turns while other moves, like gives, are less so. Exchanges may be *sequenced* so that the second pair part of a preceding exchange may serve to initiate a subsequent exchange; a turn that provides such a link is called a *continue*:

> **A:** Where do you want to go for dinner tonight?
> **B:** Let's go to the Panda Inn, O.K.?
> **A:** Fine.

Here, according to Wells et al., B's turn serves simultaneously to "give" to A's "solicit," and to "solicit" a "give" from A. Unfortunately, Wells et al. appear to confuse turns and interactional moves or acts; since B's turn contains two distinct utterance units, each of which has a different illocutionary function, the whole sequence can just as well be described as two question-answer adjacency pairs linked functionally by a precondition relation.

Another type of exchange proposed by Wells et al. revolves around an "acknowledge" utterance that simultaneously functions as a second pair part to a solicit-give exchange and the first pair part to a give-acknowledge exchange:

> **A:** What do we man by dyadic?
> **B:** Two-person.
> **C:** That's right.

Such exchanges, of course, are especially troubling to those scholars like Gazdar and Levinson who have to grapple with the issue of speech act assignment, and who are reluctant to develop formalisms that allow of both retrospective and prospective meanings. These three-utterance interchanges are staples of classroom and other unilaterally controlled types of discourse.

In general, the Wells et al. framework, while noteworthy for the notion of degrees of prospectiveness, offers little that has not been provided elsewhere, and the basic elements and units of their scheme are as ill defined as those of their competitors.

A second approach to local functional coherence is provided by Edmondson (1981b), who also relies on the functional exchange as the basic unit of conversation. Edmondson, as reported earlier, subscribes to a hearer-knows-best principle in which the function of an utterance in conversation is determined by the way in which it is treated. Like Wells et al., Edmondson also proposes that turns have retrospective and prospective, as well as "here-and-now" functions: he calls these aspects, respectively, the UPTAKER, the APPEALER, and the HEAD. The UPTAKER satisfies the preceding move of the prior speaker, the APPEALER "solicits uptake from the hearer," and what the HEAD does is not altogether clear: "the interactional function of the head derives from the type of move of which it is the head exponent" (Edmondson, 1981b, p. 84). What appears to be the case is that moves are assigned to turns rather than utterances or thought units such as independent clauses (Edmondson claims that turn-taking operates at the level of move); thus, an uptake move might correspond to a disclaimer, and an appealer move to a tag question, while the head move is sandwiched in between:

A: I understand what you're saying, but the
     El Salvador situation does have some similarities
     to Vietnam, don't you think?

This is a somewhat different view from the idea of simultaneous retrospective-prospective function, exemplified by the utterance "two-person," which in an earlier example served both as a second pair part to a solicit and as a first part to an acknowledge.

Edmondson proposes a single basic exchange as a minimal interactional unit, consisting of a PROFFER that initiates the exchange, and a SATISFY that provides an outcome in the sense of a conventional perlocutionary effect:

PROFFER   A: Why don't we take up a collection for
                  Evelyn so we can buy a place setting of
                  her silver for a wedding present?
SATISFY   B: Here's five dollars to start with.

Alternatively, a PROFFER may be met with a CONTRA or a COUNTER. The main distinction between a contra and a counter is hearer determined. Both contras and counters can themselves be "satisfied"; satisfaction of a contra terminates or resolves the exchange:

PROFFER   A: Why don't we take up a collection for
                  Evelyn so we can buy a place setting of
                  her silver for a wedding present?
CONTRA   B: I'm tired of chipping in for people I
                  scarcely know.
SATISFY   A: Yeah, me too.

The contra-satisfy pair in effect cancels the proffer. If the outcome fails to provide, at least locally, for the resolution of the exchange, the move is to be treated as a counter:

	A:	Why don't we take up a collection for Evelyn so we can buy a place setting of her silver for a wedding present?
COUNTER	A:	I'm tired of chipping in for people I scarcely know.
SATISFY	A:	O.K./
(RE-)PROFFER	A:	So how about if we buy her some nice tea towels?

The counter-satisfy pair does not cancel the proceeding proffer in this case but rather leads to a new proffer. Note that there is nothing different in the propositional content of the counter and the contra. They are assigned different functions solely on the basis of their disposition in subsequent discourse. If the satisfaction of a nonsatisfying reply to an initiating proffer resolves an exchange, then the nonsatisfying move is a contra; otherwise, it is a counter.

Other functional categories proposed by Edmondson include a PRIME and a REJECT. A PRIME is a "pre-proffer," a means of inducing one's hearer to make a proffer (1981, p. 81):

| PRIME | A: | I wish I had a cup of coffee. |
| PROFFER | B: | I'll fix one for you. |

A REJECT move denies that the preceding conversational move was legitimate; it constitutes an objection to the fact or the manner of a move's having been made:

| PROFFER | A: | Yes, hello, this is Mrs. Brown, and I'm with the Olan Mills studio and this week we |
| REJECT | B: | We don't want any. (Slam down phone) |

Edmondson proposes a number of rules, most of which turn out to be definitional, such as that the "satisfaction of a Prime" constitutes a proffer, and so on. Of particular interest is the rule that *"following a Satisfy either speaker may produce the next move"* (Edmondson, 1981b, p. 99). Although generally in two-party conversation, the sequence of alternating turns *abab* is the rule (Schegloff, 1968), the abab rule provides no resources for the allocation of turns when the issue of "who goes first" is problematic. Above the level of the exchange, turn-taking, Edmondson maintains, is a matter for negotiation and is not controlled by conversational structure. The fact that conversations have lapses from time to time may stem in part from the lack of a clear rule to guide behavior subsequent to closed exchanges.

Two types of local linkage between exchanges have been proposed by Edmondson. "Chained exchanges" are those in which the initiations seem to have the same perlocutionary intent, and the pairs of moves the same upshot or outcome. The individual proffers may be subsumed under a single global proffer; all have the same force. Similarly, each individual satisfy may be subsumed under a "macro-satisfy." Bleiberg and Churchill's *confrontation* sequence (1975, p. 274) exemplifies the notion of a chained exchange very well:

```
1   PT.   I don't want them (my parents) to have
2         anything to do with my life, except
3         (pause)// security
4   DR.   You live at home?
5   PT.   Yes.
6   DR.   They pay your bills?
7   PT.   Yeah.
8   DR.   How could they not have anything to do
9         with your life?
```

The confrontation sequence works by virtue of the fact that the chained exchanges at (4, 5) and (6, 7) have the same force as the "punchline" (Bleiberg & Churchill, 1975, p. 275), the global or macro-proffer at line 9, and especially because the implicit satisfy of the proffer in line six must have the same force as the satisfy in line 5 and 7.

Reciprocal exchanges are those in which the upshot of a subsequent exchange reverses the "speaker-hearer benefits and costs" of a prior exchange (Edmondson, 1981b, p. 111). Either party can initiate the second pair of a reciprocal exchange. For example, if B satisfies A's proffer, then either (a) B may make a similar proffer to A, or (b) A may make it for her:

```
A:   Will you do the baby bottles?
B:   O.K.
A:   And I'll go and pick her up.
G:   O.K.
              or
A:   Will you do the baby bottles?
B:   O.K. Will you go pick her up?
A:   O.K.
```

Other examples of reciprocal exchanges would include trading of names, astrological signs, and hometowns; the exchange of compliments; greetings; and closings.

Pragmatic connectives. Before leaving the issue of local functional coherence relations, we need to take a look at pragmatic connectives and disjunctives. Van Dijk (1980, p. 166) has proposed that certain connectives (if, and, but, or, unless, and so on), which we ordinarily regard as expressing only semantic relations between propositions, have functional significance as well; that is, to express the relationships between speech acts. For example, pragmatic "but" serves to herald an objection to the preceding speech act or some one of its preconditions, or to the fact or manner of its having been made:

A: So you're not sure? (about future plans)*
B: Huh uh.
A: That's bad. That's real bad.
B: Well, *but* I mean there's no- this may sound real bad
        but there's not as much pressure on- I mean like
        for guys you have to go and you know do
        somethin'

Pragmatic "or" reflects the unwillingness of the speaker to err by "establishing commitments for the hearer which may be undesired" (van Dijk, 1980, p. 171). Pragmatic "or" usually leads into an inquiry about the preconditions of a proposed action:

A: So, we're going to the movies tonight- *or*, are you
        still worried about your exam tomorrow?

Should B answer in the affirmative ("Yes, I'm afraid I am"), the pragmatic implication is to alter or even cancel the status of A's main speech act.

Pragmatic "so" connects two acts, the latter of which is a conclusion drawn from the former:

A: I have a headache.
B: *So*, not tonight, huh?

"So" may also be used pragmatically to solicit preconditions or consequences of an explicitly stated act:

A: I finally asked for that raise.
B: *So*, when do we go out for dinner?

Pragmatic "if" details the circumstances under which a main action will count; or, it inquires as to the appropriate performance of the main act:

A: I'll make you lunch, *if* you haven't eaten.
        or
A: *If* I may make a suggestion, I think we should
        meet again tomorrow.

Owen (1981) has dealt extensively with the use of "well" as a
pragmatic disjunctive; she emphasizes the essentially polite nature of
"well" in that it not only signals that a threat to the face of the prior
speaker is about to occur, but it also delays the performance of the
face-threatening utterance. "Well" may be used to preface qualified
acceptance, or rejection; or to cancel a presupposition of the action in
question (Owen, 1981, p. 109):

A: You don't like poly science, do ya?*
B: *Well* . . . yeah.
A: You do?
B: Yeah, I do.

Functional Coherence Hierarchies

We have already introduced in earlier sections the notion of a
macrostructure (van Dijk, 1980, 1981), although to date only
propositional hierarchies have been discussed. It is also appropriate
to speak of *pragmatic* macrostructures in conversation, which are
organized with respect to the representation of a *global speech act* or
macroact (van Dijk, 1981, p. 15). Van Dijk (1980, p. 11) argues that
functional macrostructures not only are needed to account for
coherence and persons' abilities to summarize conversations, but are
also required because it is primarily to the level of global as opposed
to local action that rules, norms, and conventions are linked.
Pragmatic macrostructures function to organize conversation and
provide for its convenient retrieval; they serve to reduce complex
input; and they facilitate comprehension.

A pragmatic macrostructure may be said to organize and abstract a
functional context set or common ground (Karttunen & Peters, 1979)
consisting of a set of *pragmatic presuppositions* that inform a
particular interchange (Werth, 1981, p. 131), together with the
explicit microacts that have accumulated up to that point. The
pragmatic topic, if you will, is the equivalent of the conventional
perlocutionary effect of the global act that S has undertaken; it corresponds to the speaker's goal (Jackson & Jacobs, in press). The
microacts in a pragmatic context set will vary in terms of their importance in S's overall plan; that is, some acts will be main acts and
others will be subordinate:

[T]he peculiarity of plans, which should be emphasized, is that of having their component goals structured in a hierarchical way, such that one or more dominate the others. There may be different kinds of *dominance*, but the crucial feature seems to be the self-standing character of the main goal [Ferrara, 1980a, p. 247].

Some sequences will not appear to have an explicit main act; their constituent microacts will be found to cumulatively "count" as a main or global act (Sabsay & Foster, 1982, p. 28; van Dijk, 1980). Sometimes entire sequences will be subordinate, as in contingent queries (Garvey, 1977; Sabsay & Foster, 1982):

A: Can you lend me twenty dollars?
B: 'Till when?
A: Friday.
B: Sure.

One's understanding of actions in a sequence and their relative importance will be reflected in the extent to which in the macro-structure the acts are under *pragmatic focus* (van Dijk, 191, p. 156). Like Reichman's notion of the focus levels of thematic participants, pragmatic focus refers to whether or not the function of an utterance is to establish the preconditions for successful performance of an action. When speakers' goals are met, or when those goals change, pragmatic focus will reflect those changes through the process of incrementation and/or deletion and generalization of elements in the context set. Acts directed to setting the stage for other acts will be in comparatively low focus in the macrostructure, and will be deleted altogether once satisfied, so that only the global act will be retained.

Sequences of action in conversation must cohere both locally and globally, that is, linearly or utterance-by-utterance, and as a whole. Further, linear coherence or *connectedness* is achieved if for every action there is some other action for which it is either a precondition or a result (van Dijk, 1980, p. 139). For example, a classic condition for linear coherence of an action sequence is that the "final state" of an antecedent action coincide with the "initial state" of a subsequent one (van Dijk, 1980, p. 163). Global coherence is achieved when an action sequence can be shown to have an episodic character in which the individual actions share a unity in terms of time, place, and participants (van Dijk, 1980, p. 139). Hierarchical structuring is also a source of global coherence. Actions may be ranked in importance by virtue of whether or not they are *necessary* (as opposed to merely probable or possible) ways of obtaining the global goal (van Dijk, 1980, p. 142). Further, the importance of a move varies as a function of the *relative consequences of its failure to be satisfied*. The ranking of an action might also correspond to how greatly its satisfaction is desired, or to whether or not it is accomplished in order to facilitate some other action.

Macrorules. Macrorules operate on the context set to produce a macrostructure that serves to abstract and organize the pragmatic presuppositions and microacts that constitute it. Van Dijk (1980) proposes that the identical operations performed on propositional context sets apply to pragmatic context sets: the operations of *deletion*, *construction*, and *generalization*. Actions that are merely auxiliary (for example, greetings and closings) may be deleted. Those actions that constitute the usual subunits of a compound action will be seen to construct a single global action; similarly, those actions that normally count as conditions or consequences of another action will be subject to the construction operation. In the following example, modeled after van Dijk (1980), the greeting sequences at lines (1-4) and the appreciation-minimization pair at lines (11-12) will be subject to deletion. The establishment of preconditions for the requested action (lines 5-6 and 9) will be constructed as part of the global speech act *request* that finds explicit expression in line 7 and satisfaction in line 10:

1 **A:** How ya doin'?
2 **B:** Great, and you?
3 **A:** Never better.
4 **B:** Great.
5 **A:** Listen, man, did you go to French today?
6 **B:** Yeah.
7 **A:** Great. Listen, I need to borrow your notes.
8 **B:** Well. . . .
9 **A:** Just to Xerox. I'll bring 'em right back.
10 **B:** Well, O.K. I guess it's alright.
11 **A:** Thanks. I really appreciate it.
12 **B:** Sure. No problem.

Van Dijk's generalization rule is ill defined, and we will forego a treatment of it here.

Pragmatic plans and macrostructures. The following interchange, reported by McLaughlin, Cody, and Rosenstein (1983), resulted from A's having complained that he was turned off by Christianity because one of his teachers in parochial school had taught that "Christianity was the only way to get to God." B can clearly been seen to implement a plan to reproach A for his position, using a confrontation-style strategy to induce B to indict himself for falsely generalizing from one experience:

B: Well, you know, if uh, there was one guy that was from*
      Baltimore (A's home town) that I knew before? and he was
      real uh let's say sloppy?

A: Uh huh.

B: It'd be kind of wrong for me to say that you were
      real sloppy.

A: Uh huh.

B: Right?

A: Yeah.

B: Just because you were from Baltimore.

In this example, the global goal that organizes B's utterances is never explicitly realized in talk. B has a subordinate goal (to get A to accept the premise that "B would be wrong to claim A was X because another member of the set to which A belongs happens to be X") and by analogy to accept the premise that A's reasoning in the matter of the doctrinaire nun also suffers from hasty generalization. Simply put, the structure of the sequence may be characterized by having a *global goal*: cause B to believe that q, and two *belief preconditions*: (1) B believe that p; (2) B believe that if p, then q. The former precondition is the only one to which action is explicitly directed. B trusts to A's inference processes to make the analogic leap. The sequence may be diagrammed in terms of a plan, the partial traces of which are reflected in the text (see Cohen & Perrault, 1979; also, Sabsay & Foster, 1982):

In the following dialogue, both main and subordinate actions are expicitly manifested in utterances:

A: Are you using that pencil?

B: How long will you need it?

A: About ten minutes.

B: O.K.

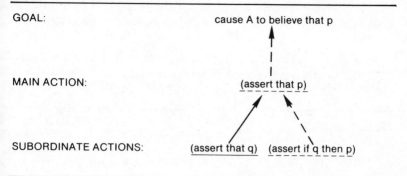

Figure   2.1

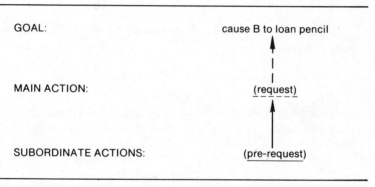

Figure   2.2

This interchange can be modeled starting with A's initial, partial plan: to inquire about a precondition of the loan, and expect that the prerequest will have the illocutionary force of a request; further, to expect that B's recognition that a request is being made will be sufficient reason for B to grant the request:

B's plan to determine if the preconditions for granting the request are favorable then intercedes. B assumes that A's recognition of her desire to know will be regarded as sufficient cause to provide an answer.

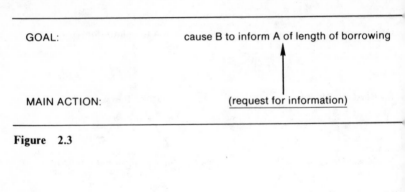

Figure   2.3

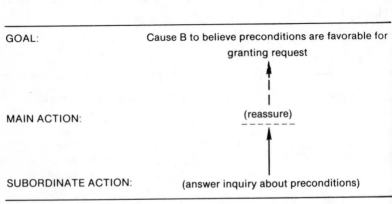

Figure   2.4

A's initial plan then requires amending; it is only a partial plan in that B cannot be sure that his response to A's request for information will meet the preconditions for A to grant B's request:

Finally, B provides the "grant," and the macrostructure of the whole interchange should look like this:

Of course the macrostructure at any point in a conversation is only temporary, altered over the course of interaction by the processes of incrementation, deletion, and generalization of the context set. One

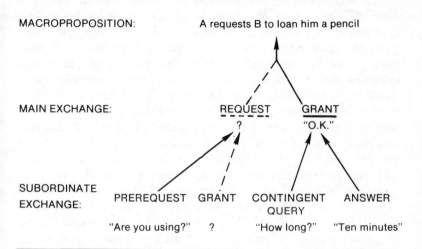

MACROPROPOSITION: A requests B to loan him a pencil

MAIN EXCHANGE: REQUEST GRANT
? "O.K."

SUBORDINATE EXCHANGE: PREREQUEST GRANT CONTINGENT QUERY ANSWER

"Are you using?" ? "How long?" "Ten minutes"

Figure 2.5

would expect that in memory the subordinate exchanges would not be retained.

The Relationship of Functional to Propositional Coherence

Very little explicit work has been done on the relationship between functional and semantic coherence. There are obviously circumstances under which the propositional content of an utterance or even the permissible range of topics is subject to functional constraints. For example, we might be in the midst of a heated argument, and have a particularly satisfying line of complaint going when our partner asks us a question, such as "So why is it O.K. for *you* to do S, but not *me*?" The demands of conditional relevance may be so great that we are forced to digress from a potentially successful conflict strategy to meet the requirements of local coherence. On the other hand, there are times when the kinds of speech acts one can perform are limited due to the constraints of the topic at hand. One may have to "work" the topic for a considerable length of time, for example, to be able unobstrusively to insert a "boast" or a "snipe." Another topical constraint on speech act organization has to do with the preconditions for performing certain kinds of actions. For example, a speaker's utterance cannot count as an *excuse* if she fails to provide a reason that absolves her of responsibility for an untoward act. An answer to a "why?" question fails as an act if it does not provide "what is culturally recognizable as a reason," even if it appears in the appropriate slot in a sequence (Foster & Sabsay, 1982). A speaker cannot *inform* a hearer of something H already knows (van Dijk, 1981, p. 185), nor can *advice* be given about actions of the speaker, about events in the past, nor without the use of action predicates (van Dijk, 1981, p. 42).

Foster and Sabsay (1982), in an extensive analysis of the propositional and functional structures in a doctor-patient interview, conclude that shifts in the structures often seem to coincide, but that the two are not, in the final analysis, identical. Van Dijk (1981, p. 199) concurs that the correlation between functional boundaries and clause-sentence boundaries is "non-trivial," but for the most part treats pragmatic and propositional structures separately.

Hobbs (1978) makes a beginning effort to tie semantic coherence relations to the functional organization of discourse. An elaboration relation may be used to fend off negative evaluations expressed by a prior utterance; a contrast relation may serve to inhibit generalization by the listener, or to express a retort; causal relations may be invoked to justify actions; and occasion relations may be exploited to sustain interaction. We shall consider these problems more fully in Chapter 4. Finally, we should note that the pragmatic connectives and disjunctives introduced in an earlier section represent at least one instance of the coincidence of semantic and functional organization.

SUMMARY

Conversational coherence, the extent to which a sequence of utterances produced by alternating speakers may be said to show relatedness, is evidenced in conversational text, in the organization of its implied and expressed propositional content, and in the structure of actions: what speakers *do* in saying.

Coherence at the level of text is usually called "cohesion." Cohesion refers to the ways in which different utterances in a discourse can be "about" the same elements or "thematic participants." Cohesion is furthered by such devices as anaphoric reference, and by conversational participants' adherence to the antecedence maxim and the given-new contract.

Propositional and functional coherence may best be understood in terms of the goals and plans of the actors, although conversation may be more or less planned. Both semantic and pragmatic coherence may be linear, or utterance-by-utterance, and global, in which each utterance is interpretable in light of its relation to a macroproposition that organizes the way the conversation is comprehended, stored, and retrieved from memory. Local propositional coherence is achieved through relating the current proposition to the immediately preceding discourse: such relations include evaluation, linkage, and expansion. Relations between conversational Issues and Events are governed by rules. Global propositional coherence results from the application of macrorules of deletion-selection, construction, and generalization to map a context set of presuppositions and explicit propositional utterances onto a semantic macrostructure. The context set is incremented locally with each new utterance, and is abstracted and organized into the macrostructure, which guides production and comprehension.

Functional coherence refers to the local and global relatedness of speech acts or illocutionary acts: acts that are produced with the desire that H recognize our intent in uttering that thus-and-so. Illocutionary acts have associated conventional perlocutionary effects that correspond to the speaker's goal in constructing an utterance or sequence of utterances. The successful performance of speech acts is associated with a set of preconditions that must be met in order for the act to take place. It is often preconditions to which explicit utterances are addressed. Speech act theory has been subject to criticism on the grounds that there is no assignment function for mapping utterances or utterance-context pairs onto actions; that is, that the rules for doing so are ad hoc.

Functional coherence at the local level springs from the conditional relevance of utterances. The idea of conditional relevance is that one speech act may establish a "slot" for a subsequent act, whose performance in the preferred form satisfies the conventional perlocutionary effect of the former act. Pairs of acts that display conditional relevance are called adjacency pairs; examples include question-answer, request-grant/deny, and greet-greet. The adjacency-pair framework has been criticized on the grounds that it lacks completeness, and its units are ill defined. There is, however, some empirical support for the importance of adjacency pairs to local functional organization. Alternatives to the adjacency-pair framework are offered by Edmondson and by Wells et al. *ignorance!*

Functional coherence occurs as a result of the organization of pragmatic context sets into pragmatic macrostructures. Actions in the macrostructure are in greater or lesser degrees of focus, depending upon their importance (status as main or subordinate acts) in the context set. Pragmatic macrorules of deletion and construction operate on the context set to produce the global structures organized around a global speech act. Goals and plans of actors determine the global acts undertaken.

Functional and propositional hierarchies often coincide, but are not always the same. Some semantic coherence relations may be seen to have pragmatic implications.

3

Turn-Taking, Gaps, and Overlaps in Conversational Interaction

◆ One of the characteristics that distinguishes ◆ conversation from other forms of discourse, for example narrative, is that during the course of interaction the roles of speaker and hearer are frequently exchanged (Edmondson, 1981b); further, that this exchange of turns-at-talk is nonautomatic (Garvey & Berninger, 1981). This "nearly the most obvious aspect of conversation" (Yngve, 1970, p. 568) has been accorded the status of a linguistic universal (Miller, 1963). Conversation may be further distinguished from other types of discourse in which speaker-hearer roles alternate—for example, interviews—by virtue of the fact that all parties at least theoretically are equally charged with the allocation of turns (Edmondson, 1981b, p. 38). Conversation, unlike, for example, debate, is further characterized by the fact that neither the size nor the order of turns is predetermined (Sacks et al., 1978).

TOWARD A DEFINITION OF "TURN"

Technical Definitions

Talk is accomplished through a series of turns. Just what is a turn? According to Sacks et al. (1978), the existence of turns implies that conversation is an economic system, and that turns are goods, possession of which entails certain costs and rewards or rights and obligations. Implicit also is a mechanism by which the scarce resource (only one to a customer) is allocated. Most scholars have been inclined to provide technical definitions for the notion of a turn. Feldstein and Welkowitz (1978, p. 335) propose that a turn "begins the instant one participant in a conversation starts talking alone and ends immediately prior to the instant another participant starts talking alone." Jaffe and Feldstein (1970, p. 19) offer a similar characterization: "the speaker who utters the first unilateral sound both initiates the conversation and gains possession of the floor. Having gained possession, a speaker maintains it until the first unilateral sound by another speaker, at which time the latter gains possession of the floor." Cherry and Lewis (1976) propose a similar definition to that of Feldstein and Welkowitz, and of Jaffe and Feldstein: a turn consists of all of the speaker's utterances up to the point when another person takes over the speaking role. All of these definitions have in common that any utterance by another speaker, including so-called back-channel acknowledgments such as "Uh huh," terminates the turn of a prior speaker and itself constitutes a claim to the floor.

Nontechnical Definitions

Other scholars offer less technical definitions of turn. Edelsky (1981, p. 403) defines a turn as "*an on-record speaking* (which may include nonverbal activities) *behind which lies an intention to convey a message that is both referential and functional.*" *Side comments,* which are "off the record," and back-channel utterances or *encouragers* such as "Mm hmm" do not count as turns, the former due to their unofficial status, the latter due to their nonreferential character. Owen (1981, p. 100) similarly insists that turns must have a functional aspect: "a turn must contain at least one *move.*" Owen describes the turn as a "structural unit into which *functional* units are slotted." Owen follows Goffman's (1976, p. 272) definition of a move, which we recognize from Chapter 2 as corresponding to a speech act: "any full stretch of talk or its substitutes which has a distinctive unitary bearing on some set or other of the circumstances in which the participants find themselves ." Turns may, in Owen's view, contain more than one speech act: a single turn, for example, may include a disclaimer, main act, and tag question, or a second pair part to a prior move by H along with a first pair part that has implications for H's subsequent turn. Owen, unlike Edelsky, does not distinguish between off- and on-record speaking. Edelsky's definition of turn derives from a particular notion of the "floor": "*the acknowledged 'what's-going-on' within a psychological time space*" (1981, p. 406).

As we shall describe in some detail later, floors may be singly or jointly held. When the floor is singly held, as, for example, in a committee meeting when the chair is reading announcements, side utterances between members such as "Do you have a Kleenex?" cannot be considered as attempts to contribute to the floor, Edelsky argues, even though they have both referential and functional content. (In support of this claim, it might be noted that should the author of a side-comment be asked to repeat her remark for the benefit of the group at large, she would quickly assert its off-record status with such remarks as "Oh, nothing," "Never mind," or "I was just asking for a Kleenex.") Edelsky proposes that technical definitions of turn fail to account both for the participant's sense of having taken a turn and for the turn-takers intentions: "a participant's sense of what counts as a turn is not necessarily the same as a research definition of a turn" (1981, p. 390).

Problems in Defining the Turn

Goodwin (1981) offers some insight into why defining the turn-at-talk has engaged the attention of so many scholars, without resulting in a consensus. First, while the "technical" group has been primarily concerned with the determination of turn boundaries, in actual talk some such boundaries are quite fluid; for example, an apparent gap may become a pause should the speaker role be taken up again by the same individual (Sacks et al., 1978). Second, the location of turn boundaries is a problem for participants as well as analysts; consequently, it may be more appropriate to regard the turn not as an "analytic tool," but rather as a conversational parameter whose negotiated status is of interest in its own right. Finally, Goodwin argues that it is inappropriate to "first define the turn and then work out how it is exchanged" (1981, p. 20); part of the process of definition involves specification of the exchange process.

For those of us whose disciplinary traditions give primacy to the message as the fundamental good of communicative exchanges, technical notions of the turn based on sound and silence patterns are not particularly appealing. Inasmuch as such definitions render equivocal the status of such interesting conversational events as gaps and overlaps, they are far from satisfactory. On the other hand, definitions like Edelsky's place enormous demands on analysts to reconstruct the underlying intent of a speaker in saying that thus-and-so, not only to determine *how* he wants his act to count, but even *if* he wants it to count. Edelsky provides little guidance in these matters. We have dealt at considerable length in a previous chapter with the difficulties of speech act assignment, and the problems attendant upon a failure to disentangle propositional and functional units. While Edelsky and others offer very compelling claims that participant sense and technical notions of the turn do not always coincide, intuitive approaches to the turn aren't particularly practical. Continuous inquiry into a participant's sense of the turn is not feasible. The analyst's own ad hoc intuitions about what a participant intends, while interesting in their own right, are not likely to contribute much to the orderly, systematic, and replicable examination of structures in talk. What the participant intends as a "non-turn" may not be treated as such in subsequent utterances; we have argued before that the best test of the function of an utterance lies in its disposition in the talk as a whole, even though the function assigned to it may appear to shift with developments in the conversation.

Clearly consensus could not be reached among the adherents of technical and intuitive approaches to the turn. It seems, however, that a proper account of the turn has to do several things: (1) specify the minimum number and kinds of *units* of which a turn may be composed; (2) clarify the status of the back-channel utterance; and (3) provide for the systematic assignment of silences and overlaps, all of these to be satisfied with an eye to the treatment of an event in talk as the ultimate arbiter of its function.

Specification of the Turn-Constructional Unit

What are some of the units that have been proposed as "building blocks" of discourse? From the previous chapter we have the notion of a locution or *utterance*, which has been described as asserting that, or standing for an assertion that, there is some entity or entities of which some relation to an attribute or other entity is predicated. The status of an utterance is accorded to each stretch of talk that can be interpreted as an independent clause, nonrestrictive dependent clause, term of address, acknowledgement, or "element of a compound predicate" (Stiles, 1978, p. 32). Included as utterances are elliptical sentences ("Great!" and "What?"), affirmations or negations that stand alone ("Uh huh," "No," "Really!"), (Auld & White, 1956) and tags ("You know," Isn't it?"). False starts that include subjects but not predicates do not count as utterances. In addition to utterances, conversational units that have appeared in earlier sections include the functional units *act* and *move*, which for all practical purposes we may treat as equivalent (although it might be argued that the move is the more global notion, in that it could be composed of several acts such as a pre-request and request). We have dealt already with the notion of *global speech act*, but since this phenomenon is not always explicit in text, its utility as a turn-constructional unit (Sacks et al., 1978) is not very great, and similary for *macroproposition*.

One controversial unit with which the reader (and doubtless most ordinary conversationalists) may not be familiar is the *phonemic clause* (Trager & Smith, 1951), "a phonologically marked macro-segment which . . . contains one and only one primary stress and ends in one of the terminal junctures" (Boomer, 1965, p. 150). Boomer found that both filled and unfilled pauses were most apt to occur just after the first word of a phonemic clause. Dittman and Lewllyn found that so-called back-channel utterances (1967) and head nods (1968) were likely to occur at the ends of phonemic clauses, with the nods occurring just slightly prior to the back channels. Dittman and Llewellyn concluded that the phonemic clause "seems to be firmly established as a unit of decoding speech" (1968, p. 82). For a case in point, Duncan's (1974) classic work on speaker- and auditor-state signals is based on the phonemic clause. Goodwin (1981, p. 27) concludes that while the unit is clearly tied to a number of aspects of conversational structure, and appears to be a natural unit of spoken discourse, the work on phonemic clauses fails to take into account how it is that the content of such a unit is sufficiently "projectable" that a hearer may produce a well-formed and encoded subsequent turn immediately upon its completion.

It is proposed here that the utterance is the most appropriate choice for the turn-constructional unit, for several reasons: (1) the utterance corresponds to a unitary, discrete segment of thought, while the phonemic clause may or may not; (2) it is utterances or utterance-context pairs that are mapped onto speech acts; (3) the intonation contours or terminal junctures of phonemic clauses have also been found to occur at utterance boundaries (Pike, 1945; Lieberman, 1967); and (4) conversational coherence both locally and globally is tied to relations among adjacent propositions and the acts superimposed upon them, and to their incrementation in a context set. Thus, the basic unit for constructing a turn may be said to be a single proposition or *utterance*. While a turn consists minimally of one utterance, it may of course contain multiple utterances.

We have dealt at length with the specification of the minimal turn-constructional unit because it is fundamental to our argument with respect to the status of back-channel communication, and also because it is fundamental to the definition of turn which will be proposed at the conclusion of the chapter. A full account of turns, however, requires that both simultaneous speech and interaction silence be dealt with. We will discuss how overlaps and gaps should be treated in a subsequent section.

THE SACKS, SCHEGLOFF, AND JEFFERSON TURN-TAKING MODEL

The most widely cited account of the turn-taking system is the complex work of Sacks et al. (1978). The authors argue that an adequate model of turn-taking must account for, among other facts, the following: (1) the occurrence and recurrence of speaker change; (2) the overwhelming tendency for only one party to talk at a time: (3)

the comparative absence of gaps and overlaps; (4) the variability of turn size, turn order, turn distribution, turn content, and number of participants (Sacks et al., 1978, pp. 10-11).

Turn-Constructional Components

The proposed model contains two basic components, one of which is called "turn-constructional," the other "turn-allocational." According to Sacks et al., the units from which turns in English may be built correspond to sentences, clauses, phrases, and lexical constructions. The main feature of a suitable unit-type is that as a hearer one is able to predict what type of unit has been undertaken, and how and when it might be expected to end.

Turn-Allocation Rules

To be allocated a turn is to be given the right, initially, to produce one turn-constructional unit (TCU); renewal is a matter for negotiation. The first possible point at which speaker change could occur is at the first projectable completion of the TCU: this point is called the "transition-relevance place" (Sacks et al., 1978, p. 12). The allocation of turns is governed by a set of rules, which are presented here in full (Sacks et al., 1978, p. 13):

1. At initial turn-constructional unit's initial transition-relevance place:
   (a) If the turn-so-far is so constructed as to involve the use of a "current speaker selects next" technique, then the party so selected has rights, and is obliged, to take next turn to speak, and no others have such rights or obligations, transfer occurring at that place.
   (b) If the turn-so-far is so constructed as not to involve the use of a "current speaker selects next" technique, self-selection for next speakership may, but need not, be instituted, with first starter acquiring rights to a turn, transfer occurring at that place.
   (c) If the turn-so-far is constructed as not to involve the use of a "current speaker selects next" technique, then current speaker may, but need not, continue, unless another self-selects.

2. If, at initial turn-constructional unit's initial transition-relevance place, neither 1 (a) nor 1 (b) has operated, and, following the provision of 1 (c), current speaker has continued, then the Rule set (a)-(c) re-applies at next transition-relevance place, until transfer is effected.

Some of the rules are constrained by others of the rules. For example, if (a) is to be operative the current speaker has to make her selection explicit in her utterance before a transition-relevance place, lest someone else self-select under option (b). Similarly, if someone other than the current speaker intends to take a turn under option (b), he must do so before the current speaker signals his intention to continue.

Accounting for the "Facts" of Turn-Taking

How does the Sacks et al. model account for the "facts" of turn-taking, for example, the facts about simultaneous talk, silences, turn size, and variable number of parties? First, gap and overlap are minimized because when transfer occurs it takes place at a predictable location—the transition-relevance place. However, overlap may occur because (1) the second allocation rule—1 (b)—allows for "competing self-selectors" (Sacks et al., 1978, p. 15); and (2) the turn-constructional unit may be extended beyond a first possible completion point, with a tag, address term, or the like. Similarly, lapses may occur because each of the turn-transfer rules is optional (Sacks et al., p. 27).

Turn size is not fixed, by virtue of the fact that several types of turn-constructional units are available, and, under option 1 (c), the current speaker may renew her right to a unit. The variability in the number of parties to the conversation is handled by the model's organizing only two turns at a time, current speaker's and next speaker's. The "size of the pool" from which they are selected is of little consequence, except in that pressure to self-select or other-nominate appreciably *prior* to a transition-relevance place is increased as the number of parties to the interaction increases.

Sacks et al. characterize the turn-taking system as "locally managed" and "interactionlly determined" (1978, pp. 41-42). By the former, Sacks et al. mean that the allocation of turns operates on a turn-by-turn basis; by the latter, that both speakers and hearers work collaboratively to determine the length of turns and the location of transfer:

> A speaker can talk in such a way as to permit projection of possible completion to be made from his talk (from its start), and to allow others to use its transition places to start talk, to pass up talk, to affect directions of talk, and so on, and that their starting to talk, if properly placed, can determine where he ought to stop talk [1978, p. 42].

THE ADEQUACY OF THE TURN-TAKING MODEL: SOME ISSUES

Defining the Turn-Construction Component

A number of serious questions have been raised about the Sacks et al. model. Edmondson (1981b) points out that the grounds for recognition of a turn-constructional unit are not clearly spelled out, nor is it clear how hearers and speakers recognize a transition-relevance place. What one may infer from Sacks et al. is that the turn-constructional unit is a syntactic unit, much like the idea of utterance that we have developed earlier. Yet, as Owen (1981) pointed out, the system seems to be functionally motivated; that is, the links between neighboring turns derive from the conditional relevance of acts. Under the Sacks et al. system, Owen argues, speaker change could follow immediately upon a question, but less automatically following an assertion, which has a lesser degree of sequential implicativeness. Indeed, Sacks and his colleagues further the impression of functional motivation by their assertion that all turns have a retrospective, a here-and-now, and a prospective aspect, and further by their recourse to the adjacency pair as a device for implementing speaker selection under rule 1 (a). It is certainly far from clear in the model how it is that hearers predict when a TCU might be terminated, other than than there are syntactic and intonational cues, and that turns must get their three "jobs" done (past, present, and future reference) before they can be considered complete. Fortunately, other scholars have provided some answers in this regard.

Duncan (1972, 1973) and his colleagues (Duncan & Niedereche, 1974; Duncan & Fiske, 1977) have given extensive attention to the signaling behaviors that occur at or near points of speaker exchange. Cues that indicate that a current speaker is willing to yield to a next speaker (the turn-yielding signal) include some or all of the following: (1) the presence of either a rising or falling intonation at the end of a phonemic clause; (2) paralinguistic "drawl" on the final or stressed syllable of the clause; (3) the cessation of hand gesturing, or the relaxation of a hand position that had been tense during the speaking turn; (4) the uttering of such expressions as "You know," "So," "But uh," and "Anyway" which Bernstein (1962) has called "sociocentric sequences"; (5) an increase in volume and/or a drop in pitch in combination with a sociocentric sequence; and (6) the completion of a grammatical clause (Duncan, 1972, 1973). Signs that the speaker intends to continue speaking subsequent to a transition-relevance place seem to include: (1) terminal filled pauses, and (2) grammatical incompleteness (Ball, 1975). When a speaker self-selects, under option 1 (b), some of the following behaviors ought to be present: (1) a change in direction of the head, (2) an audible intake of breath, (3) the initiation of gesturing, and (4) an increase in volume (Duncan & Niedereche, 1974). The combination of gesticulation and shift of head direction is usually adequate to account for the relative absence of simultaneous talk. Attempts to suppress the efforts of a current nonspeaker to take a turn have been claimed to consist primarily in the overt display of gesturing (Duncan, 1973) and gaze aversion (Kendon, 1967).

Kendon (1967) has reported that during the turn, the speaker can be expected to look away during the first few moments, and then return to gazing at the hearer as she approaches the conclusion of her utterance. This finding of a floor-apportionment function for gaze has received mixed support. While Argyle, Lalljee, and Cook (1968) found that restriction of signaling in the visual channel increased the likelihood that interruptions (i.e., non-smooth transfer of the turn) would occur, numerous other studies have failed to support the notion that gaze is used to facilitate turn transfer. For example, both Jaffe and Feldstein (1970) and Cook and Lalljee (1972) found that there were fewer interruptions under conditions of restricted gaze.

Beattie (1978) argues that Kendon's findings were based on a restricted data set of only two dyads, and that Kendon's inadequate operationalization of the turn resulted in his treating interrupted utterances and those whose termination the speaker herself controlled as the same for analytical purposes, thus increasing the likelihood that a relationship would be obtained between speaker gaze and a subsequent switch of the floor. Beattie found that gazes of greater than 1.0 seconds at the end of a complete utterance did not work to produce significantly briefer switching pauses, as the Kendon hypothesis of a floor-apportionment function for gaze would predict.

Beattie (1979) found that while gaze by the speaker at the conclusion of an utterance did not always facilitate speaker-switching, there was a trend in *hesitant* phases of speech for the longest switching pauses to occur after a complete utterance terminating with speaker gaze aversion, while the shortest switching pauses were found following complete utterances which terminated with speaker gaze. Beattie concluded that gaze played a useful role in turn-apportionment under conditions "reflecting a high level of cognitive processing" (1979, p. 392), as one might expect in conversations between strangers or partners with highly discrepant statuses.

Keller (1981) has suggested that there are conventional verbalizations associated with claim-suppression, such as "Wait a second," "Well, let's see," and "What I would say is;" the following contains a more explicit version.

A: I had a dream about taking these pictures of groups, O. K., you*
    know=

B: =Like with sorority group pictures or something?

A: Yeah, I'm gonna tell—don't stop me.

B: O. K.

A: O. K.

Keller (1981, p. 101) further proposes conventional "gambits" associated with turn-claiming ("May I interrupt you for a moment"); turn-yielding or abandoning ("That's about all I have to say on that," or "That's about it"), which we identify later on as *absolutist formulations;* and turn-avoiding (I'll pass on that").

Distinguishing Turns from "Non-Turns": Status of the "Back Channel"

A further complaint against the Sacks et al. model is that the authors fail to distinguish turns from non-turns (Edelsky, 1981). Edelsky's thesis that what goes on in conversation consists variously in turns, side comments, and encouragers has been mentioned before.

While Edelsky's characterization of the side comment as an off-record non-turn unit seems too strict, much argument has been made to the effect than back-channel utterances ought not to count as turns. Sacks et al., however, do not seem to address themselves to this issue. What is the appropriate stance?

Yngve (1970) took the position that utterance like "Mm hmm" and/or its nonverbal equivalents such as nods do not count as attempts to take a turn. Edelsky rejects such utterances as turns not on the ground that they do not constitute a claim for the floor, but rather because they allegedly have no referential content, and are merely responsive to within-turn segmentation signals.

Duncan (1973) expanded the notion of the back channel to include not only expressions like "Yeah" and "Right," but also completions by the auditor of the speaker's sentences, requests for clarification, and restatements. Although Duncan and Fiske (1977) reported that speakers do not shift their heads away while encoding back channel utterances, as they do in "regular" turns, Duncan and his colleagues have not provided a satisfactory account of the cues that distinguish "within-turn" signals from "speaker-state" signals; if anything, the former seem to be an abbreviated version or subset of the latter. Then, too, the hypothesis of the back channel derives from an analysis of psychiatric intake interviews (Duncan, 1972), in which the role and behavioral repertoire of the neutral listener is all but institutionalized.

While admittedly the kinds of behaviors Duncan and others describe as back-channel utterances may do little to advance the topic, they all can be construed as utterance-types, and they all have functional import, the nature of which may vary depending on the circumstances under which they occur. Utterances such "Uh huh," (called "minimal responses" by Fishman, 1978), amount as locutions to saying that "S has been heard"; but more importantly as *acts* have been implicated in conversational *avoidance* (Fishman, 1978) and topic *discouragement* (McLaughlin & Cody, 1982) as well as their more obvious force, as *acknowledgments* (Stiles, 1978). Furthermore, the force of an "Uh huh" or a "Yeah" varies considerably depending upon its location. A "Yeah" acknowledging a story detail is considerably different in function from the "Yeah" that follows an assertion or a question. Similarly, some sentence repetitions and sentence completions serve not an acknowledgment, but rather a confirming function, as in the following example from Bennett (1981, p. 174):

B: and y'know, it's surprising to see how much of it is more
         interrelated than people around here are willing to admit. I
         means there's a big denial from d- . . . y'know where
         they're separated and they do different things, and we're doing
         this and there's a y'know we operate in a vacuum
C: (Mhm, yeah you choose the part you want.
B: And you choose what you want.

Finally, requests for clarification can have obvious functional implications: that the other hasn't made herself clear; that the other's thinking is fuzzy; that the idea expressed by the other is unacceptable, and so forth. Certainly if a locution can be seen to have illocutionary force, we can allow it to count as a turn.

In sum, it seems the wiser course to err in the direction of conservatism and treat all utterances, with the possible exception of within-turn acknowledgments during a narrative, as being turn-constructional units. And even in the case of acknowledgments, "Uh huh" can be seen to count as a turn. If we are to accept the Sacks et al. view that turns at talk are allocated one turn-constructional unit at a time, the function of "Right" or "Uh huh" in the midst of an extended series of TCUs from a single speaker may be to reaffirm that indeed the speaker role does alternate and that S and H really are having a conversation, and to provide sanction for the speaker's numerous renewals of the TCU. That is, a back-channel utterance in this sense is a sort of *symbolic* claim to the turn.

Specifying the Cultures to Which the Model Applies

Philips (1976) has criticized Sacks et al. for failing to make an effort to delimit the cultures or situations in which the rules have force. Philips's study of the talk patterns of Indians on the Warm Springs reservation led her to conclude that the Sacks et al. model is inappropriate for the Indian culture. Philips found (1) that persons frequently spoke regardless of whether or not their doing so was ratified or legitimated by other persons (1975, p. 87); (2) that silence was easily tolerated; (3) that interruption and simultaneous speaker-starts were rare; (4) that a current-speaker-selects-next technique was rarely used to control interaction; and (5) that replies were often "widely separated" from the utterance to which they were a response.

The Importance of the Hearer's Role

Philips (1976) has further criticized the Sacks et al. article for the authors' comparative neglect of the hearer's role in the regulation of conversation. She attributes this failing in part to the fact that the data base was transcribed from audio-recordings of conversations; Philips' position is that audio tapes do not permit the analyst full access to the listener's contribution to the management of the turn-taking system. Goodwin's (1981) account of the construction of turns relies heavily on the analysis of listener (and speaker) gaze patterns gleaned from videotape recordings of interaction. Goodwin's observations have primarily to do with the implications of the following rule: *A Speaker should obtain the gaze of his recipient during the turn at talk* (1981, p. 57). One of the most interesting of such implications is that the number of turn-constructional units, or partial TCUs, and consequently the size of the speaker's turn-at-talk, is a partial function of her success in securing the gaze of the hearer.

Goodwin observed that such phenomena as pauses and restarts "provide some demonstration of the orientation of speakers to producing sentences that are attended to appropriately by their recipients" (1981, p. 59); specifically, such devices as restarts may act as a request for the hearer's attention, in the form of gaze. Evidence for this assertion is provided by the tendency of speakers to place restarts precisely at the point at which their own gaze "reaches a non-gazing recipient" (Goodwin, 1981, p. 72). Restarts may also occur when the tardy gaze of the hearer finally arrives, or when the movement-to-gaze of the hearer is observably delayed. Restarts under the first and last of these three circumstances may be interpreted as requests for the hearer's gaze.

Goodwin also presents an alternative to the Sacks et al. view that conversations lapse when first one party and then the other fails to exercise the options to speak. Goodwin emphasizes the role of the hearer in the disengagement process. The hearer may, for example, manifest signs of his intention to begin some new activity (for example, preparing to wipe his eyeglasses). This is initially accompanied by a withdrawal of gaze and a series of slow nods, resulting finally in a complete absence of engagement. Another possible role of the hearer vis-à-vis the disengagement from conversation is to maintain a posture of availability by turning slightly aside and withdrawing gaze. This display communicates to the speaker that the hearer is "on the fence": S may continue to talk, or not; H will listen if need be, but will not take on the speaker role herself. Goodwin claims that the hearer may also initiate disengagement by displaying an *eyebrow flash* at the next convenient transition-relevance place while still appearing to be attentive.

A final and very interesting point that Goodwin raises about the hearer's contribution is that the hearer's failure to meet the needs of the speaker for coordination of eye gaze may result in the speaker's lengthening of words or sounds, particularly at the ends of turn-constructional units; this phenomenon may provide a further systematic basis for the presence of simulataneous speech (1981, p. 128).

Specifying the Options in the Current-Speaker-Selects-Next Technique

Edmondson (1981b) has criticized the Sacks et al. model for failure to be explicit in detailing the techniques by which one party "selects" another to have a turn at talk. Actually, Sacks et al. present quite a few methods by which a current speaker selects the next. Obviously, a current speaker may address a question to a selected next speaker through the use of an address term, or the nonverbal equivalent of such a nomination. An unaddressed question may be seen to select a recipient if the to-be-learned matter of the question coincides with matters mentioned by a prior speaker:

A: We're paying over eight hundred a year for car insurance.
B: Girl, you can't mean it!
C: You oughta try my agent. They're a lot cheaper than any of the others I looked at.
A: Which one do you use?

Clearly, in the interchange, A's question is addressed to C, even though B is also a ratified participant. For B to be the recipient, the term "you" would have to have to be heavily inflected and accompanied by a directed gaze.

Another type of current-speaker-selects-next technique is the production of the first pair part of an adjacency pair, which will usually distinguish among possible recipients on the basis of their commonly held knowledge as to who has the resources to satisfy the move. Sometimes, however, a first pair part does not distinguish among recipients:

A: What time is it?
B: Eight-thirty.
C: (Eight thirty-three.
D: (A little after eight-thirty.

Such phenomena are more likely to characterize what Edelsky (1981) has called F2 episodes, when the floor is jointly, rather than singly, held.

The most notable gap in the Sacks et al. account is not in the arsenal of current-speaker-selects-next techniques, but rather in their failure to note characteristics of the hearer that influence the speaker-nomination process. Eder (1982) has noted in the context of classroom interaction that the often overlooked consequence of the teacher's use of eye gaze in turn allocation and student management "might be the inadvertent allocation of turns to higher status people because of greater concern about their reactions and thus more eye gaze in their direction" (p. 158). Hearers may be the recipients of more communication simply by virtue of their having initiated more. Hearers may use eye gaze to solicit or actively avoid being selected for a turn at talk. Hearers may "set up" turns for themselves by challenging or reproaching a prior speaker, so that down the line there will be a "slot" for them to evaluate the reply. Given the sensitivity of Sacks et al. to the collaborative and interactionally managed nature of conversation, their frequent neglect of the hearer's contribution is somewhat surprising.

Sensitivity to Different Types of "Floor"

Edelsky's (1981) work provides an implicit critique of the Sacks et al. model, in that she argues for two distinct varieties of conversational floor, to only one of which their view of turn-taking applies. The first type of floor, the one to which the model is relevant, is called an F1: it is the "orderly, one-at-a-time type" (Edelsky, 1981, p. 384). Edelsky claims that this view of conversational turn-taking has been the product of scholars' tendencies to construct speaker-exchange rules from what goes on in dyadic, relatively formal encounters such as client-therapist interactions or stranger pairings in a laboratory setting.

Edelsky proposes that analysis of other kinds of conversation, for example two or more than two acquaintances in comparatively informal settings, will reveal the presence of a different kind of floor, an F2, characterized by "an apparent free-for-all" or the collaborative building of a single idea (1981, p. 384).

From her study of the transcripts of a faculty committee's meetings, Edelsky concluded that F1s, which were more frequent than F2s, were characterized by the following: people took fewer, but longer, turns; there was more frequent use of the past tense; there was a greater use of the reporting function; and there were more side comments and encouragers. Generally, F1s were concerned with agenda-managing activities. F2s, on the other hand, were characterized by more turns that shared the same meaning; more laughing, joking, and teasing; more "deep" overlapping; little apparent concern for interruption; and more topics on which more than one participant was informed.

While Edelsky's notion of two kinds of floor is potentially quite useful in accounting for deviations from turn-taking rules, particularly in the matter of gaps and overlaps, one is left with the feeling that the "floors" concept lacks definition independent of the kinds of behaviors that occur within each floor, so that one is in the position of being unable to falsify any hypothesis about, say, what goes in in an F2. It would be most useful to know more about the structure and boundaries of these "free-for-all" episodes.

Violation of Turn-Allocation Rules

Garvey and Berninger (1981) have raised an interesting issue about the Sacks et al. turn-allocational rules: what happens if a speaker selected under the current-speaker-selects-next technique fails to take her designated turn? Ought there not to be another rule to cover such a contingency? Garvey and Berninger looked at children's behavior in response to just such circumstances; in general they characterized children's discourse as showing "a high degree of adaptation to the addressee, including immediate repair of breakdowns in comprehension by means of questions about prior speech" (1981, p. 31). Children who failed to receive an expected response after using a current-speaker-selects-next technique used a variety of devices to "replay" the soliciting utterance, including repetition, paraphrase, message modification, change in grammatical mood, and explicit mention of the missing response, the most common of which were repetition and change in grammatical mood. These two tactics were also the most successful, although in only about half of the sequences did the children succeed in eliciting the missing responses. Garvey and Berninger's results are such that we should posit an additional rule: *if a party selected by a current-speaker-selects-next technique fails to take his turn, and turn transfer is not effected, the rule set 1 (a)-(c) reapplies, and the first right and obligation of the current speaker is to reinstate the speaker-solicitation.* Failure to reinstate the solicitation not only means that one's extra-conversational goals will not be met, but it also has the effect that one might look rather silly to have a soliciting utterance hanging, as it were, in midair. While it is highly likely that the additional rule proposed here will be normative in dyadic interaction, it is unclear as to what extent behavior in larger groups would be subject to it. It seems probable that the right and/or obligation to replay a solicitation is distributed more generally among all ratified hearers; thus, a sequence like the following is not unlikely:

Mother: Tommy, why don't you pick up your room before
             Grandmother gets here.
                              (5.0)
Father: Tommy, your mother asked you to pick up your room.
Tommy: Oh. O. K.

That parties ordinarily do not object to such interventions is testimony to their probable interpretation of the addressed speaker's unresponsiveness as being unrelated to their own competence as a speaker; that either the nonresponse constituted a *non-hearing* (Grimshaw, 1981) or that it was a deliberate *misunderstanding*. In other circumstances, when the nonresponse can be attributed to the ineffectiveness of the solicitation strategy, such efforts on one's behalf to secure the desired second pair part might be met with resentment.

Determining What Rule Is Being Followed

Edmondson (1981b) argues that Sacks et al. have not provided adequately clear criteria for determining whether a sequence of turns as they appear in a transcript results from the fact that the turn-taking rules have been followed or whether in fact the sequence gives evidence of their violation (p. 39). Specifically, it is not always obvious whether an utterance results from self-selection under rule 1 (b) or other-nomination under rule 1 (a):

B: Andy just paid me back my fifty bucks.
A: Great. You guys wanta go out for pizza?
C: Hey B, Can you loan me ten dollars?

In this example, it cannot be entirely clear to A whether or not his solicit for dinner companions has been granted by C conditional upon B's providing the pecuniary wherewithal, or whether in fact C's request for a loan has nothing whatsoever to do with going out for pizza, and represents instead a self-selecting response prompted by B's announcement that he is flush. While subsequent conversational developments will doubtless resolve A's confusion, at the time it occurs A will be unable to determine what rule C is following, if indeed he is following a rule at all.

The Projectability of Turn-Constructional Units

A final critism that might be launched against the Sacks et al. model is that the concept of the projectability of a turn-constructional unit, and the attendent issue of prediction of transition-relevance places, is inadequately specified. We have already discussed some of the intonational and other cues associated with the exchange of speaker-hearer roles; however, not a great deal has been said by Sacks et al. on the syntactic cues to the impending completion of an utterance, or, just as important, the potential number of TCUs with which the turn will be built. One of the most obvious facts about conversation is that we are constantly signaling our intentions to our partners. Thus, there are numerous devices, documented under a variety of labels, which allow a speaker to make manifest that she wishes to claim the right to an entire *sequence* of turn-constructional units: these include *story-prefacing* statements (Sacks, 1972), *joke prefaces* (Cody, Erickson, Schmidt, 1983), and story significance statements (Ryave, 1978). Such devices indicate that the speaker wishes to reserve a "block" of TCUs of indeterminate length. Some blocks may only consist of a single additional turn-constructional unit, and some will be considerably longer. Certain of the devices can be very constraining; Creider (1981) reports that in Luo, interruptions are most likely to occur at the point at which the speaker's utterance diverges from his proposed theme, as promised in a thematization statement. Other TCU-reserving devices include *major semantic field indicators* ("I have a bone to pick with you about that"), *subject-expansions* ("And furthermore," "In a case like this,"), *subject evaluations* ("Yet on the other hand," and "But then again,"), and *action strategy* announcements ("Here's what you can do"), (Keller, 1981). One clear implication of the availability of such devices is that the Sacks et al. model is incorrect in the claim that the point at which option 1 (c) is exercised is the transition-relevance place: it is usually exercised much earlier than that.

Within turn-constructional units hearers must rely on their knowledge of syntax, semantic connectives, normal forms, and the like in order to project when an individual utterance might be complete. For instance, hearers will ordinarily presume that a subject will come first and that a predicate will follow. Although Sacks et al. underestimate the utility of semantic connectives (1978, p. 32), it is clear that a "But" at the start of an utterance will influence hearers to predict that the utterance will be over when the contrast to a prior utterance has been made. Similarly, an "If" at the beginning of a TCU will lead hearers to predict that it will conclude when a condition has been stated, and an "And" at the beginning of a TCU will lead to the expectation that the utterance will be complete when an additional element has been specified. The presence of words like "Why" or "Who" in initial positions in TCUs sensitizes listeners to the possibility of being nominated for a next turn, and increases their motivation to listen (Sacks, 1972). Key words like "including" or "only" will allow the hearer to predict the potential number of thematic participants. The issue of how the discourse cues hearers to the location of transition-relevance places is a complex one, and deserves more attention than it can be given here.

CONVERSATIONAL GAPS

Distinctions Among Hesitation Pauses, Switching Pauses, and Initiative Time Latencies

Sacks et al. have claimed that while the turn-taking system minimizes gaps between turns, nonetheless, there is systematic provision for the probability of interturn silence by virtue of the fact that taking or continuing the turn under rules 1 (b) and 1 (c) is optional. Indeed, there is evidence that in the stream of talk the presence of brief periods of silence is commonplace. One of the objections raised earlier to so-called technical definitions of the turn is that they fail to distinguish among the various kinds and characterizations of silence with which conversational parties have to cope. The usual distinction from a structural point of view is between the within-turn silence or *hesitation pause,* and the post- (or pre-) turn silence known as a *switching pause.* In most of the technical definitions, which have the indescribable advantage for the researcher that a machine can understand them, both hesitation and switching pauses are assigned as part of the current speaker's turn. The primary way of distinguishing between a hesitation pause and a switching pause is that the former is bounded on either side by current-speaker talk, while the latter is bounded by different speakers on either side. The duration of the pause is usually insufficient to distinguish between hesitation pauses and switching pauses. For instance, Garvey and Berninger (1981) found hesitation pauses in child discourse typically to be around .5 second. However, switching pauses also are typically short. Jaffe and Feldstein (1970) found that for pairs of females engaging in a 30 minute conversation, switching pauses averaged .664 seconds with a standard deviation of .165 seconds. Norain and Murphy (1938) reported a mean of .41 seconds for telephonic switching pauses. Now if we can only distinguish between hesitation pauses and switching pauses on the basis of the former's having same-speaker boundaries and the latter's having different-speaker boundaries, what are we to make of so-called *initiative time latencies?* Initiative time latencies (Matarazzo & Weins, 1967) refer to the length of time it takes A to *retake* the floor after she realizes that her partner is not going to respond.

Matarazzo and Weins found that initiative time latency is clearly different from hesitation pause duration, yet both have the characteristic that the pause is bounded on both sides by the same speaker. Are we to treat the following as one or two turns for A? (See Goodwin, 1981.)

A: When do we have our test in history?
                            (4.0)
A: Alan. When do we have our history test?
B: Friday.

The turn-assignment problem posed by initiative time latencies points up the fact that too-rigid definitions of the turn may serve to obscure rather than clarify conversational events.

Variation in Switching Pause Duration

Switching pause duration, that is, how quickly B takes up the turn upon A's completion of his own, varies from one situation and subject population to the next. Children typically have longer switching pauses than adults. Telephone switching pauses are usually shorter than those in face-to-face interaction, suggesting that some of the so-called turn transfer signals other than intonation contour and syntactic completeness confuse more than they clarify; however, the additional cues may simply take more time to monitor.

Considering children alone, Garvey and Berninger (1981) found that variations in the complexity and predictability of second pair parts had a substantial effect on the length of switching pauses. For exchanges with simple, predictable second pair parts, such as

A: Hey, Mary!
B: What?

the mean switching pause for children 2-5 was .9 seconds. For exchanges with complex but predictable second pair part types, such as

A: I got a doggy.
B: What kind?
A: Brown.

the mean switching pause was 1.2 seconds. As the second pair part in the exchange became both complex and unpredictable, such as

A: What's that?

B: I think it's maybe a zebra.

the mean switching pause duration was 1.63 seconds. Thus, switching pause is clearly a function of encoding difficulty, or the extent to which a response is readily available. It is also clear that following questions, at least, switching pauses ought to be attributed to the turn of the second speaker rather than the first, as in the technical definitions, if in fact it is appropriate to assign switching pauses to either of the speakers.

When Switching Pauses Proves Awkward

One of the most interesting aspects of conversational gaps is that, under a particular set of circumstances, switching pauses of a certain length may be experienced by parties as "awkward," in the sense that the absence of talk is perceived as a negative commentary on their respective competencies as communicators and/or the extent to which they are comfortable together. In an earlier section, several studies were reported that suggested that long latencies of response are both stereotypically and in fact associated with a lesser degree of social skill. This is not to suggest that communicative silences are perceived as awkward under all circumstances. Newman (1978) has reported that interactive silences are not troublesome provided that they are covered with some activity. Certainly, the discontinuous nature of household talk, lapses in conversation during task-related activity, and the casual engagement characteristic of stranger interactions in transitional settings such as airplanes will not pose challenges to parties' feelings of competence and relational comfort.

There are also cross-cultural differences in attitudes toward silence. Philips (1976, p. 88) reported that among the Warm Springs Indians, silences that Anglos "rush into and fill" are tolerated by the Indians. Similarly, Reisman (1974) reports that Danes, and Lapps in northern Sweden, are comfortable with silence, and in the case of Danes, are made nervous by American insistence on filling conversational gaps.

It does, however, appear that at least in American society, in social encounters where the primary focus of activity is on conversational exchange, for example the dinner date, there is considerable pressure upon the parties to sustain interaction and avoid potential gaps.

Switching Pauses as Dyadic Phenomena

In much of the more technical work on turn-taking, switching pauses have been treated as part of the turn of the current speaker (Jaffe and Feldstein, 1970; Feldstein and Welkowitz, 1978). Most of the scholars pursuing the "social skills" line of research (Arkowitz et al., 1975, Biglan et al., 1980; Dow et al., 1980) attribute the switching pause to the noncurrent speaker and describe it as a "response latency." It does not, however, appear entirely clear that switching pauses that are unusually long are to be "blamed" on an individual speaker; rather, it seems more appropriate to treat switching pauses as a dyadic phenomenon, for a variety of reasons (McLaughlin & Cody, 1982). First, switching pause duration appears to be susceptible to interactional synchrony or response matching effects (Cappella & Planalp, 1982), such that the mean response latency of an individual over the course of conversation will vary as a function of the length of her partner's response latency. Second, while it may make sense to attribute some switching pauses only to the "next" speaker, as opposed to the "prior" speaker, for example, when the next speaker is contemplating the answer to a question, given what has already been reported concerning the effects of the complexity and predictability of response requirements, we could just as easily lay the long latency at the feet of the prior speaker for making heavy encoding demands upon his partner. Third, one of the basic requirements for the smooth exchange of speaker turns is that utterances be *implicative* for subsequent turns (Jefferson, 1978); that is, that they provide the next speaker with instruction on how to proceed. If the next speaker cannot think of anything to say, it is just as likely that the prior speaker didn't give her much guidance as it is that the speaker lacked competence. Some kinds of utterances, like questions, are highly prospective and pose few problems for a next speaker making a subsequent turn; others, for example, assertions or acknowledgements, are much less implicative, and consequently make it more difficult for the subsequent speaker in constructing a next turn. Finally, conversations appear to go through natural cycles in which sections of talk are opened, developed, and closed. On the local or utterance-by-utterance level, exchanges are closed when the acts or moves that initiate them are satisfied (Edmondson, 1981b); following a closed exchange, for example, assert-agree, the question of who takes the next turn may be problematic, and similarly with question-answer pairs (Sacks et al., 1978). The same cycle of development and decay occurs with respect to the propositional structure of interaction; topics are prefaced or introduced by significance statements, worked until they are exhausted, and closed. An obvious next topic may not be at hand following closure of an old topic, nor may it be clear whose responsibility it is to find one.

The Conversational Lapse Defined

Having presented the case that the conversational lapse is a dyadic phenomenon, let us proceed to an operational definition of the lapse, and a more careful examination of the circumstances under which it occurs. McLaughlin & Cody (1982, p. 301) define a lapse as *"an extended silence (3 seconds or more) at a transition-relevance place, in a dyadic encounter the focus of which is conversation"*: specifically excluded are (1) silence following an interrogative or imperative TCU; (2) silence subsequent to turn-holding cues such as grammatical incompleteness, sustaining intonation contours, or filled pauses; (3) silence that co-occurs with activity by one or both of the parties, such as lighting a cigarette or searching for one's wallet; (4) "silence representing discretion in the presence of a third party" (McLaughlin & Cody, 1982, p. 301).

McLaughlin & Cody selected the 3-second silence criterion as an "awkwardness limen" for a number of reasons: (1) initiative time latencies (the length of time it takes for the reinstitution of talk by A following a failure by B to take a turn) are typically just over 3.0 seconds (Matarazzo & Weins, 1967); (2) the social skills researchers suggest that latencies as brief as 3.0 or 4.0 seconds significantly affect competency ratings (Weimann, 1977; Biglan, Glaser, & Dow, 1980); (3) ordinarily, mean switching pause duration appears to be less than one second (Jaffe and Feldstein, 1970); (4) Goldman-Eisler (1968) did not report any cases of persons whose hesitation pauses in spontaneous speech were longer than 3.0 seconds. While it is clear that not all interaction silences of 3.0 or more seconds will be lapses in the "participant" sense, nonetheless the researcher is not likely to have continuous access to participants' "senses" and so must resort to reasonable inferences. McLaughlin & Cody found that dyads with three or more lapses of longer than 3.0 seconds in the course of a 30-minute conversation rated their partners as significantly less competent than dyads whose conversations had fewer lapses.

Relation of Minimal Responses to Conversational Lapses

McLaughlin & Cody, looking at lapses in some of the conversations of the corpus used to illustrate this text, found that many of the pre-lapse sections of talk were characterized by patterns of *minimal response* (acknowledgements, mirror responses, and laughter) by one of the participants. They argued, using Schank's (1977) notion of how it is that utterance topics are formulated, that minimal responses do not contribute to topic advancement in that they neither reduce the old topic nor contribute new elements (Edelsky's nonreferential aspect) to the potential topic.

Support for the view that minimal responses tend to close off topics and discourage initiative comes from other quarters. Fishman (1978) found that minimal responses were used by husbands to discourage conversational initiatives by their wives. Zimmerman and West (1975) found that in 11 of their 13 observed instances of a delayed (> 1.0 second) minimal response by one conversational partner, the outcome was a "perceptible" silence on the part of the other partner. Derber (1979) describes the use of minimal responses as a way of being "civilly egocentric." According to Derber, strategies for shifting the focus of a topic from the other to one's self are either active or passive. Active strategies involve the use of carefully planned local propositional links, which appear to legitimate the shift of focus from one speaker to another:

A: You're from El Paso?*
B: Uh huh.
A: Huh! Well, what's in El Paso?
B: Lots of things! Juarez, mainly, Ha ha.
A: Oh really. Do you know Lee Trevino?
B: No.
A: He-he used to have a golf course up there.
B: Yeah, we used to ride up there. Yeah, *I* did.
A: And the he-he did some golf stuff.
B: You knew him?!!
A: Um hmm.

On the other hand, a much simpler, *passive* method for accomplishing a topic shift is to simply provide background acknowledgements as opposed to the supportive questions and assertions that normally characterize the behavior of the truly interested recipient (Derber, 1979, p. 31):

A: My dad taught me all the different things about farmin', as* far as workin'.

B: Um hmm.

A: I never did get a chance to learn any of the business part of it. I think that's one reason I was kinda interested in it, plus I figured if there was any occupation I get a degree in and still be able to farm part of the time that'd be bankin' or somethin'.

B: Um hmm.

A: Keep regular hours.

B: Um hmm.

(3.0)

Relation of Formulations to the Conversational Lapse

A subsequent pass through the same data set used in McLaughlin & Cody suggests that global as well as local coherency issues were involved in the occurrence of lapses. Many of the conversational lapses upon reexamination appear to follow immediately upon, or very shortly thereafter, a *formulation* (Garfinkel & Sacks, 1970; Heritage & Watson, 1979). Garfinkel and Sacks (1970, p. 351) characterize formulating as "saying-in-so-many-words-what-we-are-doing:"

A member may treat some part of the conversation as an occasion to describe that conversation, to explain it, or characterize it, or explicate, or translate, or summarize, or furnish the gist of it, or take note of its accordance with rules, or remark on its departure from rules. That is to say, a member may use some part of the conversation as an occasion to *formulate* the conversation [Garfinkel & Sacks, 1970, p. 350].

Formulations might be regarded as textual embodiments of macropropositions. Heritage and Watson (1979) argue that they result from and evidence the macrorule-like operations of preservation, deletion, and transformation of a whole section of talk. Formulations serve as comments on talk, providing proposed interpretations of the sense of the conversation-so-far. As proposals, they are subject to confirmation or disconfirmation; that is, *decision* by the hearer (Heritage & Watson, 1979, p. 142).

Formulations in dyadic conversations may be about B-Issues or B-Events in which case one speaker formulates his understanding of the "gist" or "upshot" (Heritage & Watson, 1979, p. 130) of the other's line of talk; they may be about A-Issues or A-Events, in which case the speaker characterizes, describes, or sums up a topic he himself has initiated and developed; less frequently, formulations may be about AB-Events or Issues, in which case either speaker proposes a "candidate reading" for some issues or event jointly known to the parties. The first two cases are described by Heritage & Watson as, respectively, "news-recipient" and "news-deliverer" formulations (1979, pp. 124-125).

Heritage & Watson propose that one use of formulations is to terminate topical talk prefatory to the launching of some new topic, or to the termination of a topic as a whole. In reexaming the McLaughlin & Cody data, formulations prior to lapses seem to have been employed either by topic initiators to acknowledge that a topic had been exhausted, or by their partners to bring the section of talk to a swift conclusion. Many of the pre-lapse conversational segments seem to contain both minimal responses and formulations. The provision and confirmation of formulations seemed to be a way in which partners signaled their mutual recognition that the topic could no longer sustain a line of talk; of formalizing at a topical level what the minimal responses had hinted at locally.

B-Issue and B-Event formulations were almost invariably likely to receive a second pair in the form of a confirmation; consequently, a lapse did not always follow immediately, but usually occurred within a few turns of the formulation:

    B: That wasn't the school I wanted to be goin' to, anyway.*
          I just went to that one cause it was close to home and
          I wasn't ready to leave.
(1) A: *Didn't want to go away from home, huh?*
    B: Uh huh.
    A: Ha ha. I couldn't wait, when I got out of high school.
    B: Well by the time I came out here I was ready to get away.
          I was goin' up the wall.

                              (3.8)

    B: He'd been here a semester longer than I had=*
                                        (   )
(2) A: Uh huh.
    B: =So I

A: *(So you thought he knew everything.*
B: Yeah. Well, I was pretty much from the sticks=
                                    ( )
A: Yeah.
B: =and I-it took me a long time to figure things out.

(7.2)

In both examples (1) and (2), none of the post-formulation talk introduces a proposition that has not already been implicit in the conversation-to-date.

Following some of the B-Event formulations, there was no apparent effort to squeeze out a few more turns; the formulation-confirmation pair led to an immediate lapse:

(3) B: And of course I have three aunts and two uncles and a*
         great-aunt and a great-uncle and all my cousins are in
         teaching.
    A: *Whole family's in it, huh?*
    B: Just about.

(3.0)

(4) A: I had a lot of tire problems. I had those Firestone 500's=*
                                   ( )
    B: Um hmm.
    A: =I had about three or four blowouts over about a four-year
         period=
                                   ( )
    B: Oh Goll-lee!.
    A: =I was
    B: *(Think I'd be changin' em!*
    A: I did. I got away from them.

(3.0)

When the topic that failed had been introduced by A, the person doing the formulating, there was a strong tendency for formulations to go unconfirmed, and to lead immediately to a lapse:

(5) A: And you can forget 'em. Anyway, now you know*
         what other people think about me.
    B: No, uh
    A: *(I'm not independent at all. I rely a whole lot on my parents
         and on my friends, and on my boyfriend, you know. I have
         to— to have to have a lot of people around me, I have
         to have a lot of people tell me what to do. I can't
         make decisions. I'm just a real baby, I guess.*

(3.8)

(6) **A:** So I was just sweatin' it out, you know. I had to get*
like 20-21 right on this final to make a—to pass the course.
I think I got 25, 26 of 'em right. And I was guessin'.
I did not know one single answer, you know. I just guessed
it.

    B: Ha ha.

    A: *It was pathetic.*

(3.2)

Those A-Event or A-Issue formulations that were confirmed tended
to result in much shorter lapses, probably because it was more
apparent to both parties that a new topic had to be found.

The most deadly of all formulations, which for want of a better term
we might call "absolutist" formulations, were only ambiguously
related to the notion of consensus on topic failure. In cases in which
absolutist formulations were produced, it was not always clear from
the discourse itself that the conversation was floundering; rather, it
appeared that the formulator unilaterally closed off the topic with an
utterance so final that virtually no coherent proposition could be
found to link to it as a next utterance. These absolutist formulations
had no "variables," no classes of thematic participants from which a
next turn could be constructed. Terms like "anything," "nothing,"
"everybody," "never," and "always" were typical of such formulations:

    B: Man, I've seen some of those guys up close, you know.*
They were so filthy, I don't see how they could stand to
live that way.

(7) **A:** I'on't know either.

    B: I wonder, you know, if they- they have a place to
live- ride around all the time.

    A: *I'on't know. There's no tellin'.*

(4.0)

(8) **B:** O. K. It's in the class.*

    A: It's where I'm supposed to be right now.

    B: Yeah.

    A: It's pretty fun, I guess.

    B: Hmmm!

    A: You don't know what to teach lot of times. *I mean, I
couldn't teach anything in business. It'd be kind of
boring, I think, to everybody else.*

(4.2)

(9)　**A:**　I think after a while they-their country's=*

　　　　　　　　　　　　　　　(　　　　)

　　　B:　　　　　　　　　　　　They're

　　　A:　=gonna go under.

　　　B:　Really.

　　　A:　You know, when it does it'll be—then *it'll be complete*
　　　　　　chaos, and nobody'll be safe, especially Americans.

　　　B:　Um hmm.

　　　A:　So-oh.

　　　B:　Hmm.

(3.3)

Although there are three minimal responses by B before the lapse, note that two of them appear *after* A's formulation.

Relation of Closed Exchanges to the Conversational Lapse

One final point that ought to be made with respect to the appearance of lapses in focused dyadic encounters is that they do not, at least in this corpus, appear to have been related systematically to closed exchanges, as Edmondson's (1981b) work would suggest. While as we have just shown lapses were likely to follow formulation-decision pairs, they were just as likely to follow formulations that were neither confirmed nor disconfirmed. The most obvious kind of conversational closed exchange, question-answer (we exclude assert-agree for the dubious implicativeness of its first pair part), was found to lead to a lapse in only four of ninety cases of lapse examined, two of those lapses coming from the same dyad. Although assumption of the role of next speaker may not be automatic following closed exchanges, there did not appear to be any evidence in the McLaughlin & Cody data that closed exchanges generally were likely to result in gaps in the conversation.

Concluding Remarks about Silence in Conversation

To say that lapses in conversation tend to be preceded by minimal responses, or formulation-decision pairs, is not to provide an *explanation* for conversational discontinuities. Minimal responses and formulations do not as a rule *account* for topic failures; rather they mark the fact that the topic can no longer sustain interaction. The roots of interactive silence in conversation must for the most part be found in extraconversational sources, such as the knowledge and interests of the parties to talk. Considerable attention to the matter on the part of a number of scholars suggests that, so far, discourse itself has provided few cues as to why conversational lapses occur.

In terms of the appropriate assignment of conversational silences, it seems fair to say that silence bounded on either side by different speakers, that is, the switching pause, should not be assigned to the turn of either speaker. Silence bounded on either side by talk from the same speaker should be treated as a hesitation pause and included in the turn of that speaker, unless an utterance immediately prior to the silence is characterized by turn-yielding signals, such as a falling intonation contour or grammatical completeness; then, the silence should be treated as separating two turns.

SIMULTANEOUS TALK IN CONVERSATION

Sacks et al. argue that the turn-taking system as they have modeled it operates to minimize simultaneous talk. Indeed, Garvey and Berninger (1981) reported that only 5% of the utterances of the children in their studies were accompanied by another's simultaneous talk. Some simultaneous talk appears to be provided for systematically by certain features of the conversational system (Sacks et al., 1978): these features include the possibility of competing self-selectors, and the fact that turn-constructional units may extend beyond their apparent first possible completion point, and the need for precision timing to avoid irrelevancy.

Systematic Bases for Simultaneous Talk

Jefferson (1973) argues that satisfaction of the "intrinsic motivation for listening" (Sacks et al., 1978), being able to predict the next possible transition-relevance place, is a systematic source of simultaneous talk in conversation. When a listener can project not only when an utterance will be completed, but especially *how* it will be completed, the loss of the motive for listening provides a reason to begin talking immediately. That is, in order for a hearer to make a credible demonstration that she already possesses information that the speaker is attempting to provide her with, or that she has in fact already assimilated the significance of the speaker's report, the hearer may be required to begin her utterance appreciably prior to a transition-relevance place, since to delay might render her contribution irrelevant and not credible.

Competently produced interruption, in Jefferson's view, demonstrates the sensitivity of the speaker to the "no sooner" and the "no later" constraints. Consider the following example (Rosenstein, 1982; Rosenstein & McLaughlin, 1983):

A: I'll pick you up at the
B: (at the gate. I know.

B's utterance is precisely placed: a fraction of a second later and B's claim to have been "told already" would be less credible; thus, we have B showing sensitivity to the "no later" constraint. If, on the other hand, B places the utterance much earlier, she takes a chance on making an incorrect projection of the remainder of A's utterance: hence, the "no sooner" constraint.

A: I'll pick you up at the
B: (at five-thirty. I know
A: I was gonna say I'd pick you up at the gate.

Goodwin (1981) suggests that a further systematic basis for simultaneous talk lies in the need of speakers to secure the gaze of their hearers. Thus, for example, a speaker might lengthen words or sounds at the end of a turn-constructional unit to coincide with receipt of the speaker's gaze. Similarly, a speaker might repeat herself in order to provide time for the hearer to bring his gaze around to a position of full engagement (Goodwin, 1981, p. 131).

Technical Approaches to Simultaneous Talk

Simultaneous talk has been approached in a variety of different ways. In the very technical definitions, for example Jaffe and Feldstein's (1970), an overlap, regardless of where in the current speaker's utterance it might intrude, is treated as part of, and in fact the initiation of, the turn of the subsequent speaker, while the overlapped portion of the prior speaker's utterance is not treated as part of anyone's turn. Schegloff's (1973) case for distinguishing between overlap and interruptions also smacks of a technical mentality:

> By overlap we tend to mean talk by more than one speaker at a time which has involved that a second one to speak given that a first was already speaking, the second one has projected his talk to begin at a possible completion point of the prior speaker's talk. If that's apparently the case, if for example, his start is in the environment of what could have been a completion point of the prior speaker's turn, then we speak of it as an *overlap*. If it's projected to begin in the middle of a point that is in no way a possible completion point for the turn, then we speak of it as an *interruption* [italics mine].

Nontechnical Approaches to Simultaneous Talk

At the other extreme, we have the approach of Bennett (1981), who does not acknowledgement the very technical definitions, and who rejects Schegloff's approach on the grounds that the major elements in his operationalization are not the "physical manifestations" in the discourse that he seems to imply. Bennett's approach to simultaneous talk and particularly interruption is "participant-sense" in the way in which Edelsky (1981) has used the term. Overlap is dismissed as a "descriptive term" about the structure of the discourse, while interruption is treated as an "interpretive category" that parties employ as a resource for sorting out their feelings and beliefs about their comparative privileges and obligations in the conversation-so-far (Bennett, 1981, p. 176). The diagnosis (or accusation) that an interruption has occurred, according to Bennett, requires that one believe (1) that the author of the intruding utterance was doing something she ought not to have been doing, and (2) that there were opportunities available to her to do something else other than interrupt (1981, p. 177). For example, in Bennett's view, if A had just related a crucial detail in a narrative and then B produced a turn about some tangential detail, for example, the address at which the central action of the narrative took place, or irrelevant characteristics of the central actor, B's comment could be classified as an interruption, at least in the participant-sense view of the term, even though no actual simultaneous talk had taken place. While it is clear that B in this case was being a bad fellow, or at least an insensitive one, Bennett's view seems to require too much inference on the part of the analyst, and a virtually continuous inquiry into the attribution processes of the affected participant. It seems that a definition of interruption that is not explicitly tied to simultaneous talk renders the task of the analyst virtually unmanageable.

What Simultaneous Talk Signifies

While Bennett's characterizations of interruptions and overlaps lack adequate definition, she is entirely correct in her assertion that how one *feels* about having one's turn intruded upon varies considerably as a function of the accounts one constructs for the other's behavior. Certainly, many persons, not the least of whom are scholars, regard interruption as an index of speaker dominance. Much of early research in which simultaneous talk featured as a variable treated interruption as a correlate of speaker dominance or power (Mishler & Waxler, 1968; Meltzer, Morris, & Hayes, 1971; Leighton, Stollock, & Ferguson, 1971; Hadley & Jacob, 1971; Rogers & Jones, 1975; Willis & Williams, 1976; Ferguson, 1977).

However, there does not seem to be evidence that not only are interruptions commonplace, but that most speakers do not regard them as significant, and take them in stride. Spelke, Hirst, and Nesser (1976) demonstrated that people can carry out several information processing tasks at a time. Garvey and Berninger (1981) found that simultaneous talk did not pose a threat to coherence: the resumption of speech and turn-transfer did not take appreciably longer than the usual speaker-pause length. While in the prevailing culture in the United States interruptions may seem to be a conversational matter of some consequence, Reisman (1974) reports that in the Antiguan village he examined not only were there no norms against interruption, but there also seemed to be a prevailing pattern of "counter-noise," such that another's talking seemed to be a good enough reason for one to begin talking himself, at the same time. Philips (1976), on the other hand, reports that interruptions among the Warm Springs Indians are extremely rare.

Temporal Parameters and Continuity
in the Classification of Simultaneous Talk

What is proposed for the remainder of this section is development of a two-pronged thesis: first, that ordinary English language users are able to distinguish between overlaps and/or interruptions that are *disruptive* in that they produce discontinuity in the current speaker's talk, and those intrusions in which the continuity of the first speaker's turn is not affected; second, that ordinary users of English are at least modestly sensitive to the issue of the precision timing of interruptions. Thus, an argument will be made on behalf of an approach to interruption that emphasizes the importance of temporal placement and speaker continuity.

A first question: How may simultaneous turns be categorized with respect to the amount of discontinuity they produce? Rosenstein and McLaughlin (Rosenstein, 1982; Rosenstein & McLaughlin, 1983) presented subjects with representative interruptions from three categories: *overlaps, forced interruptions,* and *attempted interruptions.* Overlaps referred to exchanges in which both parties talk simultaneously with neither party yielding the turn. Interruptions and attempted interruptions referred to exchanges in which one of the two parties claiming the turn yields the floor.

Samples of exchanges with simultaneous talk were selected from an interruption pool of 100 items, garnered from ten of the 30-minute conversations between strangers from which we have been drawing examples in previous sections. Prior to the presentation of the examples to subjects, trained coders had been asked to sort the examples into the three categories, with the result that intercoder reliability ranged from .55 for forced interruptions to .82 for overlaps.

Overlaps were characterized as simultaneous talk that began in the environment of a transition-relevance place, which did not interfere with the current speaker's completion of his turn. The dimension of turn-taking *outcome* (whether the current speaker keeps or yields the floor) was also used in Hoffman's (1980) taxonomy of interruptions. Below are two examples of the overlaps presented to subjects:

(1) **A:** I haven't seen a movie in (1.0) *Amityville Horror House**
was the last, or, the *Amityville Horror* was the last movie I
saw and it stunk.

    B: (I didn't see that.

(2) **A:** How long have you known him. I mean where did*
y'all meet?

   B: (I met him in El Paso.

Some of the overlaps in the sample presented to subjects were like (2), in that they represent a case in which B's reason for starting to talk is that she has grasped the significance of A's utterance already; others, like (1), were simply "near" a transition-relevance place and probably represented a turn-taking error.

Forced interruptions were cases of simultaneous talk in which the intruding utterance resulted in the "legitimate" speaker's giving up his turn:

(3) **A:** They said they were on Joe Ely's guest list. Ha ha*
ha. The owner

   B: (Under what?
Motorcycle gang?

(4) **A:** Well, I'm not from Levelland. I just- my husband*
was transferred there and so, I'm stuck here, but I'm from
Snyder which is

   B: (I
heard of Synder, yeah.

Again, some of the forced interruptions were of the "precision timing" variety, like (5), while others, like (3), simply occurred near a transition-relevance place.

The third category, attempted interruptions, contained items in which the attempt to secure the turn was successful:

(5) **A:** I mean*

   B: (No, I

   A: I mean, if you don't dance, you can't talk.

(6) **A:** Every semester something new comes up=*

   B: (I

   A: =like you need this or you needed that.

None of the attempted interruptions in the original pool was of the precision timing kind; most seemed to occur near a transition-relevance place. In these interruptions, discontinuity marked the turn of the author of the intrusion rather than that of the speaker who originally claimed the floor.

Subjects in the Rosenstein and McLaughlin study were given 18 index cards, on each of which was typed a sample simultaneous talk exchange (six items for each of the three categories). Subjects were asked to sort the items into categories on the basis of similarity. The similarities data were clustered, and the resulting cluster solution was compared with the hypothesized three categories, using the trained coder classifications of the items as a criterion. The Rand agreement statistic was .88 (Rosenstein & McLaughlin, 1983). Subjects sorted the interruption examples into two of the original categories— overlaps and attempted interruptions—and two categories of forced interruptions, one of which did and one of which did not contain the precision timing items.

Analysis of the competency ratings of "Speaker B," the perpe- trator of the intruding utterance, indicated that there was a significant but very modest tendency for overlaps to be rated as more competent than attempted and forced interruptions, presumably because they neither disrupted the continuity of the current speaker's utterance, nor represented the mild loss of face involved in the unsuccessful attempted interruption. Ratings of the domineeringness of Speaker B as a function of the type of simultaneous talk (Rosenstein, 1982) indicated strongly that the outcome of the intrusion in terms of its effect on continuity was a major factor. Forced interruptions were rated as most domineering, and attempted interruptions as least domineering, with virtually no distinction in terms of domineeringness for overlaps and the precision timing forced interruptions. In other words, the speaker who succeeded in taking the turn away from her partner was rated as being less domineering if there was a readily apparent reason for her having interrupted at the point she did. Overlaps seemed to produce the judgment the neither speaker was particularly domineering.

While the Rosenstein and McLaughlin findings were based on an analysis of patterns of simultaneous talk found in conversations between strangers—and as a result might not be replicated with samples from encounters between friends or acquantances—never- theless, it seemed to be the case that only a very few of the instances of simultaneous talk involved interruption as Schegloff defined it: an intrusion "noticeably far" from a transition-relevance place. Doubt- less, this can be attributed to the presence of politeness rules that are more constraining on the behavior of strangers.

Simultaneous Talk as a Way of Honoring Conversational Maxims

Before we leave the issue of simultaneous talk altogether it might be interesting to speculate for a moment about other circumstances, in addition to the presence of "no sooner, no later" constraints, under which simultaneous talk can be seen to be orderly or even rule-preserving in the sense that the author of the intrusion is responding to the demands of a higher-order rule or maxim than the ban on interruption. For example, one might intervene precipitously to make sure that an incorrect statement by another would not be incorporated into a plan of action by a third party, thus showing sensitivity to the Quality maxim (Grice, 1975):

A: How do I get to El Cholo?
B: Well, you go North on Western and you make a left on Olympic and then you take
C: (No, he can't take Olympic because you can't make a left turn there this time of day.

In the preceding example, for C to have waited until the projectable completion of B's utterance would have resulted in extensive reprocessing for B.

An individual might also interrupt another in order to prevent her from violating the Morality maxim (Bach & Harnish, 1979), for example, violating a confidence:

A: Esther told me not to tell this to anybody, but she said that she and
B: (I don't want to hear about it if you promised her you wouldn't tell.

If B were to wait until the end of A's utterance, her intervention at that point would be meaningless.

Turn Boundaries When Simultaneous Speech Is Present

Issues of turn outcome or continuity appear to be important in how simultaneous speech is perceived and categorized. Consequently, the location of turn boundaries in research definitions of the turn ought to reflect a sensitivity to continuity issues. Thus, in the case of overlaps, when there is no apparent yielding prior to a transition-relevance place by the speaker with the prior claim to the floor, the overlapped portions of each speaker's turn should be treated as a part of his turn. Thus, in the example below, A's turn ends with the word "Monday," and B's turn begins with the word "When":

A: I signed up for the TSO course, starting next Monday.
B: (When does it start?

Given the sensitivity of the Rosenstein and McLaughlin subjects to the precision timing phenomenon, and the numerous instances one can think of in which interruption occurs because there is no further "reason" to listen, it would be tempting to take a "hearer-knows-best" approach to the turn and say that A's turn ends when B has heard enough. To do so, however, would place a considerable burden of inference on the shoulders of the conversational analyst, since there are many cases of simultaneous speech in which the interruptor's "reasons" are simply not apparent. In taking a hearer-knows-best approach to speech act assignment, we at least have the considerable body of knowledge about conventional perlocutionary effects to guide us.

In the case of forced interruptions, the end of the prior speaker's turn must be seen to coincide with the onset of the speaker's silence. Attempted interruptions may be treated similarly, assuming that the attempt lasted sufficiently long to count as an utterance, unlike the examples on pp. 126-127.

DEFINITION OF TURN

A turn is a structural slot, within which a speaker claims one (renewable) utterance-unit. Silence bounded on either side by talk from the same speaker should be treated as a hesitation pause in the absence of turn-yielding signals in the pre-silence utterance. Silence bounded on either side by the talk of different speakers is assigned to the turn of neither speaker.

SUMMARY

Talk is achieved through a series of turns in which there is a nonautomatic exchange of the speaker and hearer roles. Turns are opportunities-at-talk into which utterances are slotted. Turns are allocated locally and managed interactionally, one turn-constructional unit at a time, with option for renewal.

The turn-taking model of Sacks et al., which introduces the basic components of the turn-constructional unit and the transition-relevance place, proposes rules for the allocation of turns through the successive exercise of options available to current and other speakers. A number of issues have been raised with respect to the adequacy of the Sacks et al. model: (1) the lack of full specification of the components "turn-constructional unit" and "transition-relevance place"; (2) the inattention to the distinction between turns and non-turns; (3) failure to specify the cultures in which the model applies; (4) neglect of the hearer's role in the management of turn-taking; (5) inadequate specification of the range of options covered under the term "current-speaker-selects-next technique"; (6) insensitivity to different floor types; (7) insufficient attention to specifying the evidence for rule-conformity and rule-breaking; and (8) inadequate specification of the nature of "projectability."

Periods of silence in conversation may be variously classified as hesitation pauses, switching pauses, and initiative time latencies. The duration of switching pauses varies as a function of context; on some occasions, switching pauses are perceived as awkward if they are long enough. Switching pauses seem to be under the control of both members of a dyad, and therefore are not rightly considered as part of either speaker's turn. Long (more than 3.0 seconds) pauses are termed lapses. Recent research on lapses suggests that they represent topic failure, and that they are marked in conversation at the local level by minimal responses and globally by formulations. Closed exchanges do not appear routinely to result in lapses.

Simultaneous talk in interaction may be said to be systematically based in such requirements of the conversational system as the need to make utterances relevant and the need to secure the gaze of the hearer. Both technical and intuitive accounts of simultaneous talk have been reported. The significance of simultaneous talk may vary considerably depending upon the context and the biases of researchers. Data on simultaneous talk generated from laboratory conversations between pairs of strangers suggest that ordinary language users are most sensitive to two dimensions; temporal placement of the intrusion and utterance continuity or interruption outcome. Little evidence was found to support the notion that interruptions are a distinct class of simultaneous talk that occur "noticeably far" from a transition-relevance place, although this apparent finding may very well be limited to conversations between strangers. Turn boundaries in research definitions must reflect the issue of the continuity of utterances.

4

Acts

♦ In Chapter 2, the idea of a speech act or ♦ *illocutionary* act was introduced. An illocutionary act was defined as one which, if "felicitously" performed, would produce "uptake" in the hearer in the sense that she would recognize the speaker's *intention* in saying that X. The illocutionary force of an utterance, as was shown earlier, consists in the recognition of the speaker's purpose in making it, not in the effect that it has on the hearer in terms of the speaker's goal. This latter is known as the *perlocutionary* effect.

CLASSIFICATION OF SPEECH ACTS

A number of scholars have approached the task of classifying illocutionary acts with respect to the conventional "recognizable intent" of the actor who utters them. One such taxonomy (Bach & Harnish, 1979) was presented in Chapter 2. In the present chapter, two further taxonomies, one from the framework of speech act theory (Fraser, 1975), and the other from a social psychological perspective (Wish, 1980), will be explored with an eye to examining the underlying features of speech acts that appear to emerge from different perspectives.

Fraser (1975) argues that speech acts are differentiated primarily by the intent of the speaker in performing the act, where the speakers's intent generally is for the hearer to recognize his orientation with respect to the propositional content of the utterance. That is, the speaker "instructs" the listener as to how his message should be categorized (Wish et al., 1980). Fraser's taxonomy thus categorizes "positions a speaker might hold toward a proposition" (1975, p. 189). Performative verbs are assigned to eight categories. The first is *acts of asserting,* which includes such verbs as claim, accuse, inform, observe, remark, state, and grant. Acts of asserting reflect both the speaker's evaluation of how the expressed proposition relates to the context and how strongly she is convinced that the proposition is true. Fraser divide assertions into two classes, the first of which contains verbs like comment, notify, reply, and tell, the second of which is characterized by such verbs as accuse, allege, concede, confess, and predict. The former category is composed of verbs that describe actions for which the preconditions for successful performance are very few. For example, in order to accomplishing informing, it is not necessary that the propositional content be anything other than new to the hearer. However, among the preconditions for successful accusation is that the proposition be pejorative, that it reference an act of someone other than the speaker, and so on (Fraser, 1975, p. 191).

A second class of illocutionary acts proposed by Fraser consists of *acts of evaluating;* some verbs included in the second category are appraise, formulate, interpret, speculate, and characterize, which reflect the speaker's basis for the assessment of the truth-value of the expressed proposition. Fraser's first two categories of assertions and evaluations are treated jointly under the label "constatives" by Bach and Harnish (1979).

A third category, *acts of reflecting speaker attitude,* contains verbs that reflect how the speaker assesses the propriety of some prior act referenced by the proposition, such as accept, agree, commend, denounce, disagree, and oppose. The reader will recognize here the Bach and Harnish "acknowledgments" category.

A fourth Fraser category is *acts of stipulating,* including verbs like identify, define, specify, and classify, which reflect the speaker's desire that the hearer recognize her favorable attitude toward the "naming convention" expressed by the proposition. Stipulations are treated as constatives by Bach and Harnish. A fifth category, *acts of requesting,* includes verbs such as beg, implore, invite, prohibit, and request, which express S's desire that H undertake, or not undertake, some action referenced in the proposition. Bach and Harnish treat these verbs as "directives."

The three final categories of the Fraser taxonomy are *acts of suggesting* (advise, suggest, warn), *acts of exercising of authority* (appoint, approve, exempt, nullify), and *acts of committing* (promise, swear, volunteer). The latter category, committing, is duplicated in the Bach and Harnish category of "commissives," but the categories of suggesting and exercising authority have no direct correlates in the Bach and Harnish scheme.

It is most instructive to compare a classification of illocutionary verbs from the point of view of a speech act theorist to the treatment of speech acts by social psychologists. Wish et al. (1980) developed a speech act classification scheme that trained coders applied to the analysis of videotaped scenes from the television series *American Family* and to other taped segments of dyadic interaction. The superordinate categories of the coding system were (1) *assertions,* (2) *evaluations,* (3) *reactions,* (4) *questions,* and (5) *requests.* These superordinate categories, with the exception of *questions,* overlap considerably with taxonomies by Fraser and by Bach and Harnish. Superordinate categories were further specified: (1) assertions were coded as to their type, from "simple event report" to "complex judgment," and to the extent of their force, from "hedge" to "strong push to convince"; (2) evaluations were coded for referent (self, hearer, others) and level (positive, negative, or neutral); (3) reactions were coded for the type of attention given to the hearer; (4) questions were coded as to form (tag, rhetorical, wh-); and (5) requests were coded for type (information, direct action, etc.) and degree of pressure. Data were also coded using Bales's Interaction Process Analysis (Bales, 1950).

The coded data were factor analyzed and five factors emerged. The first, *asking versus informing,* represented a contrast between questions and information requests, and simple assertions and reactions; that is, one pole contained elements from the *requests* and *questions* categories, the other elements from the *assertions* and *reactions* categories. The second factor, *initiatory versus reactive,* contrasted a nonreactive *assertion* to all *reactions* and to *agreeing reactions.* The third factor, *dissension versus approval,* contrasted *negative reactions* and *self-approval evaluations to other-approval evalua-tions.* The forth factor, *forceful versus forceless,* was unmindful of categories: forceful utterances of several varieties (assertions, evaluations, requests) contrasted with forceless assertions and self-evaluation. Finally, on the fifth factor, *judgmental versus nonjudgmental,* judgmental assertions and all evaluations were positively loaded, while significant negative loadings were obtained for all questions, forceless requests, all requests, positive reactions, and requests for agreement or action.

Although we cannot expect a dimensional analysis to give us the "clusters" that would allow for a direct comparison of the Wish et al. results with the categories of speech acts proposed by Fraser and by Bach and Harnish, it is interesting to note that even though the Wish group began with superordinate categories based on types of performative verbs, representatives of the categories did not load together on the obtained factors. Items appeared to be grouped together on the basis of relational or interactional factors, rather than semantic ones. Requests, assertions, and evaluations, which are treated as distinct and self-contained categories in Fraser, were found by Wish et al to "slide around" considerably as a function of their relational or interactional implications. What the traditional speech act categories seem to be lacking is any sense of a hearer-orientation, which is interesting given Edmondson's (1981a) demonstration that hearer-support and not speaker-support is lexicalized in English. It makes less difference to the hearer whether what is "done" to him is an assertion or an evaluation than it does whether what was done was responsive to what he has said, as opposed to being unaffected by his own action; whether it is approving or disapproving; whether it is judgmental or nonjudgmental. While the suggestion here is that the relational aspects of speech acts are completely missed by the linguists, the term "relational" is being used rather loosely in adducing the Wish et al. study as evidence, since the issue of relational control is reflected only indirectly in their coding scheme, in the negative evaluations and judgmental assertions subclasses. In any event, the speech act theorists clearly overlook the fact that so-called directives, for example, can be achieved through other verb forms; that assertions can carry evaluation; that the type of evaluation is an important grouping criterion; and that "acts of exercising authority" extend beyond those granted legitimacy in the lexicon. In sum, categories of illocutionary verbs may not be the most promising source for the classification of speech acts as they are realized in conversation.

While speech act theory has not been shown to provide much guidance in the matter of the classification of communicative actions, there have certainly been some successes in specifying the conditions for the successful performance of illocutionary acts (Searle, 1969, 1975). In the remainder of this chapter, we shall consider a number of such accounts of speech acts in detail.

Weiner and Goodenough (1977) have proposed that acts or moves in conversation are of two varieties, *substantive* and "housekeeping," or *management*. Substantive moves make up, if you will, the "subject matter of conversation" (Weiner & Goodenough, 1977, p. 216), or the "pragmatic topics" that will be recalled subsequent to disengaging, such as that requests were made and granted, that compliments were given and accepted, and so forth. Management moves, on the other hand, do not contribute new elements either to the pragmatic topic or to the incrementation of the propositional context set. Rather, they serve as a means by which parties provide one another with "benchmarks" so that they know where they have been, conversationally, and also where they are going. Management acts are a significant way in which conversational partners instruct one another in how to treat what has gone before, and how to proceed in subsequent talk. Weiner and Goodenough (1977, p. 216) note that management acts are most likely to occur at beginnings and endings of encounters, and/or at topic boundaries within a particular conversation.

SUBSTANTIVE SPEECH ACTS

First, let us examine some substantive speech acts. Substantive acts may be direct or indirect; by the former is meant that their literal interpretation is their intended interpretation; and by the latter, that both their literal interpretation and "something more" is intended (Searle, 1975; Clark & Lucy, 1975). We will focus first on direct speech acts.

Direct Speech Acts

Interpretations from the perspective of speech act theory have informed accounts of any number of different acts, but the *requests* seem to have aroused the most interest (although most scholars have been more intrigued by indirect requests).

Requests. Labov and Fanshel (1977, p. 78) have formulated a *rule of requests: If speaker asks hearer to perform behavior A at time T, and hearer believes that speaker believes that (1) A ought to be performed; (2) hearer would not do A unless requested to; (3) hearer is capable of performing A; (4) hearer is either obliged to or willing to do A; and (5) speaker is entitled to tell hearer to perform A, then speaker's utterance counts as a valid request for action.* The third condition (hearer can do A) is called a *preparatory* condition (Searle, 1975, p. 71). To Labov and Fanshel's rule, several other conditions must be appended: *both* speaker and hearer must believe points 1-5 (Jacobs & Jackson, 1980); both speaker and hearer must believe that speaker wants hearer to do A (the *sincerity* condition); both must believe that the speaker is predicating some future behavior A of the hearer (the *propositional* content condition; Searle, 1975, p. 71).

Requests may vary considerably in grammatical mood, in degree of mitigation, in directness, and so forth. Recent evidence indicates that the form in which a request or any directive is presented is reflective of how the speaker sums up his relationship to the target of the request (Kemper & Thissen, 1981, p. 552): "The selection of a directive form allows the speaker to mark or neutralize differences in rank, age, or territoriality, and to indicate how serious the request is and whether or not compliance is assumed or expected."

There is some support for the proposition that making a direct request occurs infrequently, and that when it does, it signifies that politeness constraints are weak. Gibb (1981), using a scenario method, found thirteen different devices for making requests; only two of the devices could be considered as direct. Despite the fact that direct requests ("Give me the salt" as opposed to "I need the salt" or "Can you pass me the salt?") are not the most popular means of meeting one's needs, directness is nontheless one of the most salient dimensions against which requests are judged (Kemper & Thissen, 1981). Kemper and Thissen had subjects make pairwise ratings of ten different request forms for two requested actions, raking the leaves and loaning money. The authors took an imperative (for example, "rake") and an associated need-assertion (leaves need raking) and combined them with affirmative or negative interrogatives ("Do/Don't you think you should"), the use of please, and other features to arrive at the different request forms. The similarities data were scaled, and the two dimensions of *politeness* and *directness* were found to underlie the judgments of request similarity. On the directness factor imperatives had high positive loadings, and were contrasted with the less direct interrogative constructions and need-assertions.

Kemper and Thissen hypothesized that direct requests would be normative whenever compliance could be assumed; for example, when a superior makes a request of a subordinate. They reasoned, therefore, that when a direct form of request was attributed to a low-status speaker, the form of the request would be recalled more accurately than if it were attributed to a high-status speaker. Their findings indicated that those requests that were most accurately remembered were those that violated conversational rules.

Replies to requests. Not a great deal of work has been done on how replies to requests are formulated—other than in the compliance-resisting literature (McLaughlin et al., 1980) that focuses on the more macroscopic *strategies* of response. Labov and Fanshel (1977, p. 86) propose that there is a *rule for putting off requests: If the speaker has made a valid request that the hearer do some action A, and the hearer addresses to the speaker (1) a positive assertion or a question about the current status of A* ("I already picked up your suit at the cleaners"); *(2) a question or a negative assertion about the time frame of A* ("I can't get around to it today"); *(3) a question or negative assertion about one of the felicity conditions associated with making a request* (such as need, ability, obligation, or rights), *then the hearer's utterance should be heard as putting off the request.* Putting off could also be accomplished by invoking the *sincerity* condition: "Wouldn't you really rather get it yourself, so you can make sure they did it the way you wanted?"

Another way of putting off requests, according to Labov and Fanshel, is by responding with a request for information:

A: Can you pick up my suit at the cleaners today?
B: Are they open 'til 6:00?

This response is usually heard as asserting that the speaker needs the information in order to deal with the request, the so-called *rule of embedded request* (Labov & Fanshel, 1977, p. 91).

Labov and Fanshel provide an interesting example of how rules, specifically the rule of embedded requests, may be exploited for strategic gain. They examine a frustrating conversation between

Rhoda, a young patient suffering from anorexia nervosa, and her mother. The conversation is reported by Rhoda to her therapist. Rhoda's mother has been staying with Rhoda's married sister, Phyllis, for a few days in order to help out with a family crisis. Rhoda feels overwhelmed by the joint burden of the household duties and her schoolwork, and desperately wants her mother to return home. However, Rhoda fears making a direct request, as to do so would be tantamount to an admission that she can't look after herself. So, she makes an indirect request, by inquiring about the time frame for performance of the desired action (Labov & Fanshel, 1977, p. 168):

Rhoda: Well, when do you plan to come home?

Her mother then expolits the rule of embedded requests:

Mother: Oh, why-y?

Although it is clear to Rhoda that the question is not a legitimate request for information, but rather a rhetorical question with the clear implication "Can't get along without me, eh?" Rhoda, being no match for her mother, behaves conventionally and treats the utterance as a legitimate question (Labov & Fanshel, 1977, p. 168):

Rhoda: Well, things are getting just a little too *much!* This is- i's jis getting too hard, and . . . I-

Since Rhoda's original request is still in force, having only been put off, Mother again exploits a rule by asserting her *inability* to return home; that is, her other daughter needs her:

Mother: Why don't you tell Phyllis that?"

Rhoda is once again led to treat her mother's utterance as a legitimate request for information, and responds with a weak, "Well, I haven't talked to her lately," when she should have challenged her mother's implications. Rhoda's inability to deal with rule-exploitation substantially limited her capacity for confronting significant challenges to her autonomy and status as an adult.

There will be much more to say on the topic of requests in the section on indirect speech acts. A further example of a direct speech act whose forms have received considerable attention is the compliment (Pomerantz, 1978; Manes & Wolfson, 1981; Knapp, Hopper, & Bell, 1983).

Compliments. To date, no one has tried to formulate a "rule" for compliments in the same spirit as they have laid out preconditions for the performance of requests. As a start, one might propose that an utterance will be taken as a compliment if both speaker and hearer believe that the speaker predicates of the hearer some positively valued attribute or property; further, in the usual sense in which compliment is used, that the positive evaluation is conveyed verbally to the hearer, and is intended to be heard; further, that the prediction is of some attribute or property of the hearer as opposed to some *good luck* that has befallen him or *success* that he has visibly achieved. Thus we may *congratulate* the groom for his marriage, and *compliment* him on his choice of bride; we may not, however, do the reverse. Finally, in order for the compliment to be performed felicitously, the speaker must believe the prediction; otherwise, the action counts as *flattering*.

Manes and Wolfson (1981) have made an intensive examination of a large corpus of compliments collected in urban areas in Virginia and Pennsylvania. The basic contention of Manes and Wolfson with respect to compliments is that they are formulaic. For example, in 546 of the 686 compliments collected, the "work" of the compliment was carried by a positive adjective. In 22.9% of these cases, the adjective was *nice;* in another 19.6%, the adjective was *good*. In all, Manes and Wolfson found that two-thirds of the adjectival compliments were carried by only five adjectives: nice, good, pretty, beautiful, and great.

Manes and Wolfson (1981, p. 120) found that compliments followed a limited number of syntactic patterns. One pattern accounted for more than half of the compliments (elements in parentheses are optional):

$$\text{NOUN PHRASE} \quad \genfrac{}{}{0pt}{}{\text{is}}{\text{looks}} \quad \text{(really) ADJECTIVE}$$

A typical realization of this pattern is "Your paper is really well written." A second pattern accounted for slightly over 16% of the compliments:

$$\text{I (really)} \quad \genfrac{}{}{0pt}{}{\text{like}}{\text{love}} \quad \text{NOUN PHRASE}$$

A typical compliment in this vein might be "I really like your shirt." A third important pattern, realized in compliments like "You are really a terrific daddy," characterized almost 15% of the sample items:

PRONOUN are (really) (a) ADJECTIVE NOUN PHRASE

The finding that they could account for 85% of the compliments in their sample with only three patterns led manes and Wolfson to the characterization of compliments as formulaic.

Knapp et al., (1983) conducted a partial replication of an earlier study by Wolfson and Manes (1980) in which they looked at the frequency with which the three compliment formulas occurred. Knapp et al. also added a fourth pattern (1983, p. 15) in which the noun phrase, linking verb, and intensifier are all optional:

(NOUN PHRASE) (linking verb) (intensifier) (ADJECTIVE) (NOUN PHRASE)

Examples of this pattern given by Knapp et al. were "The Chinese dinner you cooked was really great, Joy," and "Great shot!" The authors concluded that 75% of the compliments in their sample fit the first four cases, and that although they had found less evidence of "formulaic rigidity" than Wolfson and Manes, nontheless the evidence for the use of compliment formulas was undeniable.

Manes and Wolfson made several interesting points about the relationship of compliments to conversation generally. The first is that the Relevance maxim can usually be suspended if the irrelevant item is a compliment. The fact that compliments are in fact often independent of the context in which they occur suggests that they may be formulaic because the formulas aid in their recognition. Further, while one would be hard pressed to construe compliments as a second pair part under most circumstances, it is clearly the case that when one's self-presentation is in some way altered, for example, by a hair cut, those viewing it for the first time, and who are in a position to recognize that a change or addition has taken place, must remark upon the change favorably; the absence of comment otherwise will be taken as a negative evaluation (Manes & Wolfson, 1981, p. 130).

Pomerantz (1978) has done extensive work on the analysis of responses to compliments. Her basic contention is that there are multiple constraints that operate to fix the character of compliment replies. Pomerantz treats compliments and their responses within the adjacency pair framework. According to Pomerantz, certain kinds of responses, in particular *acceptance* and *agreement,* are "preferred" by the conversational system, while others, such as *disagreement,* are "dispreferred," and "rejection" is more or less undefined. Assuming that the hearer has recognized the illocutionary intent of the speaker, and that the hearer is being cooperative, then she ought to respond to a compliment either with: (1) an acceptance ("Thanks," "Thank you very much") that recognizes the force of the prior utterance but does not focus on the referential aspects of its expressed proposition; and/or (2) an agreement ("It is nice, isn't it") in which the hearer concurs with the assessment which is expressed in S's compliment; or (3) a disagreement ("It's not really very pretty") in which case the hearer reassesses the propositional content of the compliment and comes to a conclusion opposite to that expressed by the speaker.

Pomerantz implies that the notion of "rejecting" a compliment does not appear to be realized in actual utterances; one does not hear, for example, "No, thank you" in response to a compliment. However, "Don't try to butter me up" may come close. There is one obvious way in which a hearer may deny that a compliment has been issued, and that is to assert that the sincerity condition has not been met.

Pomerantz proposes that compliment responses take the particular forms that they do because the systematic preference for agreements and acceptances is in conflict with another constraint: the requirement that speakers *avoid self-praise.* Agreeing that one does indeed have beautiful eyes meets the demands of the preference-for-agreement constraint while violating the requirement of avoiding self-praise. Compliment responses seem to display sensitivity to these conflicting structures; Pomerantz views them as "solutions" to the problems posed by contradictory injunctions.

Communicators use a number of tactics to deal with the multiple constraints on compliment responses. One is to "scale down" their agreement with the assessment expressed in the propositional content of the compliment (Pomerantz, 1978, p. 96):

A: What a gorgeous blouse!
B: It is attractive, isn't it?

A second strategy is to distantiate oneself from the valued object or attribute; to assign credit vaguely (Pomerantz, 1978, p. 97):

A: I heard you got a paper accepted without revisions!
B: Yeah, isn't it great?

Both of the foregoing are ways of responding by diluting agreement. Disagreements may also be seen to be responsive to the conflicting demands for modesty and agreement. Recipients may downgrade the terms of compliments ("Not *that* great") or add qualifications ("Yeah, but it wrinkles a lot").

So-called *referent shifts* are a final strategy that Pomerantz proposes. Examples of referent shifts include reassigning praise ("My mother made it") or returning the compliment ("I like yours, too").

Knapp et al., (1983) were not inclined to grant that compliment responses are as problematic as Pomerantz would have us believe. They found that well over half of the responses to compliments reported by their respondents were unamended acceptances and agreements; further, that only 6%-7% of the responses were actual disagreements.

Indirect Speech Acts

Sometimes communicators choose to perform speech acts indirectly rather than directly. Kemper and Thissen (1981) suggest that in addition to the politeness constraints on the form in which requests are encoded that are imposed by the status of the speaker relative to the hearer, there is also the issue of comprehension. Indirect speech acts may be found whenever securing uptake poses a risk. Sometimes we speak indirectly so that we can retract or amend what was "conveyed" in the event that it does not meet with hearer acceptance. Direct speech acts seem to be used primarily when comprehension cannot be taken for granted, and/or when the hearer's provision of a preferred response can be taken for granted (Kemper & Thissen, 1981).

Politeness. Lakoff has observed that the demands of politeness often outweigh the requirements to make oneself clear (1975, p. 74):

> [I]t seems to be true ... that when the crunch comes, the rules of politeness will supersede the rules of conversation: better to be unclear than rude.

House and Kasper (1981, p. 157) have defined politeness as "a specifically urbane form of emotional control serving as a means of preserving face." Searle (1975, p. 64) proposes that politeness is the chief motivation for indirectness:

> [O]rdinary conversational requirements of politeness normally make it awkward to issue a flat imperative sentence . . . or explicit performatives . . . and we therefore seek to find indirect means to our illocutionary ends.

Politeness appears to be not only a nearly universal phenomenon (Ferguson, 1976), but instruction in the use of politeness formulas clearly begins at a very early age, and parents are vigilant in monitoring their children's learning and implementation of politeness routines. Grief and Gleason (1980) videotaped interactions among children, a parent, and an experimenter during the course of which the child was presented with a gift. Children's and parents' verbal behaviors during greeting and departing sequences were also observed. Grief and Gleason found that in only one of 22 cases in their sample did a child fail to produce a politeness routine ("Hi," "Thank you," or "Goodbye") without parental prompting ensuing. Furthermore, fully 50% of parents were insistent on the routine when the child failed to respond to initial urgings.

Issues of politeness are invoked whenever a speaker must perform a *face-threatening act* (Brown & Levinson, 1978). Brown and Levinson define face as "the public self-image that every member [of a society] wants to claim for himself" (1978, p. 66). Face takes two forms: *positive face* has to do with the projection of one's personality as worthy or deserving of approval, and a need for self-esteem; *negative face* refers to the claim of the individual to be autonomous and unrestricted in her actions. The demands of politeness require that communicators' mutual self-interest lies in preserving and maintaining the other's face as well as one's own. Indirect speech as well as other politeness features come into play whenever a speaker must perform an act that constitutes a threat to face—her own or the other's.

Potential threats to the negative face (claim to autonomy) of the hearer include orders, suggestions, and requests. Potential threats to the positive face of the hearer are contradictions, interruptions, disapproval, accusations, and so on. The speaker's own positive face may be threatened by such acts as confessing or apologizing; the speaker's negative face may be subjected to threat when he asks for help, accepts an offer, accepts a compliment, and so on. Speakers must balance off considerations of their own and the other's face. Generally, face-threatening acts (henceforth FTAs) ought to be performed in such a way as to minimize loss of face unless instrumental goals or a need for absolute clarity are more important.

Shimanoff (1977) found that the absence of politeness tended to have a negative affect on conversation. Her observations indicated that in routine daily encounters involving requests and other ordinary office business the most popular ways of approaching others were with positive politeness strategies directed to the hearer's positive face (seeking agreement of taking notice of the hearer), and the negatively polite strategies of hedging and indirectness.

The strategy a speaker employs to perform an FTA will reflect her estimate of the risk involved in its implementation (Brown & Levinson, 1978), risk being a function of the "social distance" between S and H, their comparative power or status, and the extent to which the act in question constitutes an imposition on H. Ferguson (1976) suggests that formulaic politeness varies along at least three other dimensions, all of which are unrelated to risk: (1) how long it has been since the communicators have seen one another; (2) how far apart they are; and (3) how many others are present.

When there is a considerable amount of risk involved in performing a face-threatening action, the speaker may elect not to do the FTA at all (Brown & Levinson, 1978, p. 65). When the estimate of the risk of loss of face is slight, or when instrumental goals have priority, the act may be performed "baldly, without redressive action." When there is a moderate amount of risk, the speaker can be expected to perform the FTA, but to take redressive action in the form of positive and negative politeness displays. Positive politeness strategies include emphasizing similarities, noticing the hearer's interests and activities, utilizing in-group membership markers, and using proximal (this, these) rather than distal (that, those) demonstratives (Brown & Levinson, 1978). Negative politeness strategies, geared to acknowledge H's need for unimpeded action and a sense of automony, include such devices as hedges, depersonalization ("It is necessary that I inform you . . . "), distantiation ("I had wanted to tell you myself that . . . "), and such conventional phrases as "Sorry to bother you, but" and "I hate to impose, but."

Many negatively polite strategies for performing face-threatening acts consist of *conventionally indirect speech acts* (Brown & Levinson, 1978), for example, asking a question about one of the felicity conditions for the performance of the face-threatening act:

S: Can you spare a dime?

In addition to conventionally indirect speech acts, which we shall shortly examine in some detail in the case of *indirect requests,* face-threatening acts may be performed *off-record* (Brown & Levinson, 1978). When there is perceived to be a high level of risk, the speaker may elect to invite implicature by violating one of the Gricean maxims, so that H's inference processes will have to take up the burden of producing the FTA. The speaker may use hints ("Boy, am I starving") that violate the Quality maxim, or violate the Antecedence maxim by invoking presuppositions, making the hearer search for an antecedent implied in the utterance:

S: How much longer will you be in the bathroom?

In this case, the hearer must search his memory to retrieve the probable span of time indexed by "longer," with the resultant inference that A is saying that "there has been a span of time," and that the upshot of it all is that the hearer ought to hurry up. We shall consider conversational implicatures in greater detail in a subsequent section.

Conventional indirectness and indirect requests. Searle has characterized indirect speech acts as those in which "one illocutionary act is performed indirectly by way of performing another" (1975, p. 60). Searle argues that most indirect speech acts could be accounted for by saying that their "essential condition" as the direct acts for which they substitute is satisfied in the reference that they make to the preconditions for the happy performance of the act—the *preparatory, propositional content,* and *sincerity* conditions (1975, p. 60). Searle (1975, pp. 65-66) lists a number of sentences that address such preconditions, which are conventional ways of performing indirect directives:

Can you pass the salt?
I wish you wouldn't do that.
Aren't you going to eat your cereal?
Would you mind not making so much noise?

The first sentence is addressed to a preparatory condition, the second to a speaker sincerity condition, the third to a propositional content condition, and the fourth to a hearer sincerity condition. Searle notes that none of the sentences contains an imperative, none is ambiguous, none is idiomatic, each has a distinct literal meaning that is *not* that H should do A, and yet all *count* as requests that H do A.

How is it that the speaker can say one thing and mean something else? Searle argues that what one needs to account for indirect speech acts are speech act theory, conversational maxims, and the presupposition of mutual contextual beliefs on the part of S and H. When H hears S utter, "Can you pass the salt?" H immediately recognizes that S has violated the Quality maxim, for S must know that H is capable of performing the action. However, given the assumption that S is cooperating, H deduces that the utterance must have some other point. H consults her knowledge of the felicity conditions for the performance of requests, and comes up with the rule that a condition for the valid performance of a directive is that the hearer can actually carry out the desired action. H further recognizes that to answer S's question affirmatively is to confirm that a preparatory condition for doing A has been met. H consults her background knowledge about salt and concludes that passing it to and fro at meals is one of the things that people do with it. Finally, H infers that the likely illocutionary upshot of S's utterance is a request to pass the salt (Searle, 1975).

Although Searle claims that constitutive rules for the performance of indirect requests are unnecessary to account for their being understood, it is not altogether clear how it is that the hearer described in Searle's series of steps above makes the inferential leaps that she does. Gordon and Lakoff (1975) bridge that gap neatly by proposing that when confronted with a literal utterance in a context that suggests that the utterance means "what it says and more," the hearer has recourse to *conversational postulates* to shortcut the process of comprehension. Conversational postulates are of the following form (Gordon & Lakoff, 1975, p. 86):

$$SAY\ (a,\ b,\ WANT\ (a,\ Q)) \longrightarrow REQUEST\ (a,\ b,\ Q)$$
$$ASK\ (a,\ b,\ CAN\ (b,\ Q)) \longrightarrow REQUEST\ (a,\ b,\ Q)$$

The first postulate says that stating a "speaker-based sincerity condition," that a wants b to do Q (for example, take out the trash) has the material implication of a request for b to take out the trash. The second postulate is that an inquiry by a as to whether b can do Q materially implicates a request for b to do Q (Gordon & Lakoff, 1975, p. 86).

Searle (1975, p. 72) does admit that there are some "generalizations" about how indirect requests may be performed, which look remarkably like conversational postulates (by asking if or stating that a preparatory condition obtains), but he does not go so far as to claim these generalizations are invoked by hearers to comprehend indirect requests.

Clark and Lucy (1975) point out that many kinds of indirect acts may be understood by invoking conversational postulates about references to preconditions, such as promises ("I can meet you at seven") and permissions ("I'm going to be able to give you the day off").

As Clark and Lucy interpret conversational postulates, what one needs to understand an indirect speech act are the literal meaning of the utterance, a context against which to evaluate it, and a set of constitutive rules. Thus, when "Can you pass the salt?" is uttered, the hearer first constructs its literal meaning, then compares that interpretation to the perceived context, which suggests that S can hardly help but be aware that H is indeed capable of passing the salt. The literal meaning must then be examined in the light of a relevant conversational postulate or rule: "if the speaker inquires about the hearer's ability to perform an action, when it is clearly evident that the speaker believes that the hearer can do so, then treat the inquiry as a request for the hearer to perform the action." Searle points out that the performance of a conventionally indirect act does not depend upon the "defectiveness" of the secondary illocution, or literal point. "Do you have change for fifty cents?" is also an indirect request, but the hearer knows that the speaker does not necessarily believe that the answer to the literal question is "Yes" (Searle, 1975, pp. 70-71). The existence of such examples suggests (a) that there must indeed be conversational postulates that are invoked to understand conveyed speech acts; and (b) that it is not essential to the invocation of such postulates that the literal meaning of an utterance conflict with its context.

Clark and Lucy (1975) were interested in establishing whether hearers do indeed respond to indirect or conveyed requests by first constructing the literal meaning of the utterance, or whether the usage of indirect requests is in fact so conventionalized that their conveyed meaning has become their literal meaning. Clark and Lucy summarized work that indicated that true-false judgments of utterances whose surface structures were negative ("I'll be sad unless you open the door") took longer than judgments of literal utterances whose surface structures were positive ("I'll be sad if you open the door"). In their own study Clark and Lucy presented subjects with displays consisting of a sentence such as, "Please color the circle blue," or "Why color the circle blue?" and a circle colored either blue or pink. The subjects' task was to determine if the color with which the circle had been filled in was the one called for in the request (1975, pp. 60-61).

Clark and Lucy found evidence that subjects did indeed construct the literal meaning of the sentences first: the sentences with negative surface polarities took much longer to process. Consider, for example, the following pairs of sentences:

(1) I'll be very happy if you make the circle blue.
(2) I'll be very sad unless you make the circle blue.

Results indicated that (2) took considerably longer than (1) to process, even though both have the same implication as a request: Color the circle blue. However, in addition to this evidence that the literal meaning was constructed first, there was also evidence that the final judgments of true and false were based upon conveyed meanings. For conveyed positive requests like (2), judgments of true were made faster than judgments of false, and for conveyed negatives like "I'll be very happy unless you make the circle blue," judgments of false were made faster than judgments of true. Clark and Lucy concluded that their evidence supported the basic account of indirect requests proposed by Gordon and Lakoff.

House and Kaspar (1981) conducted an interesting comparative study of politeness markers among native speakers of English and German, focusing upon requests, among other speech acts. Subjects were asked to act out verbally their probable behaviors in response to hypothetical scenarios; their responses were transcribed and coded into eight levels of request politeness: (1) *mild hint* ("My hamburger tastes bland"); (2) *strong hint* ("My hamburger needs salt"); (3) *query-preparatory* ("Can you reach the salt?"); (4) *state-preparatory* ("You can reach the salt"); (5) *scope-stating* ("I wish you would pass the salt"); (6) *locution-derivable* ("You should pass the salt"); (7a) *hedged performative* ("I must ask you to pass the salt"), or (7b) *explicit performative* ("I ask you to pass the salt"); and (8) *mood-derivable* ("Pass the salt"). House and Kasper found that both English and German speakers used all of the levels. For English speakers, level three, inquiring about a preparatory condition, was most typical (40.9%). German subjects were comparatively more inclined to utilize the more direct, or less polite, forms of request.

Tannen (1981) has also made an interesting cross-cultural comparison of the uses of indirectness. Tannen's thesis generally was that Greeks and Greek-Americans differ from Americans of non-Greek background in the interpretations which they assign to indirect speech. Tannen presented subjects with examples like the following (1981, pp. 227-229):

(1) **Wife:** John's having a party. Wanna go?
    Husband: O.K.

(2) **Wife:** Are you sure you want to go to the party?
    Husband: O.K. Let's not go. I'm tired anyway.

Subjects were presented with a choice of two paraphrases for the husband's turn in both examples. Tannen found that more Greeks than Americans or Greek-Americans selected an indirect interpretation of the speakers' utterances. In the case of example (1), Greeks were more likely than the other groups to see the husband's "O.K." as meaning that he is going along with his wife to "make her happy," as opposed to meaning that he really "feels like going" (Tannen, 1981, p. 229). That is, Greek respondents felt that the wife's bringing up the issue was tantamount to a statement that she wished to go. Similarly, more Greeks than members of the other groups were likely to see the husband's claim to be tired in (2) as reflecting his intuition that his wife doesn't want to go to the party, and that he is providing her with the excuse she is indirectly requesting.

Conversational implicature. We have dealt with conventional indirectness at some length. Another form of indirectness is that which is achieved by a violation of conversational maxims (Grice, 1975). Grice refers to the class of nonconventional devices associated with violations of the Quality, Quantity, Relevance, and Manner maxims as *conversational implicatures* (Grice, 1975, pp. 49-50):

A man who, by (in, when) saying (or making as if to say) that *p* has implicated that *q,* may be said to have conversationally implicated that *q,* PROVIDED THAT (1) he is to be presumed to be observing the conversational maxims, or at least the cooperative principle; (2) the supposition that he is aware that, or thinks that, *q* is required in order to make his saying or making as if to say *p* (or doing so in THOSE terms) consistent with his presumption; and (3) the speaker thinks (and would expect the hearer to think that the speaker thinks) that it is within the competence of the hearer to work out, or grasp intuitively, that the supposition mentioned in (2) IS required.

In short, the hearer, assuming that her partner in general can be expected to honor the cooperative principle and the conversational maxims, must find an implicit proposition that *does* appear to be orderly and make sense in the face of an explicit irrelevance, untruth, barbarism, and so on.

Violations of the Quality maxim are quite commonplace, as for example in *metaphors* ("Your teeth are pearls, and your lips are cherries") and *hyperbole* ("I can't wait until Christmas"). Clearly, lips cannot be cherries, nor can one "not wait" until Christmas, as it will come when it comes and not before. Most hearers, however, will have little trouble in working out what is implicated by such utterances. Violations of the Relevance maxim may be used to implicate mild rebukes, or to put off unwanted inquiries:

A: Who ya goin' out with tonight?
B: Have you seen where I put my raincoat?

Similarly, the proverbial reply to "What's my blind date like?"— "Well, she's a nice girl and is kind to animals" is more or less conventionally understood to imply that the date is not especially attractive, by virtue of the fact that it is taken as an *irrelevant* response to the implicit main concern expressed in the question: namely, what does my date *look* like?

When the speaker violates the Manner maxim, the hearer must determine why the speaker's utterance is characterized by ambiguity, obscurity, excessive verbosity, and so on. For example, deliberate ambiguities in the following implicate the proposition that the professional capabilities of Dr. X are somewhat less than spectacular:

S: This article by Dr. X fills a needed gap in the literature.
S: I cannot fail to praise Dr. X too highly.

A speaker might also violate the Manner maxim by a deliberate display of excessive verbosity; to implicate the proposition that she feels distant towards her addressee:

S: What is it that you wish to say to me?

Similarly, verbosity may be used to convey that one's request of a hearer is of considerable magnitude:

S: What would you think if I were to ask you if I might possibly borrow your car tonight?

Wilson and Sperber (1981) argue that Grice fails to see all the "implications" of implicature. Their point is that conversational maxims are used not only to work out the conveyed meaning of an utterance, but are sometimes required to construct literal meanings. Wilson and Sperber use for an example, "Refuse to admit them." The propositional content of such an utterance, it is argued, cannot be determined without recourse to the Relevance maxim, which requires that an utterance be "appropriate to immediate needs at each state of the transaction" (Grice, 1975, p. 47). Thus, in order to know what "Refuse to admit them" means, we must look at the immediately prior utterance. If it is "What should I do when I make mistakes?" then we have one interpretation; if it is "What should I do with the people whose tickets have expired?" we have another (Sperber & Wilson, 1981, p. 157). Sperber and Wilson conclude that a hearer will not only miss the conveyed implications of an utterance, but may also miss its literal meaning should he fail to use the conversational maxims as an aid to understanding.

Indirect answers. One of the most entertaining devices for provoking conversational implicature is the *indirect answer* (Nofsinger, 1976), also known as the *indirect response* (Pearce & Conklin, 1979) or the *transparent question* (Bowers, 1982). An indirect answer is ordinarily used to implicate an answer to a closed question. The implicated answer is therefore either "Yes" or "No:"

(1)   **A:**   Glad it's Friday?
       B: Does a dog have fleas?

(2)   **A:**   Ready for the test yet?
       B: Did I stay up all night to watch the sun come up?

Sometimes, however, an indirect answer can implicate an answer other than "Yes" or "No," for example, "Never:"

(3)   **A:**   When are you and Sally gonna make up?
       B: On a cold day in Hell.

Nofsinger (1976, p. 177) proposes some rules that appear to account for the way in which utterances like (1)-(3) are understood. The first indirect response, (1) B, is interpreted in accordance with a *shared existential value rule: if A asks a closed question, and B responds with a question that is irrelevant both to A's question and to the preconditions for B to provide an answer, and it is not plausible to treat the questions as referencing mutually exclusive events, then B's answer should be treated as asserting that the existential value of the answer to his own question is also the existential value of the answer to A's question.*

The indirect answer in the second example can be accounted for under a *contrasting existential value rule* (Nofsinger, 1976, p. 178): *if A poses a closed question, and B responds with a question that is irrelevant both to the speaker's question and to the preconditions for B to provide an answer, and if A can regard the events referenced in the separate questions as mutually exclusive, then B's utterance should be treated as asserting that the existential value of the answer to his own question is opposite to the existential value of the answer to A's question.*

The indirect answer type exemplified by (3) is covered by the *implausible antecedent rule* (Nofsinger, 1976, p. 177): *if, in replying to a question by A, B responds with a proposition of the form "If X, then Y," and it is implausible that X will occur, then B's utterance should be treated as asserting that in order for Y to be true, X must occur, and from this it is inferred that since X cannot occur, Y will not occur.*

Pearce and Conklin (1979) asked subjects to evaluate the appropriateness of indirect responses of the three types described above. Pearce and Conklin first were interested in whether or not such lines as "Does the Pope have a mother-in-law?" and "If the sun still rises in the East" could be heard, respectively, as the answers "No" and "Yes." They also looked at a variation represented by the response, "I always sweat like this when I'm cold," to the question, "Hot enough for you today?" (Pearce & Conklin, 1979, p. 83). Pearce and Conklin found that subjects considered the first two lines to be answers to their respective questions, but that the "I always sweat . . . " response was not regarded by the subjects as recognizable as an answer, perhaps because some of them seemed to regard it as abrasive or showing contempt for the interlocutor. There also seemed to be evidence that all of the indirect responses were regarded as more unusual and humorous, and less appropriate, friendly, and respectful than the corresponding direct approaches. As indirect answer described by the implausible antecedent rule was generally regarded as less respectful, friendly, and appropriate than those indirect answers covered under the shared existential value rules. Indirect answers generally were regarded as particularly inappropriate for use with strangers and superiors, which is an interesting exception to the general rule that one is more indirect with superiors than with peers or subordinates. Perhaps it is fair to say that the hallmark of conventional indirectness forms is their negative politeness: indirect requests, for example, are often framed in terms of inquiries about the extent of the imposition which they entail. In this sense, indirect answers are not at all polite.

Bowers (1982) conducted an empirical test of the adequacy of competing explanations of how it is that indirect responses are heard as "Yes" and "No" answers to questions. In the pragmatic view, exemplified by Nofsinger's rules, the questioner treats as an answer to his own question the answer that is clearly attributable to the "existentially unrelated" one (Bowers, 1982, p. 63). The situational explanation (Nofsinger, 1974) is that the hearer constructs her interpretation after reflection upon the context and her knowledge of the speaker, which leads her to conclude that the answer to the question is obvious and the question itself superfluous. Bowers also speculated that the interpretation of indirect answers might be a function of their syntactic-semantic form or the topic of the indirect answer. Bowers's study looked at how four independent factors—the situation, pragmatic form, syntactic-semantic form, and topic—influenced three dependent variables: (1) subjects' confidence in their judgments of the implication of the response; (2) the attitude attributed to the author of the indirect response; and (3) judgments of the respondent's competence. Bowers concluded that none of the independent variables other than the pragmatic effect (conveyed meaning under the shared existential value rules) was able to produce significant variation in attributions of the force of "Yes" or "No" to an indirect answer. Attributions of interpersonal incompetence were more likely to be made to communicators who provided a pragmatic no in a form with positive surface polarity: "Does a duck have antlers?"

MANAGEMENT ACTS

We now turn from substantive moves to a class of speech acts that serve to bracket or organize sections of talk. Some of these management acts have been presented in earlier chapters, for example, topic shift devices and strategems for alerting the hearer to the fact that a block of turn-constructional units is being claimed.

Formulations

The first type of management act to be taken up here is the *formulation*, which has been introduced earlier in the context of conversational lapses. To say that formulations are management acts may not be entirely correct; to be sure, formulations may themselves become "mentionables" (Goffman, 1976) or "conversational objects" (Heritage & Watson, 1979) and be taken up in talk as topics. However, it is their status in negotiating the *disposition* of sections of talk that is of interest here.

Heritage and Watson (1979, p. 126) have been particularly interested in formulations that "characterize states of affairs already described or negotiated (in whole or in part) in the preceding talk." Formulations operate on talk, they argue, to maintain or preserve it, to delete it, and to transform it. Consider the following example:

```
1   B:   Uh huh. Did you feel like you had*
2        to because of your brothers and sisters?
3   A:   Yeah, sometimes I did.
4   B:   Uh huh.
5   A:   Mostly about halfway through the
6        season I'd just kinda get a feeling
7        that I didn't want to run but I still
8        keep on running=
                    (        )
9   B:             Uh huh.
10  A:   =because I'd say well what will they
11       think of me.
12  B:   Oh, yeah. Oh.
13  A:   I just kept on.
                    (2.1)
14  B:   Well, at least you didn't give up,
15       you know, right in the middle of it.
                    (2.7)
```

At line 13, there is an A-Issue formulation ("I just kept on") that serves the function of preserving the central and most significant aspect of the preceding section, while *deleting* subordinate contributing elements such as the brothers and sisters. The formulation by partner at lines 14-15 serves to *transform* the account given by A from a simple unmotivated precis to a testament to A's character and endurance. The fact that formulations may serve to terminate topical talk is again evident in the silences that follow lines 13 and 15.

Heritage and Watson propose that there are two types of formulation: formulations of *gist* and formulations of *upshot*. The former have to do with "readings" of the central issues or events that have informed an immediately prior stretch of talk. A formulation may be proposed as a tentative reading of gist, which implicates a *decision* on the part of the hearer. Some formulations of gist, as in lines 7-8 below, meet with acceptance (line 9), while others, like the one in line 10, may not be received as enthusiastically, as in lines 11-12:

1	**B:**	You know, you probably know more'n*
2		you think you know.
3	**A:**	Well, I mean I just- I don't know.
4		Well, I know about it but it's just
5		that I mean I think everybody has about
6		the same opinion about it.
7	**B:**	*You're just the kind of person that*
8		*doesn't want to make a point.*
9	**A:**	Yeah.
10	**B:**	*You'd rather just listen, right?*
11	**A:**	Well, I don't think . . . see I don't
12		think people should get real radical
		about it right now . . .

While A is willing to accept B's first formulation of her position, the second is clearly less flattering and is disconfirmed obliquely by being in effect ignored with the semantic disjunctive "Well" serving to signal the incipient rejection.

Some formulations of gist have to be amended before they can be accepted. In the example below, B tried out a formulation at line 14, to which A immediately objects. When B proposes a new formulation at lines 17-19, which is more to A's liking, the formulation receives a confirmation and the topic is closed:

1	**A:**	I wouldn't join a social fraternity.*
		( )
2	**B:**	Yeah.
3	**A:**	Those are a waste of time.
4	**B:**	Well, not really. Like it helps a lot
5		when you're a freshman because you don't
6		know many people, and you get into a

7		sorority or fraternity and it helps you to
8		meet everybody, you know.
9	**A:**	I know too many guys who are goin' six years=
		( )
10	**B:**	Yeah.
11	**A:**	=took 'em six years to get out of college
12		simply because they went to a fraternity
13		their freshman year.
14	**B:**	*Yeah, but they're a lot of fun.*
15	**A:**	Yeah, they're a lot of fun but, like I said
16		I
17	**B:**	*(They spend more time playin' than they do=*
		( )
18	**A:**	Uh huh.)
19	**B:**	*=on their studies.*
20	**A:**	And the reason we're here is to study.
21	**B:**	Right.

(B switches topic to sports)

Upshot formulations seem to be much less common than gist formulations, at least in the corpus of conversations between strangers that has been presented here. In part, this may be a function of the fact that strangers are not as prone as friends to deal with the "unexplicated versions of gist" that upshot formulations presuppose (Heritage & Watson, 1979, p. 34). Many upshot formulations in the corpus were likely to be disconfirmed, which set in motion a chain of argument:

A: They probably just say that 'cause it's the most*
expensive dorm.

B: I heard it was supposed to be the higher class ladies over there, so you must be pretty high class.

A: Ha ha ha.

B: Classy little woman here. Uh- what's your dad do?

A: He's a chiropracter.

B: Really.

A: Uh huh.

B: *He's settin' you up!*

A: Ha ha. Shut up!

A: *Oh, so you're lookin' for an M.R.S. degree.**

B: No, no, no, not really.

A: Yes you are.

B: No I'm not.

A: Ha ha ha. Yes you are.

B: No I'm not. . . .

At the very least, upshot formulations in conversation put the formulator at risk of being corrected:

A: Do you think you and your girlfriend'll get back*
together?

B: No. There's no chance of that.

A: Hmm. Not a chance at all?!

B: No. We're still friends. We're friends but she was
too old for me.

A: Ha ha.

B: It's- you know.

A: There's no chance.

B: No.

A: Oh, golly.

B: Ha ha ha.

A: *To break up with someone and say, "That's it."*

B: Well, *I* didn't break up, *she* broke up. . . .

Heritage and Waston argue that formulations are first pair parts of adjacency pairs; that they implicate a decision on a subsequent turn. The data from the stranger conversations seem to indicate that many formulations simply stand on their own; that is, that the first pair part is often sufficient to do the "work" of a pair. However, it is clearly the case that disconfirmations recycle topical talk, and that in extreme cases repeated formulation-disconfirmation sequences trigger a search for a topic on which some semblance of consensus can be reached.

Scott (1983) looked at formulations in conversations between married couples engaged in routine household talk. She concluded that formulations were techniques by which couples attempted to reach consensus on relational issues. Her observations indicated (1) that formulations were usually followed, at some point, by a confirmation; (2) that formulation sequences often took an extended form, as opposed to the simple formulation-decision pair; (3) that marital partners sometimes competed with each other to be the one whose formulation was the "last word"; (4) that formulation-decision pairs did not always work to close off a topic, some topics being formulated over and over again in the same conversation; and (5) that like other adjacency pairs, formulation-decision pairs may be expanded by pre-formulation and post-formulation sequences.

Discourse Brackets

Schiffrin (1980) has proposed that there are certain kinds of utterances that have the function of *bracketing* units of discourse with coherent internal structures, such as narratives or explanations. These metalinguistic brackets may serve to indicate the boundaries of a discourse unit; for example, to open and close an argument, or to mark the beginning of an extended answer. Discourse brackets might be thought of as "parentheses," except for the fact that there may not always be a pair (Schiffrin, 1980, p. 207). Formulations can serve as brackets, but not all brackets are formulations.

Schiffrin finds that brackets that precede a discourse unit are often prefaced by "Well" or "Now," or the so-called pseudo-imperatives "Look," "See," and "Listen" (1980, pp. 207-208). Initial discourse brackets often contain a cataphoric reference to the upcoming material, while terminal brackets often refer anaphorically to elements introduced in the immediately prior section of talk. Schiffrin proposes that initial brackets have more "work" to do, in that they establish a slot or reserve a block of conversational time, as well as influence expectations about what is to follow. On the other hand, terminal brackets may be more difficult for the speaker to negotiate because they constitute a "proposal" that the foregoing section of discourse has now terminated, and hearer may not be prepared to accept that proposal at the time it is made.

While the global function of a discourse bracket is to organize talk into manageable chunks, the brackets may be observed to fulfill such specific subfunctions as *labeling* a section of talk (as a funny story, reason, or example) as in (1) and (2) below; *separating* one discourse unit from another, as in (3) below; or *instructing* the hearer as to the illocutionary point of a forthcoming act, as in (4) and (5) below:

(1) **B:** *This is kinda funny.* I heard on the news they're*
            talkin' about lettin' girls into the band, you know?
     A: You gonna get in the band?
     B: No, ha ha. This guy got on there and he said he didn't
            think they could stand up to the practicin'. That's a bunch
            of bull. 'Cause bands all over the country have girls in
            it standin' up to practice.
     A: (I know it.

(2) **A:** Oh! *
     B: Everybody puts weird things on the back in letters.
     A: That's neat! Yeah!
                                    (2.0)

(3) **B:** So. *
     A: That's really impressive.

B: *So that's why- that's why I did it- I wanted to work.*
It makes good money.

A: Yeah. *That's another thing I don't like.* I could- I could*
do it. I could run anything as long as I djdn't know
somebody was down there timing me- that's just because
I don't like running against something.

(4) A: What? Let me think. *I want to ask you somethin'.**
How far from Ft. Worth is Springton?
B: Twenty-five miles, thereabouts.

(5) A: *What I want to know is* do you remember any of*
it? Ha ha.
B: Yes, I do. I remember saying something, but I don't
know who it was to. You know, you're just kinda goin',
well, yeah, I'm here.

Although there did not appear to be any cases of *double bracketing*
(both initial and terminal brackets around the same discourse unit) in
the conversations from which the examples above were drawn, there
was an occasional instance of *back-to-back brackets,* as exemplified
in (6):

(6) B: Yeah, uh. Yeah. I think all Christians kinda believe*
that their way is the right way or else they wouldn't
believe in it, right?
A: Um hmm. Yeah.
B: But uh, but if- if there were some that uh were
derogatory=
　　　　　　(　　　)
A: 　　　　Uh huh.
B: =of other people or somethin' like that then they're
not being very Christian.
A: Christian, yeah. *That's what got me- that's what*
got me, and- *and a few other things,* you know, like
the Crusades, you know. . . .

Schiffrin (1980, pp. 218-223) also proposes that there are
evaluative brackets, which can be used to mark sections of talk in
need of repair, cancel prior formulations ("That's not the point"),
substitute new formulations ("The point is"), or comment on
collaboratively produced stretches of talk ("I'm not arguing with
you.")

Activities of Partitioning

Closely related to discourse brackets are what Rehbein (1981) has described as *activities of partitioning*. Activities of partitioning are generally formulaic utterances by means of which parties steer one another in conversation (Rehbein, 1981, p. 236). Rehbein first focuses on a group of devices that are similar to announcements, in that they preview upcoming events, so to speak. This class of partitioning activities is devoted to alerting the hearer to the functional properties of subsequent utterances. *Pre-fixed announcements* utilize speech act designating expressions such as "Let me make a suggestion," or "I have a question for you." Some examples of pre-fixed announcements were given in the immediately preceding discussion of discourse brackets: examples (4) and (5).

Rehbein's second category of activities of partitioning contains both *pre-fixations* (pseudo-imperatives like "See" and "Listen") and *announcements of paraphrase* ("In other words," "That means"). Schiffrin (1980) has dealt with both phenomena, the latter as an evaluative bracketing in which a subsequent formulation is proposed as superior to a prior formulation. Pre-fixations and announcements of paraphrase often appear to be used when an interlocutor is being a little obtuse, or impatient, or when her question contains an element of reproach. Presumably the pre-fixation signals that an account is forthcoming:

B: I mean you work twelve hours a day- whatever- you're not*
   just in the office.
A: TWELVE HOURS A DAY?!!
B: Yeah. Some days we- unless it rains
A: (SEVEN DAYS A WEEK?!!
B: Yeah. *See-* you work like that, you work two weeks and
   then you get ten days off. . . .

Connectors are defined by Rehbeim as semantic items that operate to alert the hearer that the speaker has switched to another line of action, such as "So" and "By the way." Such devices were introduced earlier (Chapter 2) in discussions of pragmatic connectives and topic shift or "disjunctive" markers. Another partitioning activity that Rehbeim reports is the *pre*—"an illocution of an announcement lacking propositional content" (1981, p. 240). Pre's include not only such nonverbal announcements as frowning for noncomprehension and clearing the throat to request the turn, but also such interjections as, "Now hold on a minute," and "Not so fast." Pre's are often associated with objections, replies, and counter-arguments:

B: Well, it could be because I'm a small town person and*

A: (You can't
raise a kid in a small community and expect him to be
intelligent.

B: *Oh, now, wait a minute,* that's an insult to me!

Another variety of partitioning device is the *pre-announcement,* which secures the attention of the hearer and characterizes subsequent sections of talk as being of interest. Pre-announcements include the "demand ticket" in a summons-answer sequence (Nofsinger, 1975), for example "Guess what?" as well as such formulaic constructions as "I'm sorry to have to tell you this, but," or "I have a confession to make." Pre-announcements are similar to Schiffrin's discourse brackets in that they both can perform a labeling function. The pre-announcement, however, "contains a demand for the hearer to give an explicit and positive point of view about the planned action and, in this way, to *enable the speaker* to make his resolution of execution" (Rehbeim, 1981, p. 243). The hearer may of course forestall the execution of a planned action by such a remark as "I don't want to hear about it."

Rehbeim also describes forms of partitioning activity that speak to the propositional character of a subsequent section of talk. In a *preceeding summary,* the speaker previews the thematic elements of an upcoming stretch of talk while simultaneously marking their anticipated order of presentation. A good example of a preceding summary would be an overview of a lecture. A *comment* reflects the speaker's attitude toward or assessment of the propositional content of the discourse unit, but does not summarize it in its entirety. The *comments* label refers to the kinds of acts characterized elsewhere as *story significance statements* (Ryave, 1978) or *joke prefaces* (Cody et al., 1983) or Issue-continuations (Reichman, 1978; Tracy, 1982). The example below is an instance of a comment that informs a discourse unit:

S: *Fanatics.* That's the word I'm lookin for. Yeah, I met a whole*
bunch of fanatics since I been down here. Always tryin' to get
you to go to this church, go to that church, you know. You
say, well, I don't know. I don't know if my past church was
right, so therefore how do I know if their churches are right,
you know.

Rehbeim's final class of partitioning activity that deals with the propositional content of subsequent discourse is the *introduction*. Introductions have the following properties: (1) they are related to an impending action by the speaker; (2) the hearer is confronted with the action as it is in the process of beginning. Introductions are usually in the form of formulaic expressions like "What I was going to say was" or "There is. . . ." or "Once . . . "; they mark the fact that a caesura between prior and subsequent discourse has already occurred (Rehbeim, 1981). In the following example, the introduction *there were* serves to mark a new discourse unit dealing with a class of thematic participants who are contrasted by a semantic connective *(but)* with a class of participants identified in a prior unit:

A: He told us about people who would come in his office and*
    interview with him, and even though they were very educated
    and they were very intelligent they couldn't speak well=

                                          (   )
B: Really.
A: =and couldn't express their thoughts. And he would just- it was
    just the big ax for them. But *there were* other people that
    weren't quite as educated- or qualified I guess you'd say-
    but they were all really able to express themselves a lot better
    so you know they'd be likely to get the job.

Passes

O.K. passes, repetition passes, and framing moves. Weiner and Goodenough (1977) considered a class of conversational phenomena whose status as speech acts or as turn-constructional units have always been debated—utterances like "Yeah," "Uh huh," "O.K.," and "So you think that X?" Weiner and Goodenough present a characterization of such utterances that provides a more formal account and a partial resolution of some of the competing claims that have been made about the function of such utterances. The authors propose first that there is a *topical continuation rule* that in effect says that *a party who has already contributed substantively to the topic may make an additional contribution on her next turn* (Weiner & Goodenough, 1977, p. 217). One way in which a conversational participant may manage a topic shift all by himself, as was pointed out by Derber (1979), Fishman (1978), and others, is to *pass up the opportunity* to make a substantive contribution. Weiner and Goodenough (1977, p. 217) describe such a *passing move* as a being a case in which under the topical continuation rule a speaker opts not to exercise her right to contribute.

Passing moves come in two varieties, the *O.K. pass* ("Yeah," "Uh huh," "O.K.") and the *repetition pass* ("You think that thus-and-so"). When a passing move takes up an entire turn slot, it is labeled a *passing turn* (lines 4, 6, and 9, below); otherwise, it is called a *framing move* (line 14):

```
 1  A:   Where if I was really tryin', where*
 2       I ran track I thought well, I can only
 3       be as good as much as I want to be=
                             (        )
 4  B:                          Right.
 5  A:   =good and it was up to me so=
                             (        )
 6  B:                          Uh huh.
 7  A:   =by doin' that you know I was able to
 8       you know satisfy you know=
                             (      )
 9  B:                          Yeah.
10  A:   =the winning instinct and all I had to
11       do was go out and try it- didn't have to
12       worry about anybody else. Just me
13       against the clock.
14  B:   Yeah. That's another thing I don't like . . .
```

With respect to the role of passing and framing moves in the management of topic, Weiner and Goodenough make the following observations: (1) if A makes a passing move and it is matched by B, it is unlikely that there will be any further substantive contributions to the current topic; (2) if the second speaker makes a framing move, it is probable that it will serve to introduce a new topic; (3) it is not necessary for a passing move to be matched for topic closure to take place.

In order for a "mirror" or reflective utterance to be classified as a *repetition pass,* it has to have a falling rather than a rising or sustaining intonation (Weiner & Goodenough, 1977). Repetition passes are more likely to be followed by additional talk on the same topic than O.K. passes. Repetitions are not as a rule followed in the same turn by a move to frame a new topic. According to Weiner and Goodenough, the implications of repetition passes in terms of interest in the topic are less straightforward than those of the O.K. pass; the latter may be regarded as an unambiguous offer to switch to a new topic. If a repetition pass is followed by an O.K. pass, it is possible that topical talk will flounder, as it is not clear from what materials a new turn should be constructed:

A: Well, what do you see as your religion?*
B: Christianity.
A: Christianity.
B: Uh huh.

(2.5)

Processing passes and conference passes. Jefferson and Schenkein (1978) have identified two other classes of passing moves in conversation that they have described, respectively, as "Processing Passes" and "Conference Passes." Consider the following conversation excerpt from Jefferson and Schenkein (1978, p. 156):

Salesboy: G'n aftuhnoon sur, W'dje be innerested in subscribing to the Progress Bulletin t'help m'win a trip tuh Cape Kennedy to see the astronauts on the moon shot. You won'haftuh pay til nex'month en you get ev'ry single day en I guarantee you ril good service. Jus' fer a few short weeks, sir, tuh help me win my trip.

Richard: Well I *live* in Los Angeles. I don'live around here but *these* fellas live here, you might- ask them, I don'know.

Richard can be seen in this turn as putting off or postponing acceptance or rejection of the salesboy's request by virtue of a Processing Pass. His appeal is based upon the presumption that a mutual contextual belief exists to the effect that out-of-towners are not proper candidates for subscription to local newspapers. His pass places the burden of acceptance or rejection of the appeal onto others whom he designates as more suitable candidates. The exchange continues (Jefferson & Schenkein, 1978, p. 156):

Salesboy: (W'd eejer- any of you gen'tuhmen be innerested in subscribing to it,
Ted: Whaddi*you* think uh Beany.
(
Steven: Na::aw
Steven: Naw. I don't *go* faw it.

Ted's action is classified by Jefferson and Schenkein as a "Conference Pass." The Conference Pass is a version of the Processing Pass in which responsibility for responding to an appeal is transferred to another using the pretext of a *consultation*. It differs from the

Process Pass in that the burden of response is transferred immediately to another party without intervention from the author of the first pair part in the form of a reinstatement.

The two kinds of passing moves that have been described differ in at least two important respects: (1) the passing moves described by Weiner and Goodenough represent the speaker's unwillingness to make a substantive contribution to *topic,* while the Process Pass and the Conference Pass are responses to demands for a *functional* contribution; (2) the passing move implies that this author is *not willing* to make a substantive contribution, while the Process and Conference passes signify that their authors are *not qualified* to do so. Note that both types of pass, however, constitute denials that preconditions for the performance of an action obtain.

SUMMARY

A taxonomy of illocutionary acts from the perspective of a speech act theorist was compared to a dimensional analysis of speech acts obtained by factor analytic methods. Results of the dimensional analysis suggested that a taxonomy of acts based on semantic similarities in English performatives is not sensitive to such important issues as the relational or command aspects of messages, or the extent to which an act is initiating as opposed to reacting.

Speech acts may be classified as either substantive or management acts. Substantive acts may be direct or indirect. Two examples of direct substantive speech acts, requests and compliments, were examined in detail. Requests appear to vary along two dimensions: politeness and directness. Requests may be put off by statements or questions about one or another of their felicity conditions. A second type of direct speech act, compliments, has been found to be formulaic, to the extent that between 75% and 85% of compliments can be seen to follow one of three patterns. Compliments are first pair parts of adjacency pairs. Preferred seconds are either agreements or appreciations. The constraint on self-praise operates systematically on replies to compliments, and conflicts with the preference for agreement.

Indirect speech acts seem to result from demands for politeness operating in situations in which face-threatening acts must be performed. Speech acts may threaten either the positive or negative face of the hearer, or of the speaker herself. When the performance of a face-threatening act poses a risk to the speaker, he may avail himself of techniques of positive and negative politeness. One way of being negatively polite is through conventional indirectness. Indirect speech acts are formed out of the preconditions for the felicitous performance of their corresponding direct forms. Evidence indicates that in understanding indirect speech acts such as indirect requests, the hearer first constructs the literal meaning of the utterance, then checks it against the context, and finally invokes a conversational postulate such as "An inquiry about H's willingness to do A counts as a request to do A" to arrive at the final representation in the form of a "conveyed" meaning. While all Western cultures seem to use indirect speech, speakers of English seem to be less direct than speakers of German, but more direct than Greeks.

Another form of indirectness results when the speaker violates conversational maxims to invite implicature: metaphor, hyperbole, understatement, and other nonliteral usages may be accounted for by this process. It has been proposed that conversational maxims are also needed to account for the understanding of the literal meanings of utterances. Indirect answers are an example of the class of conversational implicatures in which the Relevance maxim is violated. While these "transparent questions" are usually heard as answers, they may be regarded as less appropriate and less polite than more usual forms of response to questions.

Management acts serve to organize and set off units of discourse. Formulations are proposed by participants as "candidate" readings for a preceding stretch of talk, subject to confirmation or disconfirmation by partners. Discourse brackets serve to mark the boundaries of units of conversation. Partitioning activities are formulaic utterances by means of which participants "announce" to one another what is to be expected propositionally and functionally from subsequent utterances. Speakers may sometimes choose to pass when it is their turn to talk, either by declining to make a substantive topical contribution or by shifting the burden of response to a first pair part to another party than either the speaker or the hearer.

5

Sequences

♦ In Chapter 4, the rule-goverened and formulaic ♦
aspects of the production of speech acts, and some of the constraints
upon their replies, were examined. Now, it is appropriate to turn to a
consideration of larger units in conversion that have the character of
sequences; that is, a series of three or more speech acts that taken
together may be seen to constitute a self-contained unit of discourse
with a coherent internal structure. Some sequences, like *arguments,*
may be seen to involve expansions of a basic adjacency pair unit.
Others, such as openings, closings, and storytellings, may be said to
consist of subsequences within which certain "work" needs to get
done, but in the implementation of which the specific form of speech
action may be variable. We will take up first what Goffman (1971)
has called *"access rituals":* openings and closings.

RITUALS OF ACCESS:
OPENING AND CLOSINGS

Access rituals are sequences of speech acts in which parties display to one another whether and to what extent they are available for subsequent interaction; further, access rituals serve the function of indexing the state of the relationship between the parties (Laver, 1981, p. 292):

> In the marginal phases of conversation, where the use of such linguistic routines is most dense, participants conduct their social negotiations about respective status and role partly by means of the choice of formulaic phrase, address-term, and type of phatic communication.

Openings and closings can be seen to mirror one another in significant ways. First, openings involve negotiations about the prospects for increased access, while in closings, parties work out the problems attendant upon decreased access (Knapp, Hart, Friedrich, & Shulman, 1973; Krivonos & Knapp, 1975). Second, opening sequences such as greetings may function to provide comment on changes in the relationship since a previous encounter, if indeed there have been any changes; likewise, closings may serve to reaffirm that the status of the relationship will be unaffected by the absence of interaction. Finally, both opening and closing will ordinarily contain topic-bracketing moves, respectively, a topic entry and a topic exit. We shall review openings and closings in greater detail.

Openings

Schiffrin (1977) has proposed that opening sequences consist of three phases: (1) *cognitive recognition,* which can involve either recognition of the other as a member of a class or category, or biographical recognition, in which a specific individual is differentiated from other category incumbents; (2) *identification displays,* in which cognitive recognition is acknowledged by such behaviors as a smile or an eyebrow flash; and (3) *social recognition displays,* what in ordinary usage we call greetings, in which the "heightened expectations and obligations inherent in the increase in mutual access" are acknowledged (Schiffrin, 1977, p. 679).

Schiffrin proposes that the basic opening sequence consists of three steps: (1) A and B cognitively recognize each other; (2) A and B exchange identification displays; and (3) A and B greet or indicate access. Schiffrin's claim, which is not altogether uncontroversial, is that openings are begun by both parties simultaneously, and that it is the apparent prospect for increased access, rather than a unilateral "first greeting," which generates the opening sequence. This point of view seems in conflict with the no doubt commonplace intuition that mutual recognition does not always result in greetings. We are probably more likely to have had the experience of wondering if another will "speak" than to have wondered if we were recognized.

Krivonos and Knapp (1975) have provided an account of the elements of a typical opening sequence, and the order in which those elements can be expected to occur. Krivonos and Knapp observed, in a laboratory setting, verbal and nonverbal greeting behaviors of sixteen acquainted and sixteen unacquainted pairs of males. It was found (Krivonos & Knapp, 1975, p. 193) that the verbal behaviors most common to an opening sequence were (1) *topic initiations;* (2) *verbal salutes* ("Hi," "Hello"); and (3) *references to the other* by virtue of a name, nickname, or endearment. The most frequently occurring nonverbal greeting behaviors were (1) a *head gesture* such as nodding or sideways tilt; (2) *mutual glances,* and (3) a *smile.* The typical greeting sequence (Krivonos & Knapp, 1975, p. 194) for acquainted pairs was: *mutual glance, head gesture, smile, verbal salute, reference to other, personal inquiry ("How ya doin'?"), external reference, topic initiation.* The sequence for unacquainted pairs was a truncated version of the above: *mutual glance, head gesture, verbal salute, personal inquiry.* For both groups, sequences seemed to contain Schiffrin's elements of identification display (mutual glance, head gesture) and social recognition display (salute, personal inquiry).

Schiffrin describes a class of misidentification-relevant openings that she calls "recyclings," in which the joint tasks of recategorizing of identities and readjustment of recognition displays have to be achieved (1977, p. 684). In *double-takes,* only the issue of cognitive recognition needs attending to; sometimes, however, the opening sequence has progressed sufficiently far so that when the misidentification is discovered a *take-back* has to be performed: that is, the recognition display has to be canceled:

A: Hi, Stella!
B: (smiles and shakes head)
A: Oh, I'm sorry, I thought you were someone else.
B: That's O.K.

Opening sequences may be subject to alternations when one or both of the potential interactants is otherwise engaged and a full commitment to access is not possible. One such alteration (Schiffrin, 1977, p. 684) involves the *compression* of an opening sequence, in which the identification and access displays are performed simultaneously, for example with a wink or kiss blown across a crowded room. Portions of opening sequences may also be subject to deliberate *deletion*. Since opening rituals are sequential in nature, an individual can perpetrate a *snub* by being careful not to "see" an acquaintance. One cannot be criticized for failing to greet (step 3) if one has failed to recognize (step 1). A *cut*, on the other hand, involves a deliberate violation of conversation principles: one overtly refutes the other's identification display.

The nature and duration of opening sequences may vary as a function of situational constraints. Krivonos and Knapp (1975), for example, suggest that greetings become more perfunctory and less effusive after shorter absences or when the parties have an established relationship. Greetings may become problematic for persons who must routinely "reencounter" one another in the course of daily activities; greetings in such circumstances may be seen to become increasingly truncated over the course of the day, from "Good morning!" to a smile to a nod, but be reinstated in full upon the first encounter of a new day.

Laver (1981) has examined formulaic greetings in British English and concluded that the selection of a linguistic routine is determined by the formality of the setting and the nature of the relationship between the participants. Laver (1981, p. 299) has presented a decision chart for determining the choice of greeting and departing formulas. The speaker must first decide if her addressee is or is not an *adult*. If not, then "Hello" (as opposed to more formal phrases like "Good morning") is appropriate. If the addressee is an adult, then the speaker has next to consider whether or not the setting is *marked;* that is, whether special conventions such as might be found in a court of law apply; if so, then the more formal greetings such as "Good day" are appropriate. If the setting is unmarked, then at the next decision point the determination is made that an addressee is, or is not, *kin*. If so, then the less formal "Hello" is proper. If the addressee is not kin, then a speaker must determine if as a pair they could be considered well acquainted. If not, then the more formal greetings would be in order. If the pair are well acquainted, then if the addressee has higher rank, or an age advantage of 15 years, the formal greetings are used unless there has been a "dispensation." Acquaintances of approximately the same age are greeted by the less formal terms.

In addition to looking at opening sequences that revolve around greetings, a number of scholars (Schegloff, 1968; Nofsinger, 1975; Crawford, 1977) have been interested in openings that we might, for lack of a better term, call *topic-initiating*. Topic-initiating openings, for example summons-answer sequences or inquiry openers, are designed to short-circuit the social access process and provide immediately for recipient attention to matters of substance that the speaker intends to introduce. Schegloff (1968) examined a corpus of telephone calls to a police dispatcher. The first rule that Schegloff formulated to cover such calls was the so-called *distribution rule: if one answers (as opposed to places) a call, he must speak first* (1968, p. 1076). The second rule governing openings in telephone calls is that *if one places the call, then she must provide the first conversational topic* (Schegloff, 1968, p. 1078).

Schegloff treats telephone openings as a special case of the summons-answer sequence. The ringing of the telephone, like an address-term, wave, or "Excuse me," constitutes a *summons,* a first pair-part of a two-part sequence. (Actually the sequence has a least three parts, as we shall see later.) Answering "Hello" or "Police Department" upon picking up the telephone may be seen to be a special case of *answering* a summons; that is, of supplying the second pair part to the first. This is the source of the distribution rule. The second rule follows from the need for the summoner to demonstrate a *reason* for having initiated the summons in the first place. This condition is described by Schegloff (1968, p. 1081) as the property of *terminality:* "a completed SA exchange cannot properly stand as the final exchange of a conversation." Thus, exchanges like (1) a and b below are well formed, while (2) a and b are not:

		John?			(Ring-Ring-Ring)
(1)	a	Yeah?	(1)	b	Chez Henri.
		Have you seen my			Yes, I'd like to make
		cuff links?			reservations for 8:00.

	John?			(Ring-Ring-Ring)
(2) **a**	Yeah?	(2)	**b**	Chez Henri.
	(silence)			(silence)

Schegloff reported only one instance in 500 in which the distribution rule was violated. In that case, the caller spoke first because there was a pause after the telephone was picked up. In this case the appropriate thing to do was to reinstate the "summons," this time in the form of "Hello" rather than a ring. However, when the summons has been answered, it is inappropriate to reinstate it (the *nonrepeatability* property; Schegloff, 1968, p. 1082), even though we may do so inadvertently when we have a "set" that both a general and a specific summons will be necessary to reach our party, and only the latter is necessary:

A: Lawrence Jones here.
B: Professor Jones?
A: Yes.
B: I'm calling about our assignment in 365.

Summonses that are reinstated may be treated as excessively demanding if the addressee has heard both, but for one reason or another could not or would not reply to the first:

Mother: Tommy?
Tommy: (silence)
Mother: Tommy! Where are you?!!
Tommy: I'm coming, I'm coming!

According to Schegloff's *terminating rule, if a summons is not answered, there ought not to be more than three to five repetitions at most.* Note that replies in the case of reinstated summonses not uncharacteristically respond to both a first *and* a subsequent summons in the same turn.

Schegloff argues that summons-answer sequences are further characterized by the property of *immediate juxtaposition* (1968, p. 1084); that is, a summons needs to be answered on the very next turn, or else the addressee must notify the speaker that his answer will be delayed.

Nofsinger (1975, p. 2) has looked at summonses under the rubric *demand ticket:* devices that constitute "an appropriate way to begin talking to someone," which are coercive in returning the floor to their author. Nofsinger argues that demand tickets are so constraining that a person who *thinks* she might have been summoned may openly inquire, even though a negative reply may make her look foolish, if "anyone was calling me." Not only are the demands for answering a summons very strong, but the absence of a third term that discloses the reasons for the summons is treated as a source of trouble.

Nofsinger has proposed a number of constitutive rules for the well-formed demand ticket, which amount to the felicity conditions for performing one: (1) *the speaker (A) must want to have the floor to say Z, and further wants to be obligated to say it;* (2) *the speaker does not provide any apparent reason for his having uttered X;* (3) *the speaker must intend to utter Z when the hearer gives him the floor;* (4) *the speaker intends that in saying X he will obligate B to say Y, which will then obligate him (A) to say Z and require B to listen;* and (5) *the speaker intends that the hearer recognize his intent to obligate him to hear Z.* Conditions (1) and (3) are sincerity conditions, (4) an essential condition, and (5) a force condition. Condition (2) is most important, and to underscore it Nofsinger adduces (1975, p. 7) a *Pertinence maxim:* "Do not say that which is pointless or spurious." Thus, a simple address term, "Mike?", becomes a demand ticket by virtue of the fact that nothing in the context suggests a reason for its having been uttered, and yet under the cooperative principle it is assumed that the speaker's apparent violation of the Pertinence maxim implicates something other than mere address.

Crawford (1977) has looked at topic-initiating openings, specifically inquiry openings at public and semi-public inquiry stations—in a railway office and a student council office. Crawford arrived at a number of rules about how such openings are handled: (1) *if there is no line, the inquiry officer speaks first.* (Crawford found that when this rule was violated, it was predominantly by males who were dealing with a female behind the inquiry desk. The usual norm is to display politeness by waiting for the inquiry agent to acknowledge you.) A second rule was (2) *if there is a line, the person making the inquiry speaks first;* (3) *if the inquiry agent issues a greeting, it is reciprocated,* unless (4) *the inquirer has been standing in line, in which case the problem is stated without a return greeting from the inquirer;* (5) *if the inquiry agent opens with a greeting, and gets back only a greeting without the inquiry, in order to get it the agent must reinstate with another greeting;* (6) *if the inquiry agent opens with "Yes, sir?" and gets a greeting back, then the greeting must be returned before he can get the inquiry.*

These rules suggest the following with respect to summons-answer sequences: (1) that one's presence in front of an inquiry desk constitutes a summons; (2) that the presence of a line in front of an inquiry desk is testimony to the mutual orientation of agent and client to one another's presence, and thus obviates the need for either summons or answer; that is, the attention of the inquiry agent has already been obtained and thus the reason for the speaker's summons may be disclosed immediately; (3) with respect to opening sequences generally, a greeting-greeting pair is optional, or "detachable," but ordinarily reciprocation of a first greeting is mandatory, unless the greeting can be construed as superfluous, as in rule (4); and (4) finally, the rules suggest that greeting-greeting units do no other work than signaling social recognition.

Closings

Knapp et al. (1973) suggest that in taking leave of someone, there are three general functions that our behaviors fulfill: (1) signaling that there is movement towards a state of decreased access; (2) expressing appreciation for the encounter and a desire for future contact; and (3) summarizing what the encounter has amounted to. Knapp et al. were interested in specifying the elements of a terminating sequence and their ordering, and further in determining how closing sequences might vary as a function of the degree of acquaintance and comparative status of the parties to a leave-taking.

Verbal behaviors that had the highest frequency of occurrence during closing sequences were found by Knapp et al. to be (1) *reinforcement* (short agreements such as "O.K." and "Right"); (2) *professional inquiry* (questions about a partner's task role); (3) *buffing* (short sociocentric sequences like "Uh" and "Well"); and (4) *appreciation* (statement of enjoyment of the preceding conversation). Nonverbal behaviors characteristic of closing sequences were (1) *breaking eye contact;* (2) *left-positioning* (orientation toward the exit); (3) *leaning forward;* and (4) *nodding.* Interestingly enough, actually saying "Good-by" or "So long" was among the least likely of the fourteen verbal behaviors examined to occur, and similarly with the terminal handshake, although these noticeable absences might be attributed in part to the casualness and insularity of the campus environment.

A typical closing sequence in the more formal conditions (unacquainted and/or different-status partners) was as follows (Knapp et al., 1973): *reinforcement, buffing, appreciation, internal legitimizer or external legitimizer.* (Legitimizers varied according to whether they invoked an internal ("I think we've finished all the questions") or an external ("I've got to go to gym") motive for termination. In less formal circumstances, a typical sequence was: *reinforcement, buffing, welfare concern* ("Take care of yourself") *or continuation* ("See you tomorrow"). Knapp et al. found that acquaintances tended to do more reinforcing than strangers, and that in status-discrepant dyads it was characteristic of the lower-status partner to do more buffing.

Closings in telephone conversations have proven to be of interest to several investigators (Schegloff & Sacks, 1973; Albert & Kessler, 1978; Clark & French, 1981). One of the first things that must be done prior to any closing is for the parties to reach agreement that there is no further topical talk to be had. We have already described the role played by minimal responses and formulations in closing down topical talk. Schegloff and Sacks (1973) suggest further that sociocentric sequences such as "So:oo" and "Well" serve a sort of bracketing function in this regard, and can be expected to appear *after* a final topic has been formulated. If these brackets are "confirmed," then the closing sequence proper may begin.

Albert and Kessler (1978) looked at telephone conversations between twenty pairs of friends, and twenty pairs who were unacquainted. Half of the pairs were asked to engage in a structured discussion; that is, they were asked to talk about an assigned topic. The remainder of the conversations were not structured as to topic. Albert and Kessler reported that *summary* statements such as formulatons were more likely to occur early in the closing sequence (the ninth as opposed to the tenth decile of the conversation), and that they did not occur at all in the unstructured interactions. Further, summary statements were used twice as often by friends as by strangers, perhaps because friends would be more prone to formulate B-Issues or B-Events than strangers. The frequency of *justifications* for terminating (like Knapp et al.'s external and internal legitimizers) increased dramatically in the tenth decile. Justifications were used more often in unstructured conversations, no doubt due in part to the absence of obvious sources of internal (task-specific) motivation for terminating. The frequency of *continuity* statements (what Knapp et al. called continuations) increased during the tenth decile, as did the frequency of *positive* statements. Albert and Kessler proposed the following sequence as typical of closing sections: *summary statement, justification, positive statements, continuity statements, well-wishing.* This sequence is quite similar to those proposed by Knapp et al., although Knapp and his colleagues did not have a category for coding summary statements, and found that the second and third elements (justification and positive statements) occurred primarily in more formal leave-takings.

Albert and Kessler reported that there was considerable evidence that summarizations, continuity statements, and well-wishings are ordinarily reciprocated, but that justifications, for example, are not. Justifications were most apt to be followed by continuity statements. Positive statements were most likely to be followed by statements expressing hopes for continuity and expressions of good wishes.

Clark and French (1981) suggest that telephone closing sequences have three distinct subsections: a *topic termination section,* which would include the usual negotiations as to whether all topical talk has been completed, a *leave-taking section,* which includes summarizations, justifications, positive statements, continuity statements, well-wishings, and good-byes, and a *contact termination subsection,* which consists of both parties hanging up. Clark and French (1981, p. 4) argue that the whole of the leave-taking section is optional, and should *affirmation* behaviors be unnecessary, then "good-bye/good-bye" exchanges will be unlikely to occur. That is, if there is no need for parties to reaffirm their relationship with well-wishings or continuity statements, then there will be no need for good-byes either, and conversation can end with a pre-closing topic termination section (lines 4-7) that simply consists of mutual acknowledgments that the goal of the conversation has been met:

1	**Operator:**	Information
2	**Caller:**	Yes, for Jane Wilson in Pasadena.
3	**Operator:**	That number is 555-1973.
4	**Caller:**	555-1973?
5	**Operator:**	Yes.
6	**Caller:**	Thank you.
7	**Operator:**	You're welcome.

Clark and French tested their notion that "good-bye" exchanges were part of an optional leave-taking subsection by monitoring calls to a university switchboard. The support they obtained for this view was fairly strong. Callers for whom the contact with the operator was more "personal," or involving, when either the caller's requests were unusually imposing or the operator made an error, were much more likely to initiate a good-bye sequence than callers whose request for directory assistance were more routine. However, good-byes are also influenced by sequential constraints. If the operator said "Good-bye" in the slot filled by line (7) above, over 50% of the callers also said "Good-bye." If the operator said "You're welcome-Good-bye" in that same slot, over 60% of the callers provided a matching "Good-bye," which suggests that in the former case the operator's "Good-bye" was more likely to be heard as a stand-in for "You're welcome" (i.e., a second pair part), while in the latter case it was more likely to be heard as a first pair part.

If we look at the opening sequences proposed by Krivonos and Knapp (1975) for acquainted pairs (excluding the nonverbal behaviors), and at the closing sequences proposed by Albert and Kessler (1978), the idea with which we initially begin, that openings and closings mirror one another, may become self-evident:

Opening	*Closing*
Salute	Summary
Reference to Other	Justification
Personal Inquiry	Positive Statement
External Reference	Continuity Statement
Topic Initiation	Well-wishing
	(Good-bye)

Note that the last act in the opening sequence and the first act in the closing sequence both have to do with bracketing *topic*. Similarly, the next-to-last opening act and the next-to-first closing act both have to do with the *reason* or occasion for the impending increase or decrease in access. A further parallel is that the next act in the opening sequence, inquiry about the *other's welfare,* is mirrored in the closing sequence by corresponding other-orientations represented by positive statements, continuity statements, and well-wishing. Finally, the first act of the opening sequence, the salutation, has a corresponding "slot" in the optional good-bye at the end of the closing sequence.

ARGUMENTS

We now turn our attention from the "brackets" of conversation to its substance. One of the most illuminating ways of looking at the organization of speech acts in conversation is to study discourse units built around the treatment of a "troublesome" conversational event, for example, *arguments* (Jacobs & Jackson, 1979; Jackson & Jacobs, 1980; Jacobs & Jackson, in press) or *accounts* (McLaughlin, Cody, & O'Hair, 1983; McLaughlin, Cody, & Rosenstain, 1983). Looking at the management of troubles in conversation is very revealing because it provides us with some solid evidence as to what conversationalists think the rules are.

One factor that seems to have emerged very clearly from studies of talk is that the conversational system demonstrates a noticeable *preference for agreement* (Sacks, 1973; Pomerantz, 1978; Brown & Levinson, 1978; Jackson & Jacobs, 1980). It seems apparent that for many kinds of speech acts that fall within the adjacency pair framework there are preferred and dispreferred ways of providing a second pair part. We have seen, for example, in Chapter 4, how preferred responses to *compliments* are constructed. Sacks (1973) has shown that if one has to provide a dispreferred second pair part, it is typical that it be displaced as far as possible from the soliciting utterance so as to provide at least the appearance of agreement. Brown and Levinson provide an excellent example (1978, p. 119):

A: What is she, small?
B: Yes, yes, she's smallish, um, not really small but certainly not very big.

McLaughlin, Cody, and Rosenstein (1983, p. 105) proposed that interactants, particularly people who have never met, will go to great lengths to insure that "even the most outrageous and patently unappealing propositions can be confirmed, or at the very least be kept from unduly disrupting the conversation beyond the purely local level of management." The following examples are cases in point:

A: All I ever do is study. We get a hundred pages a week to read*
    in Political Science class and I- nobody else reads it. But I
    figure they assigned it, they want you to read it. But I like it.
B: Huh huh. *You- you'll learn to cheat.*
A: Yeah, well true, but-
B: Not to cheat on tests but to cheat through your reading.

A: They want you to invest more money, which will provide more*
    jobs for people and the business in essence everything will rise,
    but income will rise also, in essence everything will drop- that's
    my theory. *I just think we need more poor people in the world.*

B: I don't.

A: Huh?

B: I don't.

A: Well, that's what it is, is we give so much money to people on welfare.

B: Well, that's true. I don't believe in welfare. I don't see it. But what makes me mad are these illegal aliens.

It is not easy to dismiss the claim of the conversational analysts that there is a structural preference for agreement built into the conversational system, particularly in light of the abundant laboratory support for strong response matching effects, on a number of content and noncontent variables, variously labeled "accommodation" (Giles et al., 1973; Larsen et al., 1977; Giles, 1980), "convergence" (Giles & Powesland, 1975), "interspeaker influence" (Cappella & Planalp, 1981; Cappella, 1981), and "reciprocity" (Gouldner, 1960; Blau, 1964; Worthy et al., 1969; Cozby, 1972; Chaikin & Derlega, 1974; Rubin, 1975; Davis, 1976; Bradac et al., 1978). There is overwhelming evidence that conversational partners, particularly persons meeting for the first time, present themselves as similar to each other. Further, they seem to overestimate the extent of their similarity (Duck, 1976).

In light of the pervasiveness of the preference for agreement, there are any number of communicative events that can be seen to be directed to the management of disagreement (Jackson & Jacobs, 1979), some of which we will take up in the next chapter under the heading of "repairs." Since our interest in the present chapter is in sequences, it is appropriate at this point to consider the case of *arguments,* which are disagreement-relevant sequences built around the expansion of an adjacency pair, for example request-grant/refuse or offer-accept/refuse.

Jacobs and Jackson (1979) propose that arguments in conversation revolve around the occurrence, or impending occurrence, of dispreferred second pair parts. Jacobs and Jackson define structural preference for agreement by reference to the fact that some second pair parts conform to the conventional perlocutionary effect of the speech act that was done by the first pair part, and some do not (1979, p. 3). This structural preference seems to constrain SPPs to be grants, acceptances, and so on, and similarly, it constrains FPPs to be formulated in such a way that they will get grants, acceptances, and so forth.

Having an argument (as opposed to making one) is an outcome of the failure to provide a preferred second or to alter or cancel an arguable first pair part. Arguments are *made,* according to Jacobs and Jackson (1979, p. 3) from the preconditions for the performance of the act at issue. The prototypical case of having an argument involves the linear expansion of an overriding adjacency pair (Jacobs & Jackson, 1979, p. 4):

> [O]ne party issues a proposal or other FPP . . . which is then rejected, objected to, or countered by the other party . . . and then resupported by the first party and so on. The turn and sequence expansions elicit or supply objections or support for some aspect of either the disagreeable FPP or the dispreferred SPP, or for some aspect of already supplied objections and support.

How is it that an utterance may be disagreeable or *arguable?* An utterance may be arguable at the *propositional* level, in which case the argument turns on its truth or falsity, on its sense and reference as a proposition (Jackson & Jacobs, 1980). In the corpus of stranger interactions from which we have been drawing examples, virtually all arguments were of this variety—a hearer did not accept a speaker's assertion as correct. In the following fragment, for example, the hearer takes issue with one of the assumptions underlying the speaker's claim. She is not challenging the propriety of what he is *doing,* but rather the correctness of what he is *saying:*

A: And uh that's just a law of economics. They're gonna go*
up and then they're gonna come down. The price of gas will go up but when people stop buying

B: (Yeah, but people won't stop buying. I'm not.

A: If the price gets high enough they will.

B: Yeah, but if I had the money I'm going to spend it on it regardless.

A: Yeah, but the supply will drop off.

B: Yeah, but then it's just like the people who don't

A: (and once- when they find more the price- then they will lower the prices but the prices will come down. Europe is paying two dollars a gallon as of right now. We're getting it cheap and so-

B: Uh huh.

The example above is interesting not just in that it exemplifies a propositionally based argument so purely, but also because of the continuous operation of the preference-for-agreement constraint, which works to produce the four displaced disagreements ("Yeah, but").

The other way in which an utterance can be arguable is at the *functional* level (Jackson & Jacobs, 1980), when it appears to the hearer that one or more of the preconditions for the successful performance of the act have not been met. The hearer might, for example, attack preparatory conditions, as in (1), or sincerity conditions, as in (2):

(1) **A:** I want to get a new suit for my interview, O.K.?
     B: We can't afford it this month.

(2) **A:** I promise I'll pay you back tomorrow.
     B: You know very well I'll be out of town 'til next week.

The basic way in which arguables and responses to arguables are expanded into sequences is through *within-turn* justifications and excuses, *pre-sequences, insertion sequences,* and *post-sequences* (Jacobs & Jackson, 1979; Jackson & Jacobs, 1980). In a within-turn expansion, arguments in favor of an FPP (as in 2-4), or arguments against doing a preferred SPP (as in 5) are made in the same turn as the pair part itself:

1 **Tommy:** There's a play at school I want
2   to go go tonight, can I go, 'cause
3   we get extra credit in drama if we
4   go.
5 **Mother:** No, 'cause we're having Chuck for dinner.

Jacobs and Jackson (1979) suggest that the additional supporting information that the speakers provide may be construed as a violation of the Quantity maxim, and invoke the implication that the speaker is unsure of the reception his or her act will receive.

Another way in which disagreement-relevant pairs can be expanded is through pre-sequences (Jacobs & Jackson, 1979; Jackson & Jacobs, 1980). Edmondson (1981b) has suggested that pre-sequences are used for a number of reasons, including the fact that they represent a potential way of making the *hearer* articulate the illocutionary point of the speaker. Should it appear that the illocutionary act to which the pre-sequence is preliminary will not receive a preferred response, the intent behind the pre-sequence is still deniable:

  A: Whatcha doin' tonight?
  B: Goin' out with Jim. Why?
  A: Oh, nothin'. Just wondered.

The basic function of a presequence in conversation, then, is to check out whether or not the preconditions exist under which a first pair part such as a request, offer, suggestion, and so on can be satisfied. Of course, as was discussed in an earlier section on conventional indirectness, some pre's are so conventionalized in their interpretations that they count as a main act, and get an SPP immediately (Edmondson, 1981b).

Insertion sequences (Jacobs & Jackson, 1979) or *embedded sequences* (Jacobs & Jackson, in press) are sandwiched between first and second pair parts. According to Jacobs and Jackson (1979, p. 8), insertion sequences serve three functions: (1) they provide "objections" that will be heard as dispreferred seconds unless countered, a clear instance of the "hearer-knows-best" principle; (2) they suggest that under certain conditions, a preferred SPP might be forthcoming; and (3) as in a confrontation sequence, insertions may be used to build a structure of arguments to support an impending challenge. Most typical of an insertion sequence is the so-called *contingent query,* in which the first pair part implies that there are certain conditions that must be satisfied before a preferred second to the initial proffer can be provided. We have also discussed this strategy in the section dealing with the *rule of embedded requests,* in which one of the ways of putting off a request is to ask for further information about its entailments:

> A: Yeah. We wanted to know if you'll serve as an advisor for our chapter.
> B: What all would that involve? I mean what sorts of things would I have to do?
> A: Well, you'd have to come to chapter meetings about once a month and then help out with rush, and
> B: (We always go on vacation the week before school starts.

A further function of the insertion sequence is to encourage the issuer of the arguable FPP to modify it in some way such that the proffer can be accepted.

Finally, *post-sequences* (the placement of a subordinate adjacency pair following a second pair part of a dominant adjacency pair) may serve a number of functions: (1) reinstate the original FPP in the hope that a more satisfactory response will be forthcoming on a second trial; (2) check out the sincerity of a prior agreement; and (3) soften the effects of a prior FPP which may have been reluctantly accepted

(Jacobs & Jackson, 1979, pp. 9-10). The usual implication of the first pair part of a post-sequence is that the sincerity conditions for performing the preferred second are in doubt:

A: Would you mind dropping this off for me on your way to work?
B: Yeah, I guess so.
A: 'Cause I'm gonna be late getting off because I have to iron something to wear.
B: Well, I will if it's not too crowded.
A: O.K.

Siebold, McPhee, Poole, Tanita, and Canary (1981) developed a coding scheme for argument based on the Jacobs and Jackson model, which they applied to multiparty conversation. Their observations provided support for the notion that a preference for agreement was the underlying motive for the expansion of disagreement-relevant adjacency pairs. Siebold et al. had anticipated that the presence of multiple participants might make it difficult to sort out first and second pair parts, but actually reported that the presence of multiple interactants can increase conditional relevance constraints through the collaborative production of sequences.

In a second look at the same data set, however, Tanita, Canary, and Seibold (1982) concluded that it was frequently difficult in multiparty conversation to determine which utterances were FPPs. Furthermore, the same instance could be coded as an FPP or an SPP, depending upon its intended recipient. Finally, it was not always possible to determine upon which speech acts authors of SPPs felt their turns to be contingent. Further work needs to be done to implement the application of Jacobs and Jackson's approach to argument in other than dyadic settings.

STORIES

In this section we will examine how it is that "stories" can be recognized as internally coherent discourse units whose elements and their sequencing evidence a canonical form. There are at present at least two distinct approaches to this task, one of which emerges from the conversational analysis literature, the other of which grows out of the interest of cognitive psychologists in story grammars. We will take up the conversational analytic view of stories first.

Stories from the Perspective of Conversational Analysis

Jefferson (1978) describes the elements which constitute the collaborative activity which she terms a conversational "story-telling":

> A series of utterances which can be extracted from a conversation and identified as parts of "a story" can be sequentially analyzed as parts of "a storytelling," with recognizable story components deployed as story-entry and -exit devices, providing transition from a state of turn-by-turn talk among conversational co-participants into a story told by a storyteller to story recipient(s), and a return from the latter to the former state of talk [p. 237].

Rather than being "detachable" conversational units, stories are triggered by turn-by-turn talk, that is, they are *locally occasioned* (Jefferson, 1978, p. 220) and they are *sequentially implicative* for subsequent talk (Jefferson, 1978, p. 228). While we ordinarily think of the function of stories in conversation as illustrative, stories can clearly serve many functions. Beach and Japp (1983) suggest that stories can serve to reconstruct, justify, or evaluate events in the past; they can be used to reference or acknowledge current happenings both internal and external to the conversation; further, stories may be useful in collaborative fantasizing, to project or to pretend. Beach and Japp see stories as a way of "time-traveling," a vehicle for shifting context as conversational needs arise. Goodwin (1982) proposes that stories can be strategies embedded in the global plans of actors to manipulate the actions of others. Her case in point is what she calls "instigating," in which the storyteller reports on the behavior of a third party who is alleged to have performed actions directed against the story recipient. Goodwin argues that stories are often part of more global speech acts "embedded in social processes extending beyond the immediate social encounter" (1982, p. 799).

Sacks (1974) proposes that stories have three linearly ordered subsections that he calls the "preface sequence," the "telling sequence," and the closing or "response sequence." These labels will serve as a convenient point of departure for the next several sections.

The preface sequence. The preface sequence minimally consists of two turns, one by the potential storyteller and one by her intended recipient. The first turn by the intending teller may be seen to establish the proper conditions for the telling of a subsequent narrative. This initiating turn could contain a number of different speech acts, including offers, characterizations, stage-settings, admonitions, and so forth. In the following example, at line 1, the teller, B, makes an initial probe to determine if his hearer is familiar with the event he is about to recount. In point of fact, the preface sequence is unusually long (lines 1-9) because A and particularly B seem determined to establish A's ignorance of the event before B proceeds with his story. The preface sequence is expanded by both a contingent query initiated by A at lines (2-6) and a post-sequence initiated by B at lines (8-9):

1	**B:**	Did you see the speech that Reagan made?*
2	**A:**	Which one? I seen one of 'em- I'd
3		never seen one of 'em. Which one are you
4		talkin' about now?
5	**B:**	No. I didn't see it myself, but somebody told
6		me about- the one where he prayed, at the end.
7	**A:**	No, I didn't see that one.
8	**B:**	You didn't see it?
9	**A:**	(apparent nonverbal "No.") Guess it was
10		pretty movin'.
11	**B:**	Yeah, you know, cause
12	**A:**	(Cause you rarely see it.
13	**B:**	It was different or somethin'. He said-
14		I don't know the exact words he said,
15		"This is something I think I'd better do"
16		or somethin' like that and then he prayed.
17	**A:**	Hmm.
18	**B:**	"I'd be better off doin' than not doin'."
19	**A:**	Mm-yeah. Hmm.

In addition to securing permission for a storytelling by making sure that the event to be recounted is unfamiliar to the listener, the preface section often proposes some initial characterization of the event (Sacks, 1974). Such characterizations can range from brief "plugs" to full-fledged "significance statements" (Ryave, 1978). According to Ryave, storytellers are ordinarily sensitive to providing for their hearers an account of the import or upshot of a forthcoming narrative, in particular to stating how it is that "some assertion(s) can be appreciated and evidenced in and through the recounting of some event" (1978, p. 125). Stories are not limited to single significance statements (Ryave, 1978, p. 126); they may be formulated in different ways by the teller, or may have ascribed to them by the recipient a significance overlooked by the teller herself. In the story below, the significance statement which informs it can be found at line 4:

```
 1  A:   What do you want to teach?*
 2       Have you decided yet?
 3  B:   Fifth or sixth grade.
 4  A:   Why?!! They're terrible kids at that age!
 5  B:   No, they're not! Well, I think I can have
 6       more control over older ones like that than
 7       the little bitty ones. I don't know.
 8  A:   Why not? I remember when I was in the
 9       fifth grade I got caught for cussing.
10  B:   Uh oh!
11  A:   The teacher brought my mother in there and
12       tried to make me feel real bad 'cause I
13       was cussing on the playground.
14  B:   Ha ha ha.
15  A:   (falsetto) "Why were you cussing?" "Why
16       were you cussing?"
17  B:   Ha ha ha.
```

A third function of the preface sequence is to make some reference to the time or occasion when the event to be recounted took place (Sacks, 1974). As was pointed out in the previous chapter, in the section on introductions, the action maybe more or less "upon" the recipient before she has had a chance to prepare for it. If the preface introduces information pertinent to the *setting,* then there is ordinarily no second turn, or only a brief acknowledgment by the recipient, the teller simply forging ahead:

```
A:   One time when I was younger-see I can't even ride a motor*
     cycle-
B:   Yeah. You couldn't-
A:   One time a friend of mine had this little minibike, you know.
B:   Uh huh.
A:   Anyway, I got on it and it kept goin' around the house,
     and all these little kids were chasin' me= (       )
B:                                                 Yeah.
A:   =and I couldn't stop.
B:   Really?
A:   Yeah. I was kinda
```

B: (You're supposed to stop it with that brake
on there, you know.
A: I KNOW! but I didn't now they kept doin' like that.
B: God! Ha ha.
A: (Ha ha. And I'd go, you know, all those kids were
chasin' me. But anyway-

The devices for the type of story-entry that have been characterized
as providing a setting for a recounting are usually fairly conventionalized—for example, "Once," "One time," "There was," and
so forth.

Less often than not, the bulk of the work in the preface will be
carried by the story recipient. For example, she might ask for an
example, an accounting, evidence, or an explanation, which the teller
then supplies in the form of a story:

B: Nice shoes.*
A: Oh. Ha ha. Thanks. How'd you hurt your leg?
B: Football practice, I got hit. I'll be all right.
A: Who hit you?
B: Billy Jones.
A: Ha ha ha.

Other functions of the preface sequence include attributing a
forthcoming narrative or joke to a third party (Sacks, 1974), and
admonishing the recipient not to repeat the story (Goodwin, 1982).
In the latter case securing a preferred second to the admonishment is
necessary to conclude the preface section and move into the
recounting proper. Obviously, any time that a first pair part in the
preface receives a dispreferred second ("I've heard that one"),
whether or not the recounting takes place becomes a matter for
negotiation between the parties, and provides systematically for
expansion of the entire preface sequence (Sacks, 1974).

The recounting sequence. The telling or recounting sequence has
been described by Ryave (1978, p. 125) as "the delineation of some
event, usually requiring a number of utterances tied together by some
developing course of action." Actually, the recounting aspect of
conversational storytelling is the one about which conversational
analysts have the least to say; to find out much about story action
elements and how they are sequenced, we must turn to the story grammarians, which we will do presently.

When the conversational analysts have turned their attention to the
properties of recountings, they are as apt as not to be wrong. Sacks

(1974, p. 344), for instance, claims that the only systematic basis for recipient talk during the recounting section lies in the repair organization; questions addresssed to problems of recipient "unhearings" (Grimshaw, 1982) and misunderstandings. Sacks claims that if recipients want to say anything during a recounting sequence, they may be required to do it "interruptively." There are a number of sources of counter-evidence to this claim. First of all, some stories may be *collaboratively developed* beyond just the usual recipient acquiescing in story entrances and exits. Consider the following example.

A: How'd you feel-you came in one night and I don't think*
   you said hello.
B: Oh. Ha ha ha.
A: (Ha ha ha.
B: We'd been out in the car that night and we'd=
A: Ha ha ha.
B: =I'd mixed bourbon and (?)- we had a good time.
   Ha ha ha ha.
A: (Ha ha ha. What I want to know is do you remember
   any of it? Ha ha.
B: Yes, I do. I remember saying something, but I don't know
   who it was to. You know, you're just kinda goin', well,
   yeah, I'm here.
A: Ha ha ha.
B: (I went up straight to bed, crashed down-
A: From what I understood, you were poured into bed.
   Ha ha ha.
B: (Well, they made it sound like that, but when Liz left
   me- the person I roomed with that semester- I was coherent
   enough where I could brush my teeth, take off my make-up,
   and get under the covers, and go to bed.
A: O.K.

Although the recounting proper in the example above is concerned with what happened to A, B, the ostensible recipient, is not only involved in the preface sequence by soliciting the story and providing a setting, he also issues further solicitations, on two other occasion, in order to extract more of the details of the event from his partner; further, he supplies a formulation: "From what I understood, you were poured into bed." Thus, the conversational system can be seen to make provision for recipient talk during a recounting when the telling has been solicited by the recipient, because the "focus" of the conversation is on filling in gaps in the recipient's knowledge (see Stiles, 1978), and only the recipient can determine if and when that objective has been satisfied.

Another example of the systematic provision for recipient talk has been provided by Goodwin (1982) in her treatment of *instigating*. The main feature of an instigation is that a nonpresent party is alleged to have directed certain actions, which are recounted, against a party who is the current recipient of talk (Goodwin, 1982, p. 804). The recipient's being a character in the story provides for her sustained involvement as the storytelling unfolds and develops. Since the purpose of the instigation is to incite the recipient to action against the offending third party, recipient talk of the following variety is systematically encouraged and even solicited: (1) counters to the statements about her attributed to the offending third party; (2) pejorative statements about the third party; (3) comments on the loyalty and friendship of the teller; (4) vows that redress will be sought; and (5) rehearsals of possible confrontations with the offender, that is, *embedded stories* told by the recipient (Goodwin, 1982, p. 804).

McLaughlin et al. (1981) were interested in how recipient talk during storytelling varied as a function of the sex of the receiver. They found that, far from being interruptive, recipient talk during recounting was commonplace and varied; further, rules about such talk were sufficiently normative that males and females could be shown to differ in story reception behaviors in ways consistent with traditional sex-role stereotypes. Males and females were found by McLaughlin et al. to differ significantly on a linear combination of five recipient behaviors, three of which were recounting sequence variables: displaying *interest tokens* ("Really?" "Is that so?"), (Jefferson, 1978); *giving appreciations* ("Wow!" "How terrible!"), (Jefferson, 1978); and *adding or predicting details*. Men were more likely to display interest tokens (emphasis *tokens*) and add or predict details, while the more supportive appreciation behaviors were characteristically female. Post-conversational ratings of partner's competency indicated that males who used fewer "Um-hms" and "Yeahs" were rated as more competent.

Closing sequence. The beginning of the *response sequence* (Sacks, 1974) or more properly the *closing sequence* may be signaled in a variety of ways, including gist or upshot formulations as well as other *story-exit* devices (Jefferson, 1979). The closing of the drinking story in the previous section is marked with a "home-again" device (Jefferson, 1978):

B: I was coherent enough where I could brush my teeth, take off my make-up, and get under the covers, and go to bed.

Formulations, as was brought out in an earlier chapter, often serve
to terminate topical talk generally, and they do the same work in the
case of stories; furthermore, although significance statements usually
appear in the story preface, a formulation in a story closing sequence
may very well serve the additional function of displaying the point of
the story from the teller's perspective:

> A: Well, once she told us we're gonna debate it- that's why-*
> I didn't like it, you know.
>
> B: Yeah.
>
> A: I was never that good in P.E. and I, you know, I knew how I
> felt. I didn't like it and we didn't even have compet- competitive
> athletics but even in gymnastics and stuff I- I always felt
> inadequate- didn't feel accepted because I couldn't perform
> like the other people. And so that's what I- I didn't like
> it. And then she told us, "Well, go over to the against side,"
> and then she changed it up and told us we were gonna be for,
> and told us it was better to debate something we didn't believe
> in. Ha ha, so- we had to do a lot of research. *It hasn't changed
> my mind, but uh, you know, I still don't like the idea.*

In addition to closing down the story, a further function of closing
sequence formulations is to demonstrate for the recipient the
implication of the story for subsequent talk (Jefferson, 1978;
McLaughlin et al., 1981). The recipient is then expected to
demonstrate how the story will inform her own succeeding remarks.
Constraints to do so are strong enough, for some individuals, to
survive a lengthy pause:

> A: I went this weekend to the pet store. That's my favorite*
> store in the whole mall.
>
> B: Yeah, I like to go in there too.
>
> A: So I went in- I went in there. We were lookin' to see if we could
> find- you know- just they probably wouldn't have. We were
> lookin' to see if we could find one. 'Cause I just think- my
> dad has one and I just think they're really neat dogs.
>
> (5.2)
>
> B: They're real neat. But we don't have any pets, you know,
> we live in an apartment so it's kinda like . . .

On other occasions a demonstration of sequential implicativeness
may seem to be purely perfunctory, but nonetheless, it is still
done:

> A: Did you go to the T.C.U. game?*
>
> B: Umm hmm.
>
> A: Kind of cold, huh?

B: No, it wasn't too bad. We got a little bit down wind- there wasn't any wind at all.

A: Well, we were freezing, basically. I remember we had about four blankets=

               (   )

B: Ahh!

A: =and we had coffee=

               (   )

B: Yeah.

A: =we didn't have any sugar or anything=

                      (   )

B: Oh.

A: =we had to drink it black and it tasted like water with a little bit of coffee in there. It was terrible.

B: *We took some hot tea, I think.* What sorority are you in?

Story sequencing devices. A number of scholars (Jefferson, 1978; Ryave, 1978; McLaughlin et al., 1981) have directed attention to the devices by which the relevance of a story to the preceding talk can be demonstrated. Of particular interest are the techniques by which stories themselves may be sequenced. There are a number of ways in which a series of stories can evidence relatedness without resort to display devices; for example, they may be "about" the same topic. Frequently, however, in order to provide a simultaneous demonstration that one's partner's story was implicative for subsequent talk, and that one's own story is relevant to and occasioned by what went before, storytellers may avail themselves of *story sequencing devices.* McLaughlin et al. (1981, p. 103) list eight such devices: (1) *explicit repeat of a significance-statement,* which informs both stories; (2) *implicit repeat of a significance statement,* which connects one's story to a prior teller's; (3) *supportive story pre-fixed phrases* (Jefferson, 1978) such as "Yeah, that's true, one time I . . . "; (4) *topping* ("You think that's bad, wait'll you hear this one!"); (5) *reinterpretation* (Ryave, 1978), in which the subsequent teller's significance statement is alleged to be a more appropriate formulaton of the prior story than the one originally provided for it; (6) *disjunct markers* ("Not to change the topic, but . . . "); (7) *embedded repetitions,* in which a triggering element in a prior recounting is repeated but not marked; and (8) *marked repeats,* which explicitly cite the element that is a participant in both recountings. The last three devices were noted by Jefferson (1978). The disjunct marker actually behaves in a manner opposite to the other devices; while it is addressed to the issue of demonstrating what the relationship is between subsequent stories, what it demonstrates is that there is no relationship. As an illustration of a story sequence, an example from McLaughlin et al. (1981, pp. 106-107) is provided in which the two stories are linked by a *topping* device:

A: I just saw *Jaws* for the first time about- well, it was on*
      TV about three, four weeks ago.

(1.3)

A: That was terrible!
B: *(Well, you ought see the second one!*
A: Oh, Lord!
B: (I'll tell you, its, it's great.
A: I don't go in for those-horror movies=
B: (It's, it's great)
A: =like that.
B   I liked the heck out of it. Starts comin' up out of the water
      and this guy's tryin' to get in the boat?
A: Uh huh.
B: I guess he got knocked unconscious and these people were
      tryin' to pull him in.

McLaughlin et al. found that female storytellers were more likely than male storytellers to use the sequencing devices, particularly marked and embedded repeats; evidently they felt under a greater constraint to display the relationship of their own talk to what had gone before.

Contributions of the Story Grammar Perspective

Before examining the work of the story grammarians, a caveat ought to be issued: most of this work is within the framework of studies of reading comprehension, and most of the stories examined seem to be on the order of Aesop's Fables. The scholars who work in the area are for the most part cognitive scientists who are interested in modeling the knowledge required to interpret and produce texts. With this in mind, let us examine what this body of research has to offer the student of conversational storytelling.

Rumelhart (1975, p. 213) proposed a story grammar whose components are a set of *syntactical rules* that generate the structure of stories, and a set of *semantic interpretation rules* that correspond to them. While it is not possible to present all of Rumelhart's rules here, a few examples may suffice to capture the flavor of this work. The syntactic rules are constitutive; they specify how the major elements in the story grammar are defined. For example (Rumelhart, 1975, p. 214), Rule 1 is that *a Story consists of a Setting and an Episode;* Rule 2 is that *a Setting consists of one or more stative propositions;* Rule 3 is that *an Episode consists of an Event and a Reaction.* The semantic rules specify the nature of the relationship between elements. For example, *the relationship between Setting and Episode is ALLOW;* the setting enables but does not cause the episode (Rumelhart, 1975, p. 220). *The relationship among the states described in the Setting is AND*—simple conjunction. *The relationship between the constituent elements of Episode—Event and Reaction—is that the former INITIATES the latter.* Syntactic rules are also provided for Events, Reactions, Internal Responses, Overt Responses, Attempts, Applications, Preactions, and Consequences; their relationships are specified by semantic rules.

The overriding grammatical categories that emerge from Rumelhart's analysis are Setting and Episode, under the latter of which are embedded an Event and a Reaction to it. Embedded under Reactions are Internal Responses (Emotions or Desires) and External Responses, under the latter of which are either Actions or multiple Attempts, goal-directed actions consisting of a Plan and its Application. Embedded under the Application of the Plan are Preactions (Subgoals and their respective Attempts) and a Main Action and its Consequences. Nested under Consequences are the basic Episode constituents of Reaction and Event (Rumelhart, 1975, pp. 213-220). Rumelhart's story grammar is hierarchically organized under a global Episode; it is an argument for a representation of speech actions in terms of superordinate goals, plans, acts, and outcomes. Stein (1982) suggests that underlying Rumelhart's work (1975, 1977) is the assumption that stories are comprehended in terms of hearer's interpretations of the plans and goals of the protagonist. All of this is very familiar and typical of the global or macrostructural approach to coherence that was presented in Chapter 2.

Schemes like Rumelhart's are advocated by story grammarians as approximations to the way stories are represented in memory. The basic argument of Rumelhart, Mandler, and Johnson (1977), Stein and Glenn (1979) and others in this tradition is that stories are comprehended, recalled, and constructed with recourse to story schemata. Schemata consist of organized knowledge bases, some part of which may be described by the story grammar categories (Stein, 1982):

> A story grammar is a description of structrual regularities in a particular kind of text, best exemplified by folk tales and fables from the oral tradition. In itself a story grammar is not a story schema; the latter is a mental data structure which is used in various kinds of processing . . . At the simplest level, the rules describing the regularities in the texts can be assumed to be reflected in the story schema and its workings, but a literal translation of those rules into the head need not be, and is not, assumed [Mandler, 1982, p. 306].

A basic premise of the work on story grammars is that comprehension of stories demands knowledge in a number of different areas, one of which is the underlying grammatical structure of stories (Goldman, 1982). Like conventional rules theorists, story grammarians expect to find support for grammatical rules by looking at reactions to rule-violating stories. A typical expectations is that when texts fail to follow the canonical form, for example, when a story is opened with something other than a setting, recall of the material would be negatively affected (Stein, 1982), resequencing would be more difficult (McClure, Mason, & Barnitz, 1979), and so forth.

Sequencing of story grammar categories. Mandler and Johnson (1977) and Stein and Glenn (1979) both present a canonical sequence of story units that are trunications of the version originating with Rumelhart. Both begin with a Setting (Stein and Glenn have a Major Setting in which the characters are introduced and a Minor setting in which the conflict is described). In the Mandler and Johnson scheme, Episodes 1 through n follow, each of which may contain a Beginning (like Stein and Glenn's Initiating Event), and a Complex Reaction to the Beginning (corresponding to Stein and Glenn's Internal Response, the plans and goals of the protagonist). Both schemes feature in next position one or more Attempts by the protagonist to reach his goal, an Outcome or Direct Consequence of the Attempt, and an Ending or Reaction to the consequences of goal-oriented action (Mandler, 1982).

McClure et al. (1979) were interested in studying the effects on children's ability to resequence stories of varying the opening of the story from the canonical sequence. Three different versions of a series of stories were prepared. In one, the *setting* version, the normal placement of a setting statement as the first sentence of the story was used. In the *question* version, the first sentence was an interrogative construction whose expressed proposition was a summary of the gist of the story. In the *conclusion* version, a headline-like sentence summarizing the story was in first position. McClure et al. found that the setting version was generally the easiest for the children to resequence, and the question version was the most difficult. A developmental improvement was noted in the ability to resequence the nonstandard story forms. The McClure et al. study provided considerable support for the notion that children possess schemata for canonical story form. They ordered their sentences to fit in with an event sequence; they put setting sentences in first position even when principles of pronomialization were violated in doing so; they sequenced conclusion statements last even when they were in the present tense.

Relative importance of story grammar categories. McCartney and Nelson (1981) had children read stories about a child's typical evening at home (dinner, T.V., bath, bedtime, etc.). Their findings were that children seem to rely on schemata to recall stories, although recall was more influenced by the *importance* of a story element rather than its sequential position. The relative importance of story elements has attracted the interest of a number of researchers. Weaver and Dickenson (1982) found that the relative importance of story grammar categories in recall was very similar for both normal and disordered readers, and that the order for normal readers was as follows: (1) Major Setting; (2) Direct Consequences; (3) Attempt; (4) Reaction; (5) Initiating Event; (6) Minor Setting; and (7) Internal Response.

Omanson (1982) has also been interested in the centrality of story grammar categories. He proposes that story units can be categorized as Central, Supportive, or Distracting. Central content is "part of the purposeful-causal sequence of events" (Omanson, 1982, p. 209). Central story units include major settings in which the main characters are introduced, global actions and the states that give rise to them, outcomes, and any units that cause, enable, or disrupt a unit that has already been identified as Central by the former criteria. Excluded are subordinate actions and external responses. Motives and goals do not figure prominently in Omanson's scheme.

Supportive content includes units depicting thought and talk, including internal responses that result from events (as opposed to causing or enabling them), characterizing units, and so on. *Distracting* units include descriptions of minor characters (minor settings), interrupting events and that which enables them, and units featuring the actions of minor characters. Omanson found that (1) story units coded as Central by his scheme were independently rated as significantly more important than non-Central units; (2) the percentage of Central units recalled is about three times as great as the percentage of non-Central units recalled; (3) Distracting story units hinder rather than facilitate recall (Omanson & Malamut, 1980). Omanson claims that his approach to the processing of stories is "data-driven" rather than "schema-driven" (1982, p. 215). By data-driven Omanson means that readers account for apparently unmotivated actions in narrative, not by recourse to schema-based knowledge of conventional plans behind conventional actions, but rather that they wait for unfolding events in the story proper to supply a cause or purpose for the action. Be that as it may, be elevating global acts and major settings to Central status and regulating minor characters and their actions to Distracting status, Omanson implicitly builds in a hierarchical, top-down, schema-like framework, even though his analysis is couched more in terms of outcomes than subordinate and superordinate goals and actions (Stein, 1982). Further, Omanson's view that unfolding conversational actions will reveal the motives and purposes of apparently opaque actions presupposes the kind of social knowledge usually accociated with schemata.

Knowledge bases for story schemata. A new wrinkle in the story comprehension literature is the interest in the kinds of knowledge bases other than grammatical rule-sets that are required to process stories. Bizanz (1982) suggests that one type of knowledge involves conventional understandings about which kinds of actions result from which goals, and in what situations. Bizanz seems to assume that story recipients regard the actions of the story protagoinst as analogous to the "real-life" efforts of persons to overcome obstacles and reach the goals that they have set for themselves. Bizanz speculated that there are significant developmental differences (between college students and elementary students) in knowledge of conventional relationships among situations, plans, and actions. The knowledge bases of younger children were often insufficiently differentiated and elaborated to allow them to recognize "cues important to the application of schemata already acquired" (Bizanz, 1982, p. 272).

Goldman (1982) proposes that both content (i.e., story category) and functional (role of category in the action) knowledge are necessary for story processing. Goldman also subscribes to the view that knowledge of real-life goal behavior is brought to bear in understanding stories. Goldman proposed that there are three "plausible knowledge categories" about realistic problem solving (1982, p. 286): (1) knowledge of the *states and actions of the protagonist;* (2) knowledge of the *role of others;* (3) knowledge of the *role of the environment.* Goldman (1982, p. 295) proposed that there are three functional roles variously associated with these knowledge categories; protagonsits, others, and the environment might serve to provide *motives, means,* or *obstacles* to goal-attainment. Goldman correctly predicted that there would be developmental differences in the organization of these knowledge bases, with older subjects showing increased differentiation; that is, more situation-specific expectations about narrative content with increasing age (Goldman, 1982, p. 294). Generally, however, children seemed to have a basic core of knowledge about the kinds of function associated with different knowledge categories: the motive function was assigned most frequently to the category of the protagonist's states and actions, and least frequently to the environment; obstacles were most often connected with the role of other people, and means were primarily associated with the category role of the environment. Goldman's findings lend support to Rumelhart's original formulation of the semantic relations among story event categories.

SUMMARY

A sequence is a series of speech acts that considered together constitute a self-contained conversatonal unit with a coherent internal structure. Four kinds of sequences were examined: openings, closings, arguments, and stories.

Opening sequences that serve to bracket conversatons at their beginnings can be seen to mirror the closing sequences that serve as terminal brackets. Openings typically follow a sequence of cognitive recognition, identification display (mutual glance, head gesture), and social recognition (verbal salute, reference to other, personal inquiry, external reference), followed by topic initiation. A typical closing sequence in effect reverses the process, with a topic termination, followed by a leave-taking subsection (summarization, justification, positive statements, continuity statements, and well-wishings, followed by an optional good-bye). Both openings and closings vary in form as a function of the relative status of the parties, their degree of acquaintanceship, and situational constraints. A special case of opening sequences, the summons-answer sequence, is shown to be governed by strong demands for conditional relevance, such that its three steps of summons, answer, and topic initiation are virtually invariant, and deviations are a source of trouble in the conversation.

Arguments are disagreement-relevant sequences built around the expansion of a dominant adjacency pair such as offer-grant/refuse. Expansions are accomplished within turns or by pre-sequences, or post-sequences. Arguments may be directed to either the propositional or the functional content of an arguable. Arguments result from the appearance of dispreferred second pair parts or the refusal to alter or cancel disagreeable firsts.

Stories are sequences consisting of three major subsections. The preface sequence can be accomplished with a minimum of two turns. Its function is to assure a proper orientation of the recipient through significance statements, attributions, admonitions, characterizations, and inquiries. The recounting sequence consists of a Setting and one or more Episodes that revolve around the goals, plans, actions, and outcomes of a central actor or protagonist. In conversational storytelling, recipient talk during the recounting sequence is commonplace, and may even by systematically provided for in certain story genre. The closing sequence of a storytelling follows upon a signal that the story has concluded, such as a home-again device or a formulation. The principle task of parties in the closing sequence is to demonstrate the sequential implicativeness of the story.

6

Preventatives and Repairs

♦ In Chapter 6, the focus of interest will be the ♦
techniques and strategies that conversational participants employ to
prevent or reverse negative typifications of themselves (Hewitt &
Stokes, 1975) resulting from potential or existing violations of
conversational and more general societal rules. We will first turn our
attention to preventatives as the realization of conversationalists'
plans to circumvent the identity problems associated with the performance of own-face-threatening acts, such as making assertions
whose acceptance is in doubt. Later, we will examine the repair
organization of conversation, and the remedial work individuals
undertake to reweave the "social fabric" following the commission of
an untoward act or the omission of an obligated one.

PREVENTATIVES

Disclaimers

Hewitt and Stokes (1975) were interested in the ways in which people deal *prospectively*, as opposed to retrospectively, with possible violations of conversational and societal rules and the attendant problems of maintaining positive face. Their argument is that meaning in social encounters is organized around the *identities* of the interacting parties; further, that breaches of social understandings may produce undesired alterations in the perceived identity of the party regarded as the author of the breach (Hewitt & Stokes, 1975, p. 2):

> The thematic organization of meaning by interactants usually depends upon their ability to interpret each other's actions as manifestations of particular identities. It follows that when events fail to fit themes in interaction, identities may come into focus as problematic: if the acts of another fail to appear sensible in light of his identity in the situation, perhaps he is not who he appears to be.

Hewitt and Stokes propose that anticipation of a problematic event may result in activity by the individual who will be charged with responsibility for the problem to in effect "inoculate" other parties against the construction of negative typifications of him. One device for doing so is the *disclaimer*, which defines an upcoming action as irrelevant to the sort of typification that under most circumstances it might appear to imply (Hewitt & Stokes, 1975, p. 3). The specific function of a disclaimer is to mark an upcoming utterance as a candidate basis for negative typification, and ask for the hearer's indulgence.

Types of disclaimers. Five kinds of disclaimers are identified by Hewitt and Stokes. In *hedging*, the author of the impending speech act simultaneously (a) signals her limited commitment to it; (b) suggests her hesitancy as to how it will be received; and (c) expresses her concern that the effects of the act on how she is perceived may be substantial. Hedges include phrases like "I'm no expert, but" and "I haven't thought this through very well, but" (Hewitt & Stokes, 1975, p. 4), and the italicized items in the following examples:

A: *I don't- I've never think about these things- these* kind of things 'cause I'm not a girl, but-* guess it could be- I guess I wouldn't go back there.

B: Well, uh, no necessarily. I know that, um, *from what I* understand- I may be mistaken but,* like- like in Dallas aren't you just limited to like one thing- activity- within your high school?

Credentialling is a variety of disclaimer in which the author of an impending source of trouble suggests that dispensations are in order by virtue of his particular qualifications or credentials (Hewitt & Stokes, 1975). Implicit in a credentialling disclaimer is the speaker's conviction that the impending action would ordinarily result in a negative retypification; thus, the purpose of such a disclaimer is to show that he is not "an unknowing representative of a particular negative type" (Hewitt & Stokes, 1975, p. 5) such as a racist or sexist. Typical credentialling disclaimers are phrases like "Some of my best friends are Jewish, but."

In a *sin license*, the actor overtly asserts her sensitivity to the rule she is about to break, to avoid being typified as an "irresponsible member" of the encounter (Hewitt & Stokes, 1975, p. 5). Such phrases as "I know I'm not supposed to mix business with pleasure, but" or "I'm sorry to have to cut you off, but" are typical of sin licenses. In a *cognitive disclaimer*, the author of a potentially discrediting utterance addresses himself to issues of his own sensitivity, sanity, and rationality, to assure others "that there is no loss of cognitive capacity" (Hewitt & Stokes, 1975, p. 5). Representative cognitive disclaimers are "I know it sounds as if I'm out of touch, but" and "This may sound weird, but."

A final disclaimer category is the *appeal for a suspension of judgment*, in which the actor tries to provide a "frame" for her upcoming utterance, since it would be offensive or disagreeable if not heard in the proper context (Hewitt & Stokes, 1975, p. 6). A typical example of such a disclaimer is "Now hear me out before you get upset, O.K.?" The following fragment is an interesting case in which the user of an appeal for the suspension of judgment has his right to make the potentially discrediting utterance usurped by his partner:

A: *Don't take me wrong, I do party, but**
B: (Yeah, but I mean it's- to a point, you know, when they overdo it.

Responses to disclaimers. Very little work has been done that establishes that the use of disclaimers has a positive effect on the reception of potentially discrediting messages. One exception is the work by Cody, Erickson, and Schmidt (1983) on the use of disclaimers as prefaces to offensive jokes. Cody et al. had subjects recall recent cases in which they had been told a joke that might be considered offensive, and that could result in undesired retypification of the teller. Subjects were asked to recall both the jokes and the statements, if any, with which they were prefaced. Content analysis of prefacing statements indicated that there were four general ways in which jokes were introduced: (1) by *face-maintenance* devices, which included requests for permission to tell the joke as well as prototypical disclaimers such as "My mom told me this one, so," "I'm not anti-black, but" and "I'm Chicano, so I can tell this one"; (2) by *theme prefaces*, in which the joke appeared to arise naturally out of ongoing talk, perhaps as part of a series of jokes; (3) *disjunctively*, that is, with no preface at all, and no apparent relation to ongoing talk; and (4) by a *forewarning preface,* in which the joke-teller explicitly stated his intent to violate the hearer's negative face, typically with such utterances as "Here's a sick joke for you" or "Carol's going to hate this one."

Cody et al. (1983) examined the relation of joke prefaces to joke types, and the effects of the way in which a joke was introduced upon the nature of its reception. Cody et al. found that the jokes rated the most offensive were prefaced by forewarning tactics, while the least offensive jokes were either told disjunctively, prefaced by theme, or disclaimed. Persons who used disclaimers or who asked for permission to tell the joke were perceived as less insensitive than those who forewarned or told their joke disjunctively. Ratings of joke "amusingness" were positively correlated with the use of disclaimers and seeking permission for the joke's telling. Cody et al. concluded that disclaimers are an effective device for preventing the negative retypification associated with telling offensive jokes, although not appreciably more so than theme prefaces.

Authors other than Cody et al. who have looked at the effects of disclaimers (Lakoff, 1975; McMillan, Clifton, McGrath, & Gale, 1977; Crosby & Nyquist, 1978; Bradley, 1981) have concluded that their use results in the perception that the speaker is uncertain, hesitant, lacking in dynamism and lacking in power, and even less intelligent than others who do not use disclaimers. Such results have been regarded with considerable concern by feminist scholars, for much of the research, although not all of it, has found that women are more likely than men to use disclaimers, along with such other characteristics of the "female register" (Crosby & Nyquist, 1978) as tag questions, rising terminal intonation with declaratives, and so on. Further, there appears to be evidence that the extent to which the use of disclaimers is detrimental to the image one presents is a function of sex; Bradley (1981) found that the use of disclaimers and tag questions led to negative characterizations of female speakers, but not as a rule of male speakers.

Bell, Zahn, and Hopper (1983) point out quite rightly that most of the research in the tradition described above has looked at disclaimers in combination with one or more other deferential language variables such as tag questions, intensifiers, and so on. It was the proposal of Bell et al. to examine disclaimers independently of these other linguistic forms. In their initial investigation, a basic "transcript" was constructed, in which there were four variations on the way in which a potentially offensive utterance was presented: with no disclaimer, with a hedge, with a cognitive disclaimer, and with both a hedge and a cognitive disclaimer. There was no significant effect of disclaimer condition on the rated *competence*, certainty, or *character* of the speaker. Bell et al. concluded that the reason why their findings were inconsistent with earlier work was that the previous studies had included more than one, and usually numerous, disclaimers in each manipulation. In a second study, Bell et al. altered the Disclaimer treatment from the first investigation, so that the four conditions were: no disclaimers, two disclaimers, four disclaimers, and six disclaimers. This time, strong effects were obtained for the Disclaimer level factor. Increased use of disclaimers was strongly related to a decline in ratings of the speaker's competency and certainty, but had no effect on ratings of character. Bell et al. concluded that early studies confused the issue of the effects of disclaiming by either (1) studying disclaimer use in tandem with other deferential language features, or (2) using unrealistically strong manipulations. The latter seems a reasonable conclusion, particularly in light of the fact that at least in the corpus of conversations to which we have had recourse in this text, disclaimers are quite rare as a conversational event. The likelihood that anyone would use four or six disclaimers in a single brief interchange is extremely remote.

Licenses

Mura (1983) and Brown and Levinson (1978) have identified another variety of preventive that, unlike the disclaimer, is addressed less to the broader issues of right thinking and proper social conduct than to the specifically *conversational* issues of rules, maxims, and their observance. Mura has looked at these preventatives under the label "license," which we shall adopt; Brown and Levinson call them "hedges."

A "license," according to Mura (1983, p. 3), is a device for putting one's hearer on notice that while an impending utterance, or one whose problematic aspects are not yet clear, may appear to be in violation of one of the conversational maxims of Quality, Quantity, Relevance, or Manner, *in fact* the speaker's ultimate intent is to honor the Cooperative Principle. In a license, the speaker marks the violation and re-frames it in the light of her efforts to fulfill the requirements of cooperative interaction.

In licensing an apparent violation of the *Quality* maxim, one may mark the fact that her utterance is not literally true, but that she has no wish to misrepresent herself, by the use of paralinguistic features such as emphasis, or by reformulations signaled by phrases like "In fact," "Actually," or "Well, really" (Mura, 1983):

A: I like Texas. I've just not been to that much of Texas.*
          Just El Paso and here and I've been to Dallas once or twice,
          not very much. No, I've been there once *to tell the truth*.

Licenses of violations of the Quantity maxim may also be directed to the fact that the speaker's evidence for what she is saying is second hand or limited:

A: No, I won't be a teacher. I feel like that- I'm sure that*
          if a poll was taken that the majority of people don't follow
          their majors.
B: Really?
A: Outside, I bet they don't- *Now that's just a guess*.

A: *I don't know if they change*- see, they change laws anyway- but*
          they don't want the all-out ERA that would just let you
          walk into places that were always male- things like that.

Quality licenses are very similar to the hedge variety of disclaimer, but may appear *after* the occurrence of an item that the speaker thinks might be troublesome were the hearer to treat it as literal truth or as fully grounded in fact and supported by evidence.

According to Brown and Levinson (1978), a license for a violation of the *Quantity* maxim might be addressed to the issue of why an utterance is less informative than one might hope. Any of the following might serve as a license for a violation of the Quantity maxim:

S: *So, in a nutshell, that's why I'm asking.*
S: *I'm not at liberty to say.* (Mura, 1983, p. 15)
S: *I can't really go into it now, but . . .*

Licenses related to the Quantity maxim may also address the fact that the speaker will be long-winded: "This will take a while, but." We have already examined licenses for violating the Quantity maxim with respect to brevity in Chapter 3, in the discussion of devices for claiming a block of turn-constructional units. Mura (1983, p. 16) suggests that a further device for licensing a Quantity violation is to shift responsibility for it to the hearer by making a statement to the effect that thus-and-such is a "long story," in the hope of inducing the hearer to reply that he wants to hear all about it anyway.

Relevance licenses can exploit the same strategy mentioned above for shifting responsibility for a Quantity violation to the hearer: the speaker who wishes to recount something that is not pertinent to the talk-so-far can refer to it obliquely, but describe it as "neither here nor there" or dismiss it by saying "but that's another story," in the hope that the hearer will request that it be told (Mura, 1983). Lack of relevance may also be licensed by the devices which have been labeled *disjunct markers* in the context of topical talk and story sequencing. For example:

S: *While I'm thinking of it*, do you remember where we
        put the instructions for Biggy's medicine?

Violations of the maxim of *Manner*, for example, obscurity or ambiguity, may be licensed by statements that mark them as necessary as a function of the subject matter ("Now this stuff is complicated"). Futhermore, obscurity and ambiguity may be justified by attributing the utterance to another source ("Those are his words, not mine"), limitations of the language ("I can't find words to describe it"), and so on (Mura, 1983).

Preventatives, then are disclaimers and licenses aimed at protecting the author of a potentially troublesome speech act from negative characterization of him as an unthinking, irrational, or irresponsible member of society and/or as an incompetent communicator who either doesn't know the rules or doesn't care about them. Available data on the use of preventatives provides mixed evidence that they accomplish the ends for which they are designed.

SELF-INITIATED REPAIRS

Repairs fall into the category of actions that constitute "detours" or "time-outs" from ongoing talk. Like disclaimers, repairs are one class of a set of techniques called "aligning actions" (Stokes & Hewitt, 1976) that conversational parties use in dealing with problems or "troubles" that arise in conversation. Unlike disclaimers or licenses, however, repairs are aligning actions that are always applied *after the fact*, that is, after the problematic item has been embarked upon and is "noticeable." Preventatives are devices used to obviate the *need* for remedial action, specifically other-repair, while repairs address themselves to the fact that one or both of the parties believe that remedial work is required. Furthermore, under ordinary circumstances disclaimers and licenses are the result of "single authorship"; they are produced by the originator of the source of trouble. Repairs, however, can be the result of other-initiations, or the result of a truly collaborative effort by both parties to restore coherence and order. Some preventatives are produced "collabora- tively" in the sense that the speaker induces the hearer to supply the license. However, impetus for their instigation always comes from the speaker.

Schegloff, Jefferson, and Sacks (1977) argue that what gets *repaired* in conversation is not always error; that repair is often found when to the objective eye there appears to be nothing wrong. Repair then addresses itself to felt or *perceived* violations of grammatical, syntactic, conversational, and societal rules. An item which to the hearer was perfectly acceptable may be selected by the speaker as a candidate for repair. Similarly, an utterance that the speaker produced in all innocence may lead to a situation that the hearer sees as cause for the application of remedial action.

Preference for Self-Repair

Despite the fact that repair of a problematic item potentially can be initiated or accomplished by either party to a conversation, it appears that there is a systematic preference in the conversational system for *self-repair* over *other-repair* (Schegloff et al., 1977). By preference again is meant structural primacy: dispreferred repairs are "struc- turally delayed in turns and sequences" (Schegloff et al., 1977, p. 362).

By preference for self-repair is meant that the person who accom- plishes the repair is usually the one who produces the problematic item in the first place. This is not to say, however, that the person who accomplishes the repair is necessarily the one who initiated it. Repair may, for example, be initiated by the hearer of the "repairable," and fulfilled by its author (Schegloff et al., 1977, p. 364). The conversational system, however, seems to show a preference for both self-initiation and self-accomplishment of repair.

Schegloff et al. (1977, pp. 366-367) note that self-repairs usually occur in one of three "slots": within the problematic utterance, within a next turn-constructional unit, or in a subsequent turn, after the interlocutor has taken her turn. Other-initiations regularly occur in one slot only—immediately subsequent to the turn in which the problematic item appeared. Note that the positions for self-initiation structurally precede those for other-initiation, obviously so in the case of within-turn placements, less obviously but in fact so under the terms of the turn-taking rules (see Chapter 3) that give the current speaker the right to exercise her option to continue speaking at the end of a turn-constructional unit.

Schegloff et al. continue to build their case for the structural preference for self-repair by demonstrating that the presence of other-repairs indicates that opportunities for self-repair were not taken. First, it is argued that the vast majority of other-initiated repairs come in the next turn following the problematic one, and *not before* (Schegloff et al., 1977, p 373). Furthermore, they often come a bit past that point (that is, they may follow upon a pause,) which indicates that the hearer is supplying the author of the troublesome item with an additional chance to redeem himself. Additional evidence comes from three sources: (1) the strong likelihood that the other-initiation will amount to a simple marking of the repairable, so that the actual remedy can be supplied by the author of the troublesome item in a subsequent turn; (2) the tendency of other-accomplished repair to be "modulated"; that is, to be simply "proffered for acceptance or rejection"; (3) the fact that if the hearer is in a position to do a repair (for example supply the missing word in speaker's word search), she has enough information to produce a sequentially implicated next turn instead, and repair would be superfluous (Schegloff et al., 1977, p. 380).

Schegloff (1979) argues that not only is repair ordinarily accomplished by the author of a troublesome item within the same turn in which it was produced, but that there are structural reasons why it should be done within the same turn-constructional unit. Repair is likely to be achieved within the same turn because when the next turn is used for that purpose, "the sequential implicativeness of current turn is displaced from its primary home" (Schegloff, 1979, p. 267), and may in fact get lost altogether. Repair is likely to be attempted within the turn-constructional unit in which the problematic item is located because the projectable completion of that unit gives rise to the possibility of speaker-switch, and thus the likelihood that the repair won't get done at all.

Self-Repairs Within Turn-Constructional Units

Schegloff (1979, pp. 264-265) has described a number of different kinds of repairs that speakers can accomplish within the same turn-constructional unit as a problematic item. For example, a speaker can elaborate upon a noun phrase by inserting a descriptive clause or clauses between the NP and its planned predicate:

> **A:** There were two of 'em that uh- one was an ag econ major and*
> one was a business major- and they never did- neither one of 'em
> ever what they're, you know, 'til the last day they graduated.

Repair accomplished within the same turn-constructional unit can also convert an open-ended question to a closed-ended (yes, no) question, and vice versa:

> **A:** What do you plan to do- go back, goin' back to number six?*
> What- what do you plan to do- with your life? *Are you a- what
> type major were you again?*

A same-TCU repair can accomplish the insertion of a preventative, in the following case a license for violation of the Quality maxim:

> **A:** Of course they-re- *I heard him say* there's one senior on their*
> team, and four freshman.

Another possible use of a self-initiated repair within the TCU is to correct projectable syntactical infelicities:

> **A:** "Your attitude on politics and religion." Well, how do you*
> think-*what do you think about the-* Iran?
> **B:** Keep 'em out of Texas, that's all I can say.

Schegloff (1979) claims that repairs are very common in talk occurring at topic boundaries, particularly in topic preface or topic shift sections, and that within utterances, repairs are usually initiated just after or just before completion of the turn-constructional unit. Ongoing talk is stopped and repair initiated, as a rule, either by cut-offs or pauses, with the former attending to prior items and the latter to upcoming items (Schegloff, 1979, p. 273). *Successive* repairs seem to have an order of their own, an "orientation to progressivity"

(Schegloff, 1979, pp. 278-279) such that each repair in the series is a step further in the direction of an ultimate solution. Schegloff claims that each "try" alters some element of a previous try, as in the example below:

A: I got- think I got- I got a- Fleetwood Mac play this weekend=*

                                                          (   )

B: Yeah.

A: =in Dallas.

Of particular interest are *regressive tries,* in which the last attempt in a series of attempted repairs is the same as a much earlier one. Schegloff proposes that "regressive tries are last tries" (1979, p. 279), as the following example illustrates:

B: Do you like Campus Advance?*
A: Yeah, I like it a bunch.
B: Good.
A: Bunchy, bunchy, I'm just- huhn? - it's just- we're not, Oh, I don't know. It's just like a church group, really.

While there are no counter examples to Schegloff's claims in the corpus we have been using here (presuming we define successive repairs as three or more tries), it seems probable that counterexamples could be found.

We turn from self-initiated repair and the remedy sequences generated when the author of the item that a hearer defines as problematic has failed to initiate repair herself. We will look first at other-initiated repairs directed to the violation of specifically *conversational* rules and assumptions, and then turn our attention to repair sequences addressed to other, predominately extra-conversational violations. First, however, we need to present the notion of the repair sequence.

THE "OTHER-INITIATED" REPAIR SEQUENCE

Remler (1978, p. 398) has identified a series of steps that she regards as basic to the accomplishment of a repair initiated by other, and we shall see in subsequent sections that most other-initiated repairs conform to this canonical sequence. The steps include a *request for repair* or an utterance that indicates that something is amiss; a *remedy*; and an *acknowledgment.* The basic sequence can be and almost always is expanded by the kinds of within-turn justifications and excuses, pre-sequences, insertion sequences, and post-sequences that were discussed in Chapter 5 in the context of conversational argument.

A repair sequence can be seen to be a special case of a *side sequence* (Jefferson, 1972), in which parties detour from ongoing talk to deal with some side issue raised by that talk. The variety of side sequence which is relevant to the problem of repair Jefferson calls a *"Misapprehension Sequence,"* whose elements are a problematic statement; a demonstration or an assertion that the statement was misunderstood or not fully understood (like a *request for repair)*; a clarification (like the *remedy*); and a statement of "satisfactory termination" (like the *acknowledgment*). In the conversational excerpt below, which is addressed to a violation of the maxim of Quantity (A doesn't say enough for B to establish a unique antecedent), the repairable is at line 5, the request for repair at line 6, the remedy at lines 7-9, and the acknowledgment at line 10.

1	**B:**	How can you say that?*
2	**A:**	Because it's a proven fact. I mean like
3		I read it.
4	**B:**	Well, what do you base this on?
5	**A:**	On this magazine.
6	**B:**	What magazine?
7	**A:**	Uh, *D*.
8	**B:**	*Big D,* the Dallas magazine?
9	**A:**	Yeah, *D* magazine.
10	**B:**	Yeah, yeah, Huh.
11	**A:**	They said not now, but a few-many years ago-
12		five years ago.
13	**B:**	Yeah, maybe. Yeah.

Jefferson (1972, p. 305) formulates the following rule to cover the way in which the remedy of such repairables is regulated: *"if a statement is made and is followed by a demonstration/assertion that a hearer did not understand, then the one who made the statement may/must provide a clarification."* Side sequences involve the "must" form of this rule; the request for repair serves as a first pair part to the remedy, and the remedy serves as a second pair to the request and a first pair part to the acknowledgment.

Side sequences generally and repair sequences particularly have the property that the author of the problematic item probably did not intend to set up a reason for the remedial activity; nor can she be the one to determine that the sequence is in fact concluded and that the prior topical talk may be resumed (Jefferson, 1972). The rule is that *opening and closing moves in a side sequence are the responsibility of the party who "calls" the violation.*

Repair Addressed to the Violation of Conversational Rules and Assumptions

A convenient way of looking at other-initiated repair is to inquire as to the rules or assumptions that the repair seeks to reinstate. While not much work seems to have been done on repairs addressed to the conversational maxims of Quantity or Manner, studies of the remedy of violations of the Quality, Relevance, and Antecedence maxim are available.

Unfortunately, most of the work on violation of conversational rules and assumptions has been limited to studying either solicitations for repair or the repairs themselves, but not the full repair-relevant sequence. The exception has been in the work by Jefferson and Schenkein (1978) on "Correction Sequences," which may be seen to be specifically addressed to violations of the Quality maxim.

Violations of the Quality maxim. Jefferson and Schenkein (1978) describe and present an example of what they call a Correction Sequence, in which the request for repair is directed to some aspect of an interlocutor's utterance that is regarded as false, lacking in support, or based upon very limited experience. In Jefferson and Schenkein's representative case, an adolescent boy takes violent issue with what he regards as his mother's overestimate of his weight. However, virtually any "energetically controversial matter" (Jefferson and Schenkein, 1978, p. 165) could provide the impetus for a Correction Sequence. The basic steps in a Correction Sequence, according to Jefferson and Schenkein, are a Correction Solicitor, a Correction, and an Acknowledgment. In its expanded version, a second Correction Solicitor initiated by the author of the problematic item may be inserted between the first Solicitor and the Correction, much like a contingent query or embedded request:

A: Why did you tell Kevin I was coming in on Thursday?
B: Well, aren't you?
A: No, on Wednesday.
B: Oh, O. K.

In this case, the author of the troublesome item does get to terminate the sequence, but only by virtue of the fact that she initiated a new Correction or side sequence of her own; in this regard, the example is quite rule-conforming.

Repairs directed to violations of the Quality maxim need not involve a Correction in the "request-for-repair" slot; any indication that the prior speaker's utterance is problematic with respect to its claims or warrants will qualify as initiating a repair sequence of this type. In the following example, the initiator requests repair by virtue of a series of demonstrations of his skepticism:

1	**A:**	Well, we didn't have T.V. where I was*
2		until last year.
3	**B:**	*Really?*
4	**A:**	Yeah.
5	**B:**	*You kidding?*
6	**A:**	Huh uh.
7	**B:**	*Golly. Did you live in a log cabin or some-*
8		*thing?*
9	**A:**	No. It was because the mountains blocked us
10		from getting reception to our house.
11	**B:**	Oh. Yeah.

The repair sequence above conforms to the canonical form, with requests for repair at line 3, 5, and 7-8, a remedy at lines 9-10, and an acknowledgment at line 11.

Violation of the Relevance maxim. Violations of the Relevance maxim fall under the heading of what Remler (1978, p. 396) calls "information link repairs," which "occur when the listener shares the identities of referents with the speaker but does not completely understand how certain bits of information in the utterance are related to other information on various levels of the topic structure." Remler suggests that there are three types of repairs directed to the issue of relevance. In a *frame* repair sequence, the initiator is concerned with an apparent lack of relation between an utterance and the topical macrostructure. A typical request for repair would be "What's that got to do with anything?" (Remler, 1978). In a *figure* repair sequence, the initiator of the sequence is perplexed as to how some element or character in the utterance fits into the larger picture. The repair request might be, "Where does *she* come into it?" In a *focus level* repair (Remler, 1978), it is not clear as to which referent some predication attaches. In the following example, it is not clear whether B's "Why?" and its implicit proposition "There is a reason for X," attaches to A's alleged mental state or to B's attribution to A of that mental state:

B: I think you came to work in a bad mood today.

A: Why?

B: Why? I don't know. Probably because you had another fight with your wife.

A: No, I mean why did you decide that I must be in a bad mood?

Vucinich (1977) was interested in examining the kinds of Relevance-related remedy sequences that followed the production of totally noncohesive and partially noncohesive turns. A totally noncohesive turn was one which exhibited no relationship whatsoever to the ongoing conversational topic; for example, having a confederate introduce the utterance "Monopoly is a really fun game" into a discussion of the hardships of final examinations (Vucinich, 1977, p. 235). Partially noncohesive turns were created by manipulating the local proposition links between utterances. Confederates supplied an utterance with an improper cause, effect or identity relationship to the immediately prior turn. For example, the B turn in the following asserts an improper *identity* relationship:

A: My children never give me a minute's peace.

B: Yeah, it's like with nuclear weapons.

While a reply could be formed that might integrate the B turn into the current topic (for example, "Yeah, they should both be banned"), it would require considerably more than the usual amount of cognitive effort.

Vucinich examined the effects of fully and partially noncohesive turns on subsequent responses, using the following as indices: the presence of requests for repairs; the latency of response; and significant internal responses (i.e., recall; Vucinich, 1977, pp. 236-238). Vucinich also coded post-irrelevancy responses into one of four topic reference categories: (1) *focus*, in which the noncohesive turn informed subsequent talk, and all talk about the pre-irrelevancy topic was abandoned; (2) *die,* in which a new topic unrelated to either prior talk or the noncohesive turn was taken up; (3) *ride,* in which the noncohesive turn was ignored, and talk resumed on the former topic; and (4) *contribute,* in which the hearer found a way to incorporate the topic of the irrelevancy into the former topic.

Vucinich found that for fully noncohesive turns, post-irrelevancy latencies were significantly longer than were latencies following cohesive turns; more requests for a remedy were initiated; talk about the pre-irrelevancy topic was significantly more likely to be abandoned; and fully noncohesive turns were significantly more likely to be recalled (Vucinich, 1977, pp. 240-242). For the partially cohesive turns (turns with an improper unit relationship to a prior), results were quite similar, although the old topic was not as likely to be abandoned as it was following a wholly noncohesive turn. there was no significant difference among effects of the improper-unit-relationship types of post-irrelevancy responses.

Violation of the Antecedence maxim. Remler (1978, p. 395) has described a class of discourse level repairs that she calls "information structure repairs": "misnegotiations of the given-new contract," in which the request for a remedy is directed to the fact that what the speaker has presented as "old," or "given," is in fact without a unique antecedent in the hearer's awareness. Remler proposes that there are three varieties of repair sequences addressed to violations of the antecedence maxim. In the first, the speaker fails to supply the identity of a specific referent:

A: I saw Roseanna at the conference and she said
B: (Who's Roseanna?

In the second category, not only does the hearer have no unique antecedent for the referent, she has no idea to what class of phenomena it might belong:

A: How could you do that to me!
B: What did *I* do?

Finally, in the third variety, what is missing is a bridging proposition to link the new information to the hearer's prior knowledge:

A: Congratulations!
B: You mean I got it?

Repairs Addressed to Violations of the Turn-Taking System

Repairs may be addressed not only to violations of conversational maxims, but also to failures related to the turn-taking system. The presence of gaps and overlaps is a possible source for the generation of repair sequences, as is failure to obey the requirements of conditional relevance and take a turn when summoned.

There does not appear to have been much work done on repair sequences subsequent to *interruptions,* perhaps because such repairs occur so infrequently as to be of little interest. As was demonstrated in Chapter 3, ordinary language users are quite sensitive to the issues of timing of interruptions and the extent to which interruptions produce discontinuities in the talk of the speaker with a legitimate claim to the floor. Reardon (1982) reported that even very young children seemed to be sensitive to turn-taking rules, and that their ability to account for hypothetical others' violations, such as interruptions, increased with age and with greater complexity. What was of most interest in Reardon's findings is that many of the children, even the more complex ones, predicted uncooperative outcomes and additional interruptive behavior for subsequent interaction between the hypothetical partners. Given the comparative absence of indications that violations of the "one-party-talks-at-a-time" rule are routinely impaired, the children's response suggests they are insufficiently mature to realize that even in cooperative environments interruptions are commonplace and generally provide little threat to coherence.

McLaughlin and Cody (1982) were interested in the effects of conversational *lapses*, of which we spoke at length in Chapter 3, on subsequent strategies for restoring connected talk. McLaughlin and Cody hypthesized that the most obvious way to reinstate talk subsequent to a lapse was for one of the parties to pose a *question,* since a question would be implicative for at least one additional turn. While it was not suggested by McLaughlin and Cody that this was a good strategy, since it guaranteed only a minimum of two turns, and guaranteed almost exactly that if the question were of the closed-ended variety, nonetheless it was hypthesized that this would be the device of choice.

McLaughlin and Cody found that many of the post-lapse sequences in their sample contained a *question-answer* adjacency pair. Generally speaking, the person who first took a turn *after* a lapse, whom we shall call "B," was not the last person who spoke, so that the "burden" of the lapse, in effect, was laid at the feet of B, and the lapse treated as his latency. Considering only those cases in which a question was the first post-lapse utterance, the last speaker before the lapse was more likely to be the first speaker after it, although not significantly so. The most common question-answer sequences subsequent to a lapse were (1) lapse, A questions, B acknowledges; (2) lapse, A questions, B edifies; (3) lapse, A questions, B questions; (4) lapse, B questions, A discloses; and (5) lapse, B questions, A edifies. Below are presented examples of sequences (4) and (5):

B: I had a good time. They thought I spoke Spanish well. I'd*
       like to get down there and put it to good use, maybe
       some kind of business related stuff.

(   )

A: Uh huh.

(4)

(13.3)

B: Do you li- do you enjoy sports or anything?

A: Yeah, I love to play sports.

A: Yeah. I think that's what it was.*

B: Boy, that's a young team, too. Sure is.

(5)

(4.5)

B: Who do you think'll take the title in college basketball?

A: Probably DePaul.

It is worth noting that in both of these examples, another lapse occurred within a few seconds of the previous one, suggesting that the closed-ended question strategy could not be counted on to sustain talk for any length of time.

Merritt (1982) has addressed herself to another violation of turn-taking rules: *the absence of a response to a summons.* We have described in the previous chapter the strong demands for a response that the summons places upon its addressed recipient. Merritt, however, has described an environment in which the usual require-ments of conditional relevance apply very weakly—the elementary classroom. Merritt was interested in looking at how elementary students gain the attention of their teachers; specifically, she examined *replays* of the original summons which occurred after a child had failed to gain the teacher's attention on a first try. The problem was described by Merritt as one of conflicting activity domains: "the teacher has a special interactional role which is reflected in the control she exercises over the vector of activity that she is engaged in, and the extent to which students seek to engage her in their individual vectors of activity" (Merritt, 1982, p. 142). Merritt found that, in contrast to Schegloff's rule that an unanswered summons is repeated no more than three to five times (see Chapter 5), children who failed to engage their teachers in their own activities could be extremely persistent in replaying the solicitations (a fact that Schegloff, 1968, noted to be very annoying to adults). In one of Merritt's examples, a child replayed the same summons fourteen times before he was able to engage his teacher's attention. What Merritt's work suggests is that not only do children not observe the terminating rule, but adults operate on the assumption that a child's initial summons can safely be ignored if need be, as she will be sure to continue reinstating it until her solicitation receives a reply. On the other hand, Merritt's data could be read as suggesting that adults regard children as nonpersons whose utterances are implicative for their own only when it is convenient for them to be. Clearly, only a person who was mad, bad, or deaf would ignore fourteen summonses in a row from another adult in the same room with him. In fact, the teacher's behavior in ignoring a child's repeated solicitations can be seen to be part of the socialization process, in which a child is taught that the "demands" of conditional relevance, which she learns very early (Foster, 1982), are superseded by the requirements of cooperative action: the need to wait one's turn, not interrupt, and so forth. Merritt's work is a good example of the case in which one party's efforts at repair are rebuffed by virtue of the other's concern for higher-order rules.

Illocutionary repairs. Before we leave the topic of repairs addressed to violations of conversational rules and assumptions, we might consider a class of repairs directed to violations of constitutive rules, which Remler (1978) has called "illocutionary repairs." In a request for an illocutionary repair, either hearer or speaker can be understood to be making the claim that each of them may have a different understanding of the force of some particular prior utterance. Illocutionary repairs may be addressed to force conditions, sincerity conditions, propositional content conditions, and so on. In a *force* repair request, the speaker asserts that the purpose behind her utterance was misunderstood (Remler, 1978, p. 397):

A: When is the dinner for Alfred?
B: Is it at seven-thirty?
A: No, I'M asking YOU.
B: Oh. I don't know.

In a *sincerity* repair request, the speaker questions whether or not the author of the repairable believes in the truth of what he has said:

A: I think this is one of the best papers you've ever written.
B: Do you mean that, or are you just being nice?

In a *propositional content* repair, the speaker can be understood as claiming that the proposition expressed was inappropriate for the kind of speech act its author intended it to be:

A: You think just like a man.
B: Is that supposed to be a compliment?

Repairs Addressed to Extra-Conversational Violations

In this section, we will examine repair sequences in which the request for repair is addressed to something other than violation of a conversational maxim; for example to some idea or belief that an actor has stated, to which the hearer takes exception; some untoward act or *offense* (Blumstein, 1974) that the actor has committed; or some obligation that the actor has failed to fulfill. These exceptionable behaviors (real and imagined) may all be lumped together under the rubric *failure events* (Schonbach, 1980; McLaughlin, Cody, & O'Hair, 1983).

The management of failure events: account sequences. Schonbach (1980) has presented a taxonomic scheme for the stages of failure events, in which he has drawn upon earlier work by Scott and Lyman (1968), Sykes and Matza (1957), Harré (1977), and others. According to Schonbach, each episode related to a failure event may be said to consist of four stages: the *failure event* itself, the *reproach*, the *account*, and the *evaluation*. What Schonbach describes here is clearly in conformity with the canonical form of the repair sequence presented earlier, where the reproach corresponds to a request for repair, the account corresponds to the remedy, and the evaluation corresponds to the acknowledgment.

McLaughlin and Cody and their colleagues have done a series of studies (McLaughlin, Cody, & O'Hair, 1983; McLaughlin, Cody, & Rosenstein, 1983; McLaughlin & Cody, in press) on the management of failure events, specifically looking at the effects of different forms of reproach on the choice of strategies for accounting, and the effects of the accounting strategy on the ultimate disposition of the failure event. The first study in this series was based on subjects' recollections of how they and some other individual, usually a close friend, parent, or employer, had collaboratively managed a failure event episode. Subjects in the McLaughlin, Cody, and O'Hair study were asked to describe the circumstances surrounding the episode, including how they were reproached, how they dealt with the reproach, and how they evaluated each of the following: (1) the intimacy of their relationship with the reproacher; (2) the relational consequences of the accounting strategy they chose; (3) the extent to which the reproacher was the dominant one in their relationship; (4)

the importance of getting their account accepted; (5) the importance of maintaining positive face; (6) the importance of maintaining the relationship; and (7) the severity of the failure event (McLaughlin, Cody, & O'Hair, 1983, pp. 216-217). Subjects' protocols were also coded for the degree of guilt expressed by the actor with respect to the failure event.

In coding the data on how people were reproached for failure events, McLaughlin et al. found that these requests for repair were of six varieties: (1) *silence*—for example, a policeman pulling a speeder over, asking for his license, but saying nothing further; (2) *behavior cues*—for example, frowning or looking disgusted; (3) *projected concession*—for instance, speaking as if an admission of guilt or an apology were forthcoming; (4) *projected excuse*—for instance, indicating that the actor was probably going to deny responsibility for the failure event; (5) *projected justification*—for example, indicating that the actor would probably try to defend the failure event or minimize its severity; and (6) *projected refusal*—for example, implying that the actor would refuse to admit guilt. Using Labov and Fanshel's (1977) notion of the "aggravating" and "mitigating" forms of the performance of speech acts, McLaughlin, Cody, and O'Hair speculated that implying that the other owed an apology, or was likely to try to minimize severity or deny guilt were highly aggravating forms of reproach, and that they might be expected to be met with more aggravating forms of reply during the accounting stages of the failure event episode.

McLaughlin, Cody, and O'Hair (1983) proposed that possible responses to reproaches were of five varieties, the first four of which are from Schonbach (1980): *concessions*, which may include acknowledgments of guilt, apologies, or offers of redress; *excuses,* in which the actor admits that the failure event occurred, and that it was harmful, but denies personal responsibility for it (Scott & Lyman, 1968); *justifications*, in which the actor accepts responsibility for the failure event, but denies that it was serious, or unwarranted; *refusals*, in which the actor denies guilt, denies the existence of the offense, or challenges the reproacher's right to request repair; and *silence*, by which the reproached individual avoids referring to the failure event in any manner whatsoever (McLaughlin, Cody, & O'Hair, 1983, pp. 209-210). Examples of concession, excuse, justification, and refusal and presented below, in that order. They are from a data set collected by McLaughlin, Cody, and O'Hair:

I said it wasn't that I didn't think about writing or calling- I did- but I had so much on my mind- I was just doing the things I had to absolutely get done. Contacting you was very important to me. *I'm sorry you got the wrong impression.*

I came into work 20 min. late and my boss looked at me as if she expected me to say something. I felt that 20 min. late was a lot of time, therefore, I should have already been at work. I said, *"The dryer broke down so I had to go somewhere to dry my uniform."*

I related to him the incident that had caused me to be up very late the night before my absence. He agreed that it was justifiable and excused me. *The reason I was out so late is that a friend of mine left a suicide note and some of us went to find her.*

In accounting for the acquisitions [sic] made against me, I simply told the warehouse man to check the inventory and note that I had listed the crib as being broken. He then just blew off the fact that I had listed the crib as being broken and made a comment suggesting that I was lying. *I then told him to check the inventory and not to accuse me of doing something I had nothing to do with.* The conversation ended there.

Account strategies were viewed by McLaughlin, Cody, and O'Hair as falling along a continuum with concessions being most mitigating, followed by excuses, justifications, and refusals, which were regarded as defining the aggravating end of the continuum (1983, p. 212).

McLaughlin, Cody, and O'Hair found that the way in which a reproach was done was an excellent predictor of the actor's choice of repair strategy: "mitigating reproaches led to mitigating account behavior, and aggravating reproaches evoked aggravating strategies in response" (1983, p. 222). This could be explained in part by reciprocity effects, and in part by the presence of interlocking preconditions (Searle, 1975) for the performance of the respective acts. The examples below are instances of the effects of aggravating reproaches in eliciting aggravating accounting behaviors. The examples are from the data set collected by McLaughlin, Cody, and O'Hair.

They both said, "Why haven't you come by to see us?" "Couldn't you have called?" "You have gone by to see everyone else!" I told them that they could have come to see me. I was the one who had come home for a visit. Why didn't they make an attempt to call or come by to see me?

She said, "What the heck are you doing with my boyfriend at 1:30 in the morning when you said you'd be up 2 hours ago?" I answered: "We're only talking and it happens to be about you. Charlie (her b-friend) just needed someone to talk to and so here I am. You really ought to know me better by now.

Tupperware!?!? He said it rather loudly, as if "what a dumb thing to buy." My response: "Your best friend's wife had a Tupperware party and I had to buy something."

Another variable that predicted to the choice of repair strategy was the degree of guilt expressed in the protocol, with the "more guilty" being more likely to concede. Severity of the event was a good predictor of the use of mitigating strategies. A low orientation to instrumental goals was associated with the use of justifications or silence. Relational variables such as intimacy and desire to maintain the relationship were poor predictors of the choice of strategy to manage a failure event.

In the second study in the series on the repair of failure events, McLaughlin, Cody, and Rosenstein (1983) looked at repair sequences in conversations between strangers. It became immediately apparent that while these episodes conformed to the canonical form of the repair sequence, the specific characteristics of the early portions of the sequence, involving the perceptions and claims of the reproacher, were different from the failure events reported in the first study. In the McLaughlin, Cody, and O'Hair study, virtually all of the failure event episodes took place in the context of relationships such as parent-child or employer-employee in which there was a well-established network of corresponding sets of rights and obligations (McLaughlin, Cody, & O'Hair, p. 103). The kinds of repair sequences found in conversations between strangers dealt not with violations of rights and failure to fulfill obligations, but with issues of similarity and dissimilarity, agreement and disagreement. Most of the "offenses" were relatively nonserious. What in the case of stranger interactions the reproacher seemed to be doing was either (a) dealing with an apparent dissimilarity or disagreement as a potential threat to mutual liking and current relational comfort; or (b) exploiting the dissimilarities as an interactional resource, in the sense that disagreements may serve as a basis for conversational expansion (McLaughlin, Cody, & Rosenstein, 1983, p. 103).

McLaughlin, Cody, and Rosenstein (1983, p. 103) proposed that account sequences in conversations between strangers consisted of a minimum series of three turns: a reproach, an account, and an evaluation. While they found that the accounting strategies used in the stranger interactions fell into virtually the same categories as those found in the recall data from the earlier study, the strategies for reproaching were different, primarily in that they were less inclined to *project* the form of the account that was to follow. This no doubt was a function of the fact that, being strangers, there was not much of a knowledge base from which the parties could make predictions. Furthermore, strangers were less inclined to attempt overt guilt manipulations, as in a projected concession, presumably because there were no feelings of relational indebtedness to exploit (McLaughlin, Cody, & Rosenstein, 1983, p. 109).

Four categories of *reproach* or request for repair emerged from the data. In the first, an expression of *surprise or disgust*, such as "You're kidding!" or "What??" or a mirror question, the reproacher performs what Remler (1978) has called a "pseudo-repair": her utterance does not reflect a sincere misapprehension of the putatively repairable utterance, but is used rather to express disagreement, disbelief, or negative evaluation:

A: Well, I'll probably work Christmas Day.*
        I-
B: (*CHRISTMAS DAY?!!*
A: I worked Thanksgiving Day, see.
B: Oo-o. Ha ha.
A: See, we're open- it's cotton season=
                                    (   )
B: Yeah.
A: =shipments are right now- we're open
        twenty-four hours a day, you know, so=
B: =you have to be there.
A: Yeah.

A more subtle form of reproach involves an implicit comparison between the moral or intellectual character of the reproacher and the target of her reproach. The reproacher "suggests that someting about the other's taste, lifestyle, work habits, or current mode of interacting is not quite up to his or her own high standards" (McLaughlin, Cody, & Rosenstein, 1983, p. 109). This reproach form was labeled "moral-intellectual superiority"; some examples of it are presented below.

B: No- its' too much of an individual effort.*
I get more joy out of teamwork than individually.

A: I always liked the individual. *I never liked
to depend on other people for my success.*

B: Well, I don't DEPEND on them, but it just
helps to have other people helpin' you'n
everything.

A: I'm not into money.*

B: *Why don't you want to be something else
besides a teacher?*

A: Well, see, my major was business=

$$(\quad)$$

B: Oh!

A: =but I didn't know what I wanted to be.

B: *What's it like when you feel that gettin'
married'd be the best thing?*

$$(1.0)$$

A: I don't know.

B: *I mean what is it like?*

A: I don't know.

A third form of reproach that was common to interactions between
strangers was a *direct request for an account*, in which the reproacher
explicitly asks for an explanation or justification for the repairable:

B: What are you gonna be doin' once you*
graduate?

A: I have no idea.

B: *What's this gonna get ya?* I mean,
you know, hundreds of good courses here-
*I mean good majors. But what'll speech comm
do?*

Finally, reproaches in conversations between strangers appeared
as *direct rebukes*, in which the reproacher provides an explicit,
negative characterization of some aspect of the other revealed in
his talk:

B: I work four to twelve on Fridays and eight*
to six on Saturday mornings, eight to six
on Sundays=

$$(\quad)$$

A: Hmm.

B: =and Mondays to six in the evening.

A: *You don't want too much social life, do
you?*

B: I do all right.

A: I don't like it. Too many Mexicans in there.*
B: Oh. *You're prejudiced.* (McLaughlin, Cody, &
        Rosenstein, 1983, p. 110)

The way in which an account was *evaluated* seemed to fall into one of four categories. In the most favorable form, *honor*, the author of the reproach acknowledges her acceptance of the account, with agreement, endorsements, laughter, and so on. In the short sequence below, we have a *surprise-digust* reproach at line 6, a *justification* at line 7, and an *honor* at line 8:

1 **A:** What's your major?*
2 **B:** Ag education.
3 **A:** Oh, really? Are you gonna be a teacher
4   or
5 **B:** (I don't know.
6 **A:** Ha ha. You don't KNOW?!! Ha ha.
7 **B:** Ha ha. Who knows?
8 **A:** Yeah, really.

In a slightly less favorable form of evaluation, but one that nonetheless is equally suited to closing off the repair sequence, the reproacher *retreats* from her original position after an account has been provided. In the following example (McLaughlin, Cody, & Rosenstein, 1983, p. 112), B withdraws from his implicit earlier suggestion that A is responsible for the tension they are experiencing, and blames it on the fact that their conversation is being recorded:

B: No- we not- we need to talk now.*
        It's not relaxed in here.
A: (I know. Well.
B: *Just tension. It's this thing* (recorder)
        runnin' here. (McLaughlin, Cody, & Rosenstein, 1983, p. 112)

Retreating may also be accomplished by the reproacher's "agreeing to agree" with some side issue or entailment of the original repairable.

In the third evaluation form, the reproacher does not provide even partial honoring; rather, he *rejects* or *takes issue* with the other's account, or he *reinstates the reproach* as if to cancel or erase the account. In the example below, A has just reproached B for watching soap operas, to which B has replied for the second time that "It's just like readin' a book," a claim wich A *rejects* at line 1. An elaboration on the book theme is immmediately *rejected* at line 3, and an example developed whose ultimate formulation is an *reinstatement* of the moral-intellectual superiority reproach with which A originally began: "I have enough problems of my own without gettin' all involved in some little fictional problem" (McLaughlin, Cody, & Rosenstein, 1983, p. 110):

1	**A:**	No-o. Ha ha. Not for me.*
2.	**B:**	I mean they got stories, you know.
3.	**A:**	Oh, they just drag and drag, Well, we were
4		at the lake with his parents- and his mother
5		and little sister- we would be out (swimmin')
6		or Dan and I would be out in the boat, you
7		know, skiin' and everything, you know- his
8		mom and little sister were in the cabin
9		watchin' the soap operas.
10	**A:**	Oh. Ha ha.
11	**B:**	*I couldn't hardly believe it. People can*
12		*get so hung up on those.*

Finally, the evaluation was sometimes omitted entirely, as the parties simply *dropped* the subject or *switched topics* immediately after the account. This happened in about a quarter of the cases. In the example below, A rebukes B at line 4 for finding her dull, B rejects her reproach at line 5 and the issue is then dropped.

1.	**B:**	'Scuse me- I'm yawnin'.*
2	**A:**	Ha ha- gonna fall asleep.
3	**B:**	No-o. Ha ha.
4	**A:**	(Ha ha, I'm not exciting to talk to.
5	**B:**	Oh man, Yeah you are.
6	**A:**	Hmm. How many more minutes?

McLaughlin, Cody, and Rosenstein found that the selection of a strategy for accounting was determined both by the nature of the offense and the type of reproach used. For example, excuses were apt to be offered for "offenses" having to do with personal tastes:

A:	I like soap operas! Oh! I just=*
A:	(You do?!!!
A:	=watch them all too often.
B:	(Ha ha ha.
A:	Ha ha. I like, uh, *Days of our Lives,* things like that.
B:	(nonverbal display of disagreement)
A:	You don't? *That's about the only- we don't watch it at night- we're just so busy, 'n we just- you know- are studyin' or something.*

Failure to account was associated with moral-intellectual superiority reproaches and direct rebukes. Refusals were associated with offenses of taste, attitude, belief, and with rebukes or imputations of superiority to the reproacher.

Reproachers were likely to honor excuses overtly, but did not necessarily do so for concessions, probably because apologies or admissions have to be "accepted" in such a way as to preserve the other's face; to accept them directly is to appear smug. Accepting a concession or admission is usually done by minimizing the offense or making excuses for the offender. Concessions and justifications were likely to be followed by retreats. Justifications, refusals, and failures to account were significantly likely to be followed by rejection statements or reinstitution of the reproach, as the example below illustrates. A opens with a surprise-disgust reproach at line 3, reformulated at lines 5 and 7. B fails to provide any substantive account for her offense, and so at line 11, A escalates to a moral-intellectual superiority reproach, albeit a camouflaged one, in which A implies that B is incautious. B then initiates a defense with a justification, at line 12, which still fails to convince A, as we see at line 21, where she challenges one of the underpinnings of B's line of argument. Finally, A addresses herself to this subpoint, and B performs a retreat, accepting the subpoint but not the entirety of A's whole line of talk.

1	**A:**	You all plannin' on gettin' married?*
2	**B:**	Yeah, in about a year.
3	**A:**	Really??
4	**B:**	Uh huh.
5	**A:**	A year after high school?!!
6	**B:**	Uh huh.
7	**A:**	Wow!
8	**B:**	Yeah, and a semester after high school
9		(?) and he's only got a semester left.
10		He's a junior.
11	**A:**	I think I- I don't know- I'm pretty chicken.
12	**B:**	It depends- it depends upon who you met. Like
13		you met somebody, like we've been dating over
14		a year and you know, we thought about waiting
15		until after we graduated but he may have to leave
16		here for five or six months to go off to New
17		York or somewhere, that's it. It doesn't make
18		any difference if we were married. It would

19		be the same- it wouldn't change that much the
20		way we lived (?).
21	**A:**	Really?
22	**B:**	Well, not all the time. I go over there and
23		study all the time and we're always together.
24	**A:**	Yeah, I see. That's good.

A final determination with respect to the antecedents of the reproacher's evaluation was that if no account whatsovever was provided, that is, if the reproached individual failed to demonstrate uptake of the reproach, in addition to reproach reinstatement, there was a significant likelihood that the issue would simply be dropped.

Apologies and Dismissals

Apologies and dismissals represent elements of the repair organization of social interaction that have not received the extensive scholarly attention that has been directed toward "accounts" in the narrow sense, that is, toward excuses and justifications. Yet, work by McLaughlin and Cody and their colleagues clearly indicates that conceding and refusing are commonplace strategies in dealing with charges that one's statements or behaviors are in some manner exceptionable. Let us look first at apologies.

Apologies

Fraser (1981) has laid out the preconditions for the felicitous performance of an apology, in terms of a set of sincerity conditions. In order to believe that a speaker is apologizing, a hearer must believe that the speaker believes (1) that some act was performed in the past; (2) that the act was personally offensive to the hearer; (3) that he (the speaker) was responsible for the offense, at least in part; and (4) that the (the speaker) sincerely experiences regret for his actions (Fraser, 1981, p. 261).

Edmondson (1981c) proposes that apologizing is an example of a speech act that must be performed directly; to support his point, Edmondson compared COMPLAIN and APOLOGIZE, both of which involve for the same offense, the same actors, and a set of interlocking preconditions. An APOLOGY "counts as an attempt on the part of the speaker to cause the hearer to withdraw a preceding COMPLAIN" (Edmondson, 1981c, p. 280). For COMPLAIN, however, directness is not lexicalized, but for APOLOGIZE it is; "I APOLOGIZE that I did X" (Edmondson, 1981c, pp. 278-279). Edmondson attributes this property of apologies to the hearer-supportive, speaker-suppressive maxims examined in earlier chapters.

Schlenker and Darby (1981) propose that an apology is a way of splitting off the "bad self" that was responsible for an offense, from the "real self," which would not have undertaken such an action had it not been for thus-and-so. Schlenker and Darby (1981, p. 272) have identified five components of an apology: (1) a statement of apologetic intent (that is, the kind of act described above by Fraser and Edmondson): (2) an expression of "remorse, sorrow, and embarrassment"; (3) an offer of redress; (4) pejorative statements about the self; and (5) requests for forgiveness.

Schlenker and Darby hypthesized that the greater one's responsibility for an event and the more serious its consequences for the "victim," the more likely it is that multiple apology components will be deployed. Schlenker and Darby had subjects read scenarios about a "bumping" incident in which the actor had either very little or a great deal of responsibility for the event, and in which the consequences of the event appeared to be either minor, moderate, or serious for the victim. Schlenker and Darby found that both severity and degree of actor responsibility had an impact on the apologies selected, in that as responsibility and severity increased, more apology components were added. Schlenker and Darby obtained "completeness" ratings for apology elements, and found that apologies could be ordered from least complete (a perfunctory statement of apologetic intent, such as "Pardon me"), through a perfunctory statement of regret ("I'm sorry"), a self-castigation ("I'm sorry, I feel foolish"), an expression of remorse ("I'm sorry, I feel badly [sic]"), an offer of help ("I'm sorry, can I help"), to the most complete form, a request for forgiveness ("I'm sorry, please forgive me"), (1981, p. 277).

Fraser (1981) found that when infractions were more serious, apologies were likely to be accompanied by excuses and justifications. In the most serious cases, offers of redress were common. When apologies were made in formal situations, the performatives (I apologize for X") or pseudo-performatives ("I must offer you an apology for X") were the norm, while in intimate relationships performatives were less common than utterances like "Oops" or

"I'm an idiot," which are more on the order of omissions than anything else (Fraser, 1981, p. 268).

Dismissals

Whereas apologies represent the most mitigating class of stategies that can fill the "remedy" slot in a repair sequence, dismissals are representative of the most aggravating form of remedy—the dispreferred form, if you will. Wagner (1980) has suggested that there are a number of ways in which persons may respond to attacks upon their character, intellect, and human worth. *Dismissing,* as Wagner describes it, involves a collection of techniques for refusing such an attack, that is, for canceling it or causing it to be withdrawn. A number of Wagner's techniques can be seen to have parallels in disclaimers, and are addressed to the same sources of discredit. For example, attacks may be dismissed by claiming that the attacker is misinformed, or ignorant. Similarly, attacks may be forestalled by a hedging disclaimer, by admitting that one might be misinformed or ignorant. An attack may be dismissed be referring to the other's "dark side" and "potential for ill will"; that is, one can claim that the other is just the "sort of person who attacks" (Wagner, 1981, p. 615). Similarly, credentialling disclaimers can be seen to be addressed to forestalling attacks on these grounds: for example, "I'm not a prude, but" or "I'm no racist, but."

Dismissals may also be constructed by claiming that the attacker is crazy, just as "cognitive disclaimers" are used to ward off charges that the author of a dubious utterance may be crazy. Other of Wagner's dismissals strategies can be seen to have parallels in apology components. An attack may be dismissed by claiming that the attacker has unfairly attributed to the "true" self what in fact was properly attributed to some "diminutive or foreign part of it" (Wagner, 1981, p. 610). Similarly, an apology can be fashioned by proposing that the blame for an untoward act is properly placed with the "bad" part of the self, and that the true self is untarnished.

SUMMARY

Preventatives and repairs are, broadly construed, responses to the presence, or potential presence, of negative typification arising from violation of conversational and societal rules. Preventatives include devices like disclaimers and licenses. In a disclaimer, the author of a potentially discrediting utterance hedges or prefaces the utterance with statements designed to establish her as a thoughtful, responsible, rational member of society, despite the probability that the impending utterance will give evidence to the contrary. Disclaimers are regarded by some scholars as facilitative in the prevention of discrediting, and by others as having a detrimental effect on perceptions of the communicator's competence. Licenses are speaker-initiated devices used to elicit approval and understanding, and prevent other-initiated repairs, or violations of the maxims of Quality, Quantity, Relevance, and Manner.

Repairs are addressed after the fact to violations of grammatical, syntactical, conversational, and societal rules. Repairs may be either self-accomplished, other-accomplished, or collaboratively achieved. The conversational system seems to demonstrate a preference for self-initiated over other-initiated repair, as the slots for self-initiated repairs are structurally prior to the slots for other-initiated repair. There is also a systematic preference for self-repair to be accomplished within the same turn-constructional unit as the problematic item.

Other-initiated repair may be directed to violation of conversational rules and maxims or to extra-conversational offenses. The canonical form of a repair sequence for an other-initiated repair consists of a three-turn series: the request for repair, the remedy, and the acknowledgment. Repair sequences constitute a special case of the side sequence, in which parties detour from ongoing talk to deal with some side issue raised by the talk. Repairs addressed to violations of the Quality maxim (for example, information structure repairs), have been documented. Repairs may also be directed to turn-taking violations such as lapses and failure to answer a summons.

Repair sequences may also be addressed to extra-conversational violations. The canonical form of such sequences is identical with conversation-internal repair sequences, but the labels reproach, account, and evaluation are usually employed in the case of extra-conversational repairs. Considerable evidence exists that the form in which a reproach (request for repair) is formulated has a strong influence on the type of account that will be provided: aggravating reproaches such as direct rebukes tend to elicit like responses, that is, aggravating account forms such as justifications and refusals. Apologies and dismissals are the extreme and opposite forms of the kinds of acts that can be placed in the remedy slot. Apologies are remedies whose complexity (number of components such as remorse, redress, etc.) increases as offense severity and actor responsibility increase. Dismissals are shown to be addressed to the same sources of discredit as apologies and disclaimers.

7

Significant Issues in Research on Conversation

◆ The search for a set of rules that can account ◆
for structure in conversational interaction has engaged the energy and
imagination of scholars in a number of disciplines. The diverse
methodological commitments that these scholars have brought to the
pursuit of the conversational rule preclude our presenting in this final
chapter issues particular to any specific methodological stance;
consequently, there will be no treatment of such problems as
transcriber reliability, coding scheme validity, static versus sequential analysis of data, and so forth. However, there do seem to be a
number of issues related to the actual doing of research on conversation that pertain regardless of discipline or perspective, to wit,
issues of *observational and explanatory adequacy* (Chomsky, 1965;
Grimshaw, 1974). In making a claim that there is a rule that accounts
for structure, the researcher regardless of his or her theoretical and
methodological predispositions must be prepared to demonstrate not
only that all the pertinent data have been collected, but that the
proposed rule or rule-set is consistent with an empirical generalization
about significant patterns or regularities in the data set, and that the
proposed rule is a better explanation of the observed regularities than

an alternative plausible rule or perhaps some law-like governing mechanism. Let us first consider the issue of *observational adequacy*.

ISSUES RELATED TO THE ADEQUACY OF OBSERVATION

The first responsibility of those who would make a claim to have discovered a significant aspect of conversational structure is to demonstrate that all of the perinent facts have been assembled:

> Observational adequacy implies that all relevant data needed for adequate structural description and for the discovery of rules are collected, whether those data be speech utterances, kinesic accompaniment to speech, knowledge of social relationships, intended ends of speech events, or whatever [Grimshaw, 1974, p. 420].

The Conversation as a Data Base: Standards of Adequacy

The most fundamental data base will of course consist of a corpus of conversations or conversation excerpts held to be representative of the domain of interest. Grimshaw (1974, p. 421) has noted four data types that appear to be used with some frequency in ethnographic studies of speaking: (1) "naturalistic" conversation in everyday, ordinary settings; (2) "natural" speech obtained in laboratory or other controlled environments; (3) samples of specific speech behaviors that are elicited as the result of a direct request from the researcher; (4) samples of "spoken" discourse taken from literary and/or historical sources. To this list we might add a fifth source, (5) examples of spoken interaction "constructed" by the researcher herself.

There seems to be little consensus as to the types of data most suitable for conversational analysis. While Sacks and his colleagues Schegloff and Jefferson have been criticized for what Edmondson (1981b) describes as their "highly selective" approach to data, that is, their use of conversation excerpts particularly well suited to show-casing their constructs, the same data sets have generated admiration because of the diversity of the topics and participants and the apparent naturalness of the settings in which they were recorded. Nor does there seem to be much agreement as to how many examples are required to demonstrate a regularity, much less a rule. While traditional empiricists strive to record and examine as many examples as possible, conversational analysts following the "method of analytic induction" (Jackson, 1982) may apparently make their case for a particular rule with only a few examples, provided that they can make credible the claim that no counterexamples could be found, or that the examples themselves are counterexamples to the only plausible or logical alternative to the proposed rule.

Examples of conversation from literary materials. Just what are the relative advantages and disadvantages of each of the five types of data noted above? It is probably fair to say that recourse to literary materials, while exceedingly convenient for the researcher, is nonetheless the least advisable way to proceed. While the application of analytical tools developed for the study of conversation may lead to new insights about literary structure or substance, it seems unlikely that the contrived discourses of a play or novel will offer up many useful leads to the organization of everyday conversational interaction. For example, take the case of the speech act *request*. It is extremely common to the dramatic form that characters use the imperative or explicit performative in trying to gain compliance from others. Yet work by Searle (1975) and by House and Kasper (1981) and others suggest that in routine daily encounters imperatives and performatives are rare and that speakers ordinarily use more circuitous routes to their goals. In plays and novels, dialogues are developed in furtherance of specific issues of plot and subplot; they are more likely than our routine daily conversations to be characterized by conflict; both propositional and functional structures of literary discourse are likely to be "compressed" to facilitate an economical development of character, setting, and action. Literary dialogues generally are suspect as sources on the grounds that they differ significantly in form and content from actual conversational interaction.

Hypothetical examples of conversation. Jackson (1982, p. 3) has argued that examples that are recalled or contrived by the researcher serve "as well as or better than natural talk," pointing to the successes achieved by Grice (1975) and Searle (1975) from a hypothetical data base. Jackson argues that (1) restricting usable data to naturally occurring conversation imposes "restrictions on the kinds of discoveries that will be made"; (2) conversation from natural settings is needed only to describe how language is used; (3) the contrived example, like natural discourse, "presents us with facts to be explained"; and (4) hypothetical talk is not noisy with "speaker idiosyncrasies or contextual peculiarities" (Jackson, 1982, p. 3).

While indeed, as Jackson argues the works of Grice on conversational maxims and Searle on indirect speech acts have been enormously successful, those successes have been due not to the fact that either author provided a rigorous demonstration of his claim using hypothetical examples, for certainly neither did, but rather to the simplicity and broad applicability of their central constructs, together with the absence of any clear indication as to how their claims might be falsified. How, for example, might one *disprove* that indirect speech acts are built out of the preconditions for the felicitous performance of an action, when the construct is not defined independently of the properties claimed for it? Falsifiability aside, the conversational maxims and the notion of action preconditions have been invoked by their authors to account for *interpretive* procedures; both Searle and Grice were proposing not surface rules, but rather a set of underlying dimensions of *some* of the processes that hearers go through in understanding the utterances of others. The widespread popularity of the Gricean maxims and Searle's preconditions must be said to be due in part to the fact that the basic constructs are sufficiently broad and undefined that they may be applied in a multitude of situations, and seem to be capable of the virtually effortless generation of new "discoveries." The credibility of the claims of Searle and Grice have nothing whatsoever to do with their use of hypothetical examples, and in fact are successful in spite of their lack of a solid data base because of the simplicity and intuitive appeal of the ideas they propose.

Jackson's argument that restricting the data set to naturally-occurring samples of talk restricts the sorts of things we can learn is true in part, particularly if we operate under the usual requirements of traditional empiricism and the object of interest is a relatively rare conversational phenomenon. For example, as was brought out in the previous chapter, naturally occurring talk might not provide as many examples of disclaimers as we might need to be able to make a compelling claim, and similarly with such interesting but relatively scarce phcnomena as "transparent questions" ("Is the Pope a Catholic?"). Granted that such problems do occur, still the researcher need not rely solely on his own contrivances; techniques such as asking subjects to role-play a situation in which the phenomenon of interest would be likely to occur, or asking for subject's recollections of pertinent examples could help to supplement the researcher's own hypothetical ones.

Jackson further argues for the acceptability of hypothetical examples as evidence by proposing that naturally occurring conversation is needed for the data base only when our goal is *description* (1982, p. 3), and that hypothetical talk is quite suitable for the purpose of theorizing. On this point, one can only note that a theory growing out of an observationally inadequate data base would not be acceptable in many branches of the social sciences. The further claim that hypothetical examples propose a set of "facts" to be explained (Jackson, 1982, p. 3) is correct only if the researcher is unconcerned with whether or not the "facts" of his own imaginings happen to coincide with the "facts" of the experience of others. If such a coincidence exists, then we have something that it is worth our while to examine.

The final argument is favor of the researcher-contrived example as evidence that Jackson makes is that these examples don't bother us with anomalies attributable to a particular speaker or context. Yet, elsewhere in the same paper (1982, p. 10), Jackson argues that "deviations from a rule are an important source of the evidence for the existence of a rule," and that demands of completeness require that every example available to the researcher be consistent with the rule at some level.

Ultimately, the success of an account of conversational structure based upon researcher-contrived examples will depend upon the breadth and yet the ordinariness of the researcher's experience. Some people make themselves open to certain kinds of communicative phenomena; for example, they may hear a lot of indirect answers because they ask a lot of obvious questions. Similarly, they may close themselves off to the reception of other kinds of speech acts, such as jokes or threats to negative face. In the final analysis, the researcher himself as the only source of evidence is simply not an adequate source. Consider, for example, the case of research on compliance-gaining messages. Early "arm-chair" taxonomies of influence tactics developed by French and Raven (1960) and Marwell and Schmitt (1967) have been found by subsequent researchers (McLaughlin, Cody, & Robey, 1980; Cody, McLaughlin, & Schneider, 1981) not only to contain strategies that virtually no one uses, but also to omit strategies that are very common.

To summarize, it seems that the arguments in favor of the use of hypothetical examples as evidence (as opposed to illustration) are not sufficiently compelling to regard them as a substitute data base for naturally occurring talk.

"Elicited" examples of conversation. Sometimes researchers will elect to collect samples of a conversational phenomenon by making a direct request for the subject to produce it. Under this general heading we can include a variety of techniques that range from asking subjects to recall a particular type of interaction, as McLaughlin, Cody, and O'Hair (1983) did when they had subjects recall what they said and what others said relative to a failure event, to having a pair of subjects work collaboratively with the researchers to arrive at a verbatim reconstruction of a specific interchange, as Jackson and Jacobs (1981) did with recollected examples of arguments, to asking subjects to role-play certain speech acts under a variety of hypothetical conditions, as House and Kasper (1981) did in their study on requests. Most of the research on compliance-gaining messages has used pencil-and-paper elicitation techniques in which the subjects are presented with a scenario and asked to construct a compliance-gaining message. Gibbs (1981) used this strategy in his study of indirect requests. A refinement of this technique is to present subjects with a hypothetical message to which they are to produce an appropriate response.

Elicited samples of conversation are free from at least two of the drawbacks attributed earlier to literary and hypothetical materials. First, they are more realistic by virtue of the fact that they are not in service of a plot, nor are they particularly required to be interesting, dramatic, economical, or significant in any way. Second, elicited samples relieve the researcher of the burden of having to rely solely on her own creativity and experience, which may be limited or biased in some of the ways suggested earlier. However, elicited data may be flawed in a number of important ways. First, recall in those studies that call for it is unlikely to be entirely accurate, although the Jackson and Jacobs method of collaborative recollection by both participants is a significant advance in that regard. Meichenbaum and Cameron (1981), in overviewing significant issues in cognitive assessment, suggest that in obtaining self-report data of any kind, accuracy of recall and reconstruction is facilitated if the reports are obtained as soon as possible after the events of interest, in a nondirective manner so as to avoid setting up any demand characteristics, with an instructional set that maximizes the importance of a complete and an accurate recounting.

Even under optimum conditions, however, if pencil-and-paper techniques are used to obtain recollections, as they usually are in furtherance of increasing the sample size, they can be expected to evidence considerable signs of editing simply by virtue of the transition from the oral to the written medium. Written messages will probably be briefer, will have few if any false starts, repetitions, hesitation pauses, lapses, overlaps, and so on, and will probably have fewer infelicities of syntax than the oral messages that they purport to represent. Oral recall may of course be similarly affected.

Finally, the accuracy both of recall and role-play may be affected by a tendency of subjects to paint themselves in a flattering light; the extent to which this occurs may depend upon how recall is prompted. For instance, Sudman and Bradburn (1974) found that, when compared against retail sales figures for their geographical area, persons' self-reports of alcohol consumption tended to be underestimates. Open-ended questions that probed the issue of alcohol consumption indirectly tended to pose less question "threat" than items that asked for a direct report, say, of the number of beers consumed per week. Similarly, Cody (1982) and Cody, O'Hair, and Scheider (1982) found that having subjects write essays about what they might say in a hypothetical scenario yielded better results than asking them to rate the likelihood that they would select a particular message among a set of messages, for, in response to the latter strategy, subjects tended to over-report their preferences for prosocial messages and underreport their preferences for negative or self-oriented messages.

"Natural" conversation in controlled environments. One of the most common strategies for obtaining conversational data has been to record interaction in a laboratory setting. Subjects may be told openly that their conversation is to be recorded; that is, they may be made explicitly aware that the object of the experimenter's interest is their interaction itself (McLaughlin et al., 1981; McLaughlin & Cody, 1982; McLaughlin, Cody, & Rosenstein, 1983), or their interaction may be recorded while they are ostensibly "waiting" to begin what they have been led to believe is an experiment on some other topic unrelated to their current conversation (Krivonos &

Knapp, 1975). While a data base collected by either strategem has the obvious advantages over the previously reviewed sources of being independent of the artistic purposes of an author, the insularity of the analyst, and the inaccuracy of the recaller, there are certain problems associated with the laboratory setting itself that are worth noting. The subject in the controlled research environment cannot help but be alert to the fact that some aspect of her person, character, or performance will at some point be subject to scrutiny. Not only will she be likely to have developed hypotheses about what will be expected of her, but she may also have developed suspicions that things are not what they appear to be. Under such circumstances, subject behavior can be expected to be more than usually prudent and cautious. What this increase in circumspection entails is the probability that conforming behaviors will be more than usually apparent; thus, we might expect that the indices of pattern or behavioral regularity that we obtain represent an upper bound on the strength of the context-behavior relationship covered by the rule in question. Additionally, we can expect that normative constraints will be even more compelling if the interacting parties are unacquainted with one another.

A further problem that might arise in both laboratory study and in research on conversation in more natural environments is that of the potential for reactivity of the recording procedures. Weimann (1981) examined the effects of four levels of videotaping obtrusiveness, from "obvious" to "covert," on a set of nonverbal behaviors that are ordinarily thought not to be under the conscious control of the subject, such as forward lean, object manipulation, reclining posture, and number of turns, variables usually associated with the dimensions of *anxiety* and *responsiveness*. Weimann found that knowledge of being videotaped did not produce speech act differences in conversational behaviors that were out-of-awareness, nor did the obtrusiveness of the procedure make a difference. In fact, subjects for whom it was made quite apparent that they were being videotaped were more responsive and relaxed than those who were unaware that they were being taped. Anticipation of being videotaped did not appear to increase anxiety or suppress responsiveness. A decline in anxiety means over the course of interaction suggested that the effects of videotaping could be expected to dissipate over time. Weimann concluded that at least for the out-of-awareness behaviors that he observed, there was little need to resort to covert recording to avoid reactivity problems, although he suggested that less obtrusive measures might be in order, since the increased responsiveness of subjects in the "obvious" condition, in which a camera and microphone were clearly visible, indicated that they put on a bit of a "show" for the experimenter compared to subjects in the other conditions. Weimann accounted for his finding that the covertly taped subjects displayed more anxiety by proposing that they had not had the benefit of the reduction in situational ambiguity that the overt presence and/or knowledge of recording equipment could provide. One limitation of the Weimann study in dealing with the issue of reactivity is that we don't really know how far we may generalize from the out-of-awareness behaviors that served as dependent variables. It seems probable that such variables as topic, speaker-switches, politeness, and so on would not be unaffected by the presence of recording equipment, although whether those effects would persist over time is anyone's guess. For most of us, however, the advantages of covert recording are offset by the ethical problems it presents.

"Natural" conversation in uncontrolled environments. In general it can be said that the most desirable data base is a corpus of conversations collected in a wide variety of natural, noncontrived settings, such as in a restaurant, at the beach, at the kitchen table, and so forth. Provided that the researcher follows some sort of replicable procedure for collecting his materials, so that the conversations represent more than just a sample of convenience or a collection of "interesting" excerpts, then the acquisition of data in noncontrolled settings may be the most appropriate way to proceed. Inasmuch as it is desirable in the interests of rigor to make every effort to find counterexamples to a proposed rule, the search for conversation materials should be as wide as possible, and sample as many settings as is consistent with the aims and purposes of the researcher. Sampling from a wide variety of situations also contributes to the ability to narrow the range of circumstances in which the rule applies, or to make definitive exclusions of those classes of context in which it does not seem to apply.

The issue of reactivity that we examined in the context of laboratory observation is of course relevant in naturalistic settings as well, and perhaps even more so. Weimann (1981) speculated that one of the reasons that he found so few differences in the out-of-awareness nonverbal behaviors as a function of recording obtrusiveness had to do with the already considerable potential for reactivity present in the laboratory setting itself; that is, the obvious presence of a recorder may not have produced a significant increase in arousal given that the situation itself was already adequate to produce high arousal. In more natural settings, however, the differences between obviously recorded and unrecorded conversational behaviors may be more dramatic. There is, to this writers' knowledge, no convincing evidence on this point one way or another.

The Importance of Nonverbal Behavior to the Data Base

The best argument for the use of "naturalistic" samples of conversation, regardless of where they are obtained, is that examples of any other kind (recalled, literary, constructed) will not be accompanied by appropriate nonverbal behaviors. Our treatment of the nonverbal aspects of conversation has been quite sketchy in the text so far, and this is not less than an accurate reflection of the attitude that most contemporary adherents of a "rules" approach to conversation have taken. There are some notable exceptions, as for example in the work of Goodwin (1981) on the effect of hearer gaze on the processes of turn construction and exchange. Although some of the conversational analysts make an effort to measure hesitation pauses and switching pauses and to indicate intonation contour and emphasis on their transcripts, for the most part nonverbal behavior is not regarded as being worthy of note unless it in some way conflicts with what's going on at the verbal level. There have been a number of recent studies, however, that suggest that the linkages between verbal and nonverbal behavior in conversation are too complex to justify the continued neglect of the latter.

Heeschen, Schiefenhovel, and Eibl-Eibesfeldt (1980) found that among the Eipo of West New Guinea, the acts *requesting, giving,* and *accepting* tended to be accomplished nonverbally. The Eipo appear to operate under a rule according to which a comment on another's possession is tantamount to a demand for a share of it, and thus such comments are to avoided. Heeschen et al. found that direct verbal requests rarely resulted in compliance; rather, the usual response of the target to a verbal request was to turn away, change the topic, or make a formal statement of rejection such as "begging forbidden" (1981, pp. 154-155). Had the authors examined only the transcripts of verbal interactions, they would have missed altogether how acts of requesting are accomplished. Among children, requesting a share of another's portion of sweet potatoe, a prized commodity, was achieved through such movements as "repeated proxemic shifts into body contact" (Heeschen et al., 1981, p. 151), or head-tilting solicitation gestures. *Offering* was accomplished by a movement in which the arm of the potential giver is held in a rather hesitant position (bent at the elbow), as if to express uncertainty as to whether the offer would be accepted. *Refusing* to give was accomplished by physical withdrawal from bodily contact and/or gaze aversion. Among adults, strategies that increased the likelihood of compliance with a request included adopting submissive paralinguistic features like nasality or a whining tone while stroking the beard or chin of the target of the request, or, while in close proximity to the target, establishing eye contact and audibly breathing in air in a sound that might convey anticipation. Heeschen et al. noted that there appeared to be no apparent demand in the communicative system for an immediate response to a request—an apparent failure of the notion of conditional relevance to apply cross-culturally.

A study by Rosenfeld and Hancks (1980) was similarly devoted to uncovering the nature of the linkages between spoken and unspoken aspects of conversation. Rosenfeld and Hancks were interested in the class of verbal behaviors that some scholars have described as backchannel utterances, and that they called "listener responses," "brief verbal commentaries" that were "preceded and followed by at least five seconds of undisputed floorholding by the speaker" (1980, p. 196), such as "Mhm," "Yeah," or "Right, right." Rosenfeld and Hancks scored listener responses in conversations for *complexity, audibility,* and the extent to which they implied *attention, agreement,* and *understanding.* It was found that the more complex the listener response, the more audible it was, and the more likely it was to be characterized by nonverbal *acknowledgments* (head nods) and expressions of *interest* (forward lean, evidence of visual attention, and eye flash); further, it was found that the audibility of the listener response was a function of active efforts by the speaker to obtain a reaction from the listener without yielding the floor; and, finally, it was shown that judgments of listener attentiveness, understanding, and agreement were significantly correlated with the listener's use of head nods, forward lean, and visual attentiveness behaviors. Rosenfeld and Hancks also found that the behaviors they had earmarked as listener responses were indeed relatively lacking in "indicators of complex speech encoding."

Listener responses were found to be characterized by eye movement away from the partner in only 9% of the cases, while the speaker-state turns (the longer floor-holdings) were accompanied by such gaze aversion in 42% of the cases. Rosenfeld and Hancks concluded that the distinction between listener and speaker roles could be made on nonverbal as well as verbal grounds. While the Rosenfeld and Hancks findings suggest that utterances may differ in certain nonverbal features from other utterances, and that the two classes of utterances differ by virtue of whether the person who made them is in the "speaker mode" or the "hearer mode," their findings are not strong enough to warrant a wholesale rejection of our earlier contention that so-called back-channel utterances ought to be treated as turns. However, the Rosenfeld and Hancks study is important in that it indicates some ways in which a single lexical item, for example, "Yeah," could be used to convey several different speech acts such as agreement, encouragement, or discouragement, as a function of variation in its audibility and a multitude of other nonverbal characteristics. Information of this nature is vital in resolving issues of speech act assignment.

Other recent work on the relationship between verbal and nonverbal communication suggests that nonverbal behaviors may provide important cues to conversation structure. Kendon (1980, p. 222) has made some convincing arguments that patterns of gesticulation may, "in various ways, make visible the organization of the discourse." For example, if a speaker were to plan a discourse whose structure might be said to be that of a list of features, or members, of some superordinate class, a not uncommon accompaniment might be a "ticking off" of the members of the class one at a time, with the left hand palm up in a sustained position while the fingers of the right hand strike it successively with the onset of mention of each new member of the class. The sustained position of the left hand could be seen to represent on an analogic level the macroproposition of the discourse segment—that "there is a class of persons who . . . ," while the successive "tickings off" represent the subordinate propositions 1 through n that "X is a member of the class of persons who . . ." (Kendon, 1980, p. 222).

Kendon regards gesticulation as a "second output of the process of utterance," which is usually organized and displayed *prior* to its verbal counterpart (1980, p. 221). Indeed, upon reflection it is clear that gestures that occur after their corresponding verbal referents are extremely rare, and, when they do occur, have the effect of making the speaker appear comical. Kendon attributes the temporal priority of gesticulation to the fact that the same idea may be expressed more quickly and economically in gesture than in words, although this point is debatable. In any event, if Kendon is correct in his conclusion that gestures are temporally prior outputs of the same system that produces utterance, then clearly gesticulation is an important source of *guidance* for the listener, and may be of considerable utility in his task of projecting the nature and duration of his partners' utterances.

Since there is evidence that nonverbal behaviors may play a critical role in such features of conversational interaction as the communication of illocutionary point, the management of the turn-exchange system, and the overt symbolization of the propositional macrostructure, it is important that nonverbal aspects of a recorded interaction at least be available for inspection, and for this reason, videotaping is recommended, even though for most conversation researchers it has not to date been the technique of choice.

Sources of Evidence for Inferring
the Presence of a Conversational Rule

Assuming that the researcher has gathered a sufficiently large corpus of conversations such that claims for thoroughness can be made credible, what evidence should he or she put forward in support of a contention that a particular conversational rule is operative? It appears that there are a number of sources of evidence, both within and external to the conversation itself, which may be exploited in defense of a proposed rule. The first and most obvious is *behavioral conformity:* is there a regularly occurring relationship between some particular communicative behavior and a context for which it is claimed to be the appropriate action?

Behavioral conformity to the proposed rule. We have noted in earlier chapters that there are rules that virutally no one honors, and that norm and rule are not identical constructs. Indeed, Ganz (1971, p. 78) has argued that a rule can still be a rule even if it is unfulfilled; that it needn't be "regular, frequent, consistent, or anything of the like." Further, Ganz argues that any given behavioral event could be made out to conform to a variety of different rules, even though the actor was in fact unfamiliar with any of them. Nevertheless, if our ultimate interest is in accounting for *structure* in conversation, then we will wish to confine our attention to those context-behavior relationships that occur with sufficient frequency that they can be claimed to constitute an organizing feature of conversational interaction. Thus, the first source of evidence for the presence of a regulative rule is that, in the conversational corpus that constitutes our data base, there is a significant co-occurrence between the presence of some antecedent context and the subsequent enactment of the behavior of interest. In the case of constitutive rules, what is required is a demonstration that a speech act satisfying some particular set of preconditions is routinely treated as a request, an offer, an apology,, and so on by its hearers. While the presence of behavioral conformity is the most basic source of evidence which the researcher can adduce in support of the proposition that a proposed rule is accounting for structure, to be able to make the claim that thus-and-such a behavior is "treated" as an apology, or that this-and-so always occurs given context C, requires us to meet certain standards of descriptive accuracy first, for example, that our coding and classification procedures are valid and reliable. Furthermore, the demonstration must be made at some point that there is a behavioral regularity *in the absence of logical necessity* (Pearce, 1976). We will consider issues related to how such a demonstration might be made when we take up the question of explanatory adequacy along with such issues as accounting for regular deviations from the rules.

While the following position clearly reflects the author's bias in favor of traditional empiricism, it seems fair to say that no one espousing a method other than the use of statistical tests of significance has provided a rigorous *procedure* for the demonstration of the presence of a behavioral regularity, although there have been some successful demonstrations in isolated cases for particular rules (Schegloff, 1968). Every known method of research on conversation relies on the (more or less) implicit proposition that the proposed rule-conforming behavior occurs regularly in the "slots" in which it is supposed to occur, and that it does so in a fashion that is unlikely to have resulted by chance. For example, Schegloff's (1968) claims in his study of telephone opening sequences were made credible in part because of his finding that only one of his 500-odd cases failed to conform to the rule, and he was able to account for that failure by reference to the absence of a normal input condition. Similarly, most conversational analysts working outside traditional social scientific empiricism who have had any success have done so by virtue of an implicit comparison process in which the reader aligns his own experience with that of the author and finds that, indeed, he can think of few if any counterexamples to the proposed rule. While the ultimate value of any demonstration that X-Y is a behaviorly regular co-occurrence depends on the exhaustiveness of the data base itself, there seems to be no compelling reason why the researcher ought not go the whole mile and provide the most rigorous and scientifically acceptable demonstration possible that the alleged regularity does in fact constitute a significant, nonrandom phenomenon.

In support of the argument that a rigorous, data-based defense of one's claims is desirable, let us consider a case in point. Schegloff, Jefferson, and Sacks (1977) asserted that in cases where repair seemed to be in order, repairs *initiated* by others "overwhelmingly" resulted in self-repair, although no frequency data were reported. However, Zahn (1983), in an analysis of eighty cases of "successful repair," found a significant interaction between source of *initiation* of repair (Self, Other) and source of *accomplishment* of repair (Self, Other) such that other-initiations were significantly more likely to lead to self-repair *only* for conversants for whom there was a previous history of acquaintance; for initial interactions, other-initiations usually resulted in other-repair. Zahn's findings suggest that claims that are not backed up with a rigorous demonstration of their validity must be considered tentative at best.

The actor's knowledge of the proposed rule. An additional source of evidence for the operation of a proposed rule is that actors *know* it in some fashion (Ganz, 1971; Collett, 1977; Adler, 1978). This is not to say that absence of explicit rule-knowledge implies the absence of a rule; rather, the presence of rule-knowledge in some form is supportive evidence given that the presence of a behavioral regularity has already been established. The rule-knowledge issue really involves two questions: (1) Is the rule "known" in some sense to an actor whose behavior appears to conform to it? (2) Is knowledge of the rule widely held in the population of which the actor is a member?

To answer the first question, we might attempt to determine if the actor can *articulate* the rule which governed her behavior in a particular context; if not the exact rule, then perhaps a sentence which is "co-extensive" with it (Ganz, 1971). For example, we might ask a person why she said "Pass the salt" to her eight-year-old son, but "May I have the salt, please?" to her employer. Lindsay (1977, pp. 166-167) has argued against the articulation criterion on two grounds. First, Lindsay suggests that an actor's ability to articulate a rule which seems to fit a given instance of behavior does not justify our attribution of the rule as the generative mechanism underlying the behavior. Indeed, work by Nisbett and Wilson (1977) and Nisbett and Ross (1980) indicates that people's ability to provide accurate explanations for their own behavior is not particularly good: "the accuracy of subjective reports is so poor as to suggest that any introspective access that may exist is not sufficient to produce generally correct or reliable reports" (Nisbett & Wilson, 1977, p. 233). While other scholars have regarded the claims of Nisbett and associates as exaggerated (White, 1980; Genest & Turk, 1981), nonetheless it is apparent to even the most charitable observer of human inference proceses that our ability to reconstruct why we behave as we do should be viewed with some skepticism.

Lindsay also argues that most actors simply cannot articulate a rule that will fit their behavior. Lindsay proposes two very stringent tests for inferring that a rule generated a particular behavior: (1) that there ought to be *no* cases in which the actor was unable to articulate a rule which fit the behavior; (2) that there ought to be data establishing that variation in how the rule is articulated (i.e., the "version" of the rule proposed) corresponds to differences in the behavior called for by the rule. While the former test seems much too rigid—it is doubtful, for example, that many ordinary language users could articulate Crawford's (1977) rules governing the complex effects of the presence or absence of a line on who speaks first at an inquiry desk—the latter criterion, that behavioral variability ought to correspond to variation in rule version, seems quite reasonable. Along these same lines, Adler (1978, p. 436) has proposed that regularly occurring context-behavior relationships ought to be demonstrably higher for those who can articulate the rule than for those who cannot.

It appears to be a rather commonly held view among rules theorists that an actor who is unable to articulate a rule may nonetheless be said to "know" it in the sense that he will in some fashion demonstrate an awareness of it when it is broken. There are a number of strategies open to the researcher to tap this dormant knowledge. For example, an actor who has been observed to engage in rule-fulfilling behavior but who has not been forthcoming with the proposed rule as the mechanism generating the behavior might be presented with deviant or abnormal sequences and asked if she can recognize "what's wrong with the picture." A rule-statement might be elicited more easily when the prompt is its breach, as opposed to its honoring. Similarly, the actor who was incapable of articulating the rule from a simple inspection of her own behavior might be able to formulate it if she were first required to generate some inappropriate responses to the eliciting context.

A demonstration that an actor whose behavior conforms to the proposed rule does in fact know the rule, in some sense, is strong circumstantial evidence that the rule was the mechanism generating the behavior in question, although to be sure the behavior may be required by other rules that the actor knows, but neglected to mention. An alternative way in which rule-knowledge may be used as evidence in support of a claim is by a demonstration that knowledge of the rule is widely held in the subject population from which the examples have been collected.

There appear to be several possible indices of social knowledge of a rule. Among these are (1) the ability of actors as observers to recognize an infringement of the rule (Pearce, 1976; Collett, 1977); (2) the disruption of conversational coherence in the event that a rule is broken or violated; (3) the presence of comment or repair in the event of a breach; (4) the negotiation of new rules in the event of an infringement (Morris & Hopper, 1980); (5) the application of sanctions following a violation of the rule (Collett, 1977); (6) the use of the rule in accounts and explanations (Harré & Secord, 1972); and (7) the presence of rules in projections of future behavior.

To demonstrate that actors as observers recognize an infringement of the rule, subjects from the population from which the conversation samples were drawn could be asked to classify sequences, some of which are deviant, as to the appropriateness or competence of the speaker's behavior. A variation of this strategy was used by Planalp and Tracy (1980) to tap social rule knowledge in their study of topic shift devices. Another strategy for demonstrating wide social knowledge of a rule is to establish that its violation produces a disruption of conversation coherence. Vucinich (1977) used this method in his study of violations of the Relevance maxim, in which he observed that the unilateral topic shifts in which he had his confederates engage often resulted in topical and even conversation discontinuities. The researcher could also look for the presence of efforts at repair, the application of sanctions, or even simple comment as indicators that a rule had been broken, which of course presupposes that the rule indeed exists. For example, the conditional relevance of an answer upon a question might be demonstrated by the presence of any of all of the following in response to a confederate's failure to provide anything interpretable as an answer to a naive subject's question: (1) reinstatement of the question, with either an explicit repeat or a paraphrase (Garvey & Berninger, 1981; Merritt, 1982); (2) expressions of annoyance or irritation; (3) attempts to uncover the reason for the failure to respond.

Another way to test for widespread rule-knowledge is to elicit *accounts* or explanation of behavior that is described as having taken place in a context where the rule is expected to be operative. For example, suppose that a researcher were interested in establishing that rules could be hierarchically organized such that conditional relevance constraints were at a lower order of priority than, say, the so-called Morality maxim (Bach & Harnish, 1979). Evidence in support of such a claim could be obtained in the following manner: present subjects with a scenario like the following, in which A inquires, "Did Victor tell you how much his merit increase was?" and B replies "Do you remember where I left my sunglasses?" Next, ask the subjects to explain or account for why B behaved as she did. If in fact the rule that a question be answered with a relevant response is superseded by the maxim that one not ask others to disclose that which they ought not to, then the accounts of B's behavior which the subjects provide ought to say something like "B didn't think it was proper to repeat what Victor told her, so instead of answering she changed the topic." Similarly, one could present subjects with an excerpt from Merritt's (1982) elementary classroom transcripts and ask subjects to describe the teacher's behavior with respect to the child's repeated summonses, and to account for why the teacher did what she did. Subject protocols should reflect the priority of turn-taking rules over local demands for conditional relevance. Tannen (1981) used a variation on the method of accounts to buttress her argument that Greeks, Greek-Americans, and Americans of non-Greek descent have different constitutive rules for certain indirect speech acts.

Consensual knowledge of particular rules may also be evidenced by a demonstration that the rules figure in projections or *predictions* of behavior. For example, one might test for knowledge of the Reichman rule that it is inappropriate to digress from a digression to introduce a new topic (1978, p. 374) by having subjects predict what B would say in a scenario like the following:

A: My daughter called me yesterday and said she'd gotten a
      promotion and she'd be transferred next month to the office in
      Santa Barbara. She'll be the only woman in the office, she said

B: Santa Barbara, is that south or north of Los Angeles? My cousin used to live there.

A: It's about eighty miles north.

B: Is that on the coast?

A: Uh huh.

B: I see. *(What will B say now?)*

Responses could be examined for whether or not they introduced a new topic unrelated either to the digression or to the prior topical talk about Mrs. A's daughter's job transfer.

Actor's intention to conform to the rule. Another source of support for the proposition that a particular behavior is rule-governed would be evidence that the actor *intended* to conform to it, although again it is not *necessary* that such a demonstration should be made. However, it is necessary that data be adduced to the effect that the behavior was under the control of the actor—that he chose to do it rather than that he had to do it. Shimanoff (1980) suggests that the primary way in which one makes such a demonstration is by showing that it is physically possible for the actor to exercise control over her behavior. What this amounts to is having the actor demonstrate that there were other kinds of responses that conceivably could have been made given the particular set of circumstances in which the alleged rule-governed behavior was emitted. For most conversational behaviors, demonstrating the actor's capacity for choice constitutes an exercise in the obvious; clearly, we can choose not to answer questions, we can make abrupt changes of topic, and we can ignore attempts to claim the floor. In some areas, however, the line between rule-governed behavior and law-governed behavior seems to be fuzzy, and care should be taken to see to it that possible generative mechanisms other than rules are taken into account. For example, Jefferson's (1973) assertion that the apparent "precision timing" of a certain class of interruptions is a function of the interrupting speaker's goal of making a credible demonstration that the current speaker's topic is already known could not survive the finding that there is physical incapacity or at least "dispreferredness" to listen simultaneously for the nearest transition-relevance place *and* cope with the processing demands which the speaker's utterance-so-far has already set in motion. For many conversational phenomena it may turn out that what we think are rule-governed behaviors are in fact related in some systematic, law-like way to the limitations of our cognitive processes.

If it can be shown that a behavior was intentionally performed in order to achieve a goal in some particular context, then such a demonstration can be counted as strong evidence that the actor, at least, thinks that there is a rule. What is required is a demonstration that the actor had a *plan*, however rudimentary it might have been; that is, that the action undertaken was what is normatively "done" in such situations, and that the actor consciously undertook it because she believed it would result in the realization of some goal (von Wright, 1971). Von Wright (1971) argues that the actor herself, who by all appearances is the only possible source of verification on this latter point, is nevertheless an unreliable source because she might respond either untruthfully of inaccurately. While the work of Nisbett and Ross (1980) has provided a certain amount of support for the inaccuracy of self-reports, Hewes and Planalp (1982) argue that subjects are aware of their biases to some extent, and try to compensate for them. Louden (1983) has reviewed the literature on conditions affecting the veridicality of self-reports of cognitive processes, and has reported several factors that appear to influence how accurately subjects can reconstruct not only what they did, but how and why they did it. Work by Langer (Langer, 1978; Langer & Weinman, 1981) indicates that much social behavior is carried out "mindlessly," according to scripts or cognitive representations of the usual sequence of events in a recurring social episode. For example, some years ago, the author had to undergo a tonsillectomy (something of an ordeal for an adult), and was not at all pleased with the bedside manner (not to speak of the bill) presented to her by the physician who performed the surgery. As a reflection of this displeasure, I pointedly neglected to thank him upon my departure from the last post-surgical interview. However, our leave-taking ended like this:

Patient: Good-bye.
Doctor: You're welcome.

The doctor's mindless responding protected him from this tiny parting shot. The mindlessness characteristic of many conversational routines such as greeeting, parting, thanking, and excusing oneself is counterproductive of accurate recall and antithetical to the notion of conversational planning.

Louden (1983) also reports that such factors as the *objective self-awareness* (Duval & Wicklund, 1972) and *private self-consciousness* (Fenigstein, Scheier, & Buss, 1975) of the actor have been found to influence his ability to reflect on his own cognitive processes. Generally, there seems to be support for the notion that accuracy and insight increase as the actor becomes more focused on self. The body of literature on objective self-awareness suggests that actors might be more effective at recalling their plans and intentions with respect to conversational issues if they were first presented with something to increase awareness of their own interaction behavior, such as a videotape or transcript of the conversation about which recall is desired.

Evidence that the behavior varies with context. Shimanoff (1980) suggests that one of the main tests for identifying whether or not a behavior is rule-governed is to check for changes in the emitted behavior as a function of changes in the context. This suggests that the researcher ought to have data establishing that a particular behavior is not an invariant output of a given actor, but rather a unique response to a particular situation or class of situations. The extent to which it is actually possible for the researcher to make a convincing demonstration on this point is debatable; clearly there is a limit to the number of situations through which one can "run" a subject, even using pencil-and-paper methods, and it is not practical to assign research assistants to follow subjects around and record changes in their behaviors as they move from one context to the next. It is, however, possible to narrow the range of contexts in which the behavior of interest can be observed, and to exclude some of the situations in which the rule is not operative, and then generalize to the larger classes that those situations seem to represent.

Erickson and Schultz (1977, p. 6) find that social contexts "consist of mutually shared and ratified definitions of situation *and* in the social actions persons take on the basis of those definitions." Because of the interactional constitution of context, it is extremely difficult to try and recreate it using only broad situational dimensions such as relationship intimacy, degree of formality, distribution of power, and so on. Not only are there rules whose if-conditions correspond to these broader aspects of context, but more global rules are often supplemented or even supplanted by specifically conversational regulative rules that govern such phenomena as replies to requests, responses to compliments, and so forth. No analysis of context could be complete without incorporating the highly specific but essentially provisional characteristics of the pool of propositions, acts, and presuppositions that constitute the conversation as it has unfolded. Any conversational behavior that one would hope to link to a broader context, such as formality, must first be examined in light of how it fits "locally" with the immediately prior talk, as well as more globally with the functional and propositional macrostructures that organize the discourse.

Erickson and Schultz (1977, p. 9) have proposed a procedure for detecting changes in conversational context that they believe to be "congruent with the ways participants in interaction must be construing interaction as it happens, attending first to longer segments as gestalts and then to shorter ones embedded within the larger frames." Their procedure involves the reconstruction of context junctures from verbal and nonverbal cues emerging from repeated viewings (by the researchers and the participants) of the videotaped interaction. The underlying thesis is that at principal junctures between contexts or occasions, "major reorientations of postural configurations (positions) occur among participants, and that across the duration of a principal part, these positions are sustained collectively" (Erickson & Schultz, 1977, p. 6). Other features such as changes in rate, inflection, speech style, topic, direction of gaze, and so forth can also serve as contextualization cues (Gumperz, 1976).

Erickson and Schultz list several types of evidence for a shift in context: (1) at those points that have been identified by the researcher's theoretic perspective as transitional from one context to another, objectively definable changes in contextualization cues are taking place; (2) after a point that has been independently identified as transitional, there are major changes either in the relative frequency and/or the sequential position of significant verbal or nonverbal behaviors from that which characterized them prior to the transition. (For example, there might be a significant decrease in group laughter or joking following a period in which there was a transition from "group orientation" to "task activity." The shift in context might be co-extensive with and heralded by shifts in group members' nonverbal behaviors such as greater forward lean, more erect posture, more direct body orientation, and so forth); (3) after the juncture, participants act as if the rules about what is or what is not proper have changed; for example, behaviors resulting in repair or sanction prior to the transition no longer seem to be treated the same way after the juncture. Thus, joking that might be frowned upon during "task activity" would once again be well received during the "back-patting" or reinforcement stage of the group session. Erickson and Schultz also regard it as important that participants who view film of the transition point and the activities on either side of it can confirm the kinds of analyses made in the three earlier steps.

When the presence of rules is inferred from less direct sources of evidence than audiotapes or videotapes of conversational interaction (for example, when evidence is elicited by asking subjects "what they might say" in such-and-such a situation), the researcher will probably want to use some version of a "scenario" method (Gibbs, 1981). For example, in studying the formulation of requests, Gibbs used scenarios like the following (1981, p. 433):

Psychology Dep't Office

You are taking a course in the Psychology department which you think is terrible. So, you decide to drop the class during the drop-add period. You need to have your drop-add card stamped by one of the people at the Psychology department office. You walk into the office and say to one of the people working behind the counter . . .

The strategy of presenting subjects with a description of a hypothetical situation that varies along some significant set of contextual dimensions has been used extensively in research on compliance-gaining and compliance-resisting messages (Miller, Boster, Roloff, & Seibold, 1977; McLaughlin et al., 1980; Cody et al., 1981). The researcher using this method is urged to pretest the scenarios extensively prior to her main study to determine that the hypothetical situations do indeed differ on the dimensions along which they are claimed to vary, and that they do not differ in other significant ways that are not accounted for in the researcher's model. Scales for the reliable and valid measurement of the situational variables *apprehension, intimacy,* and *dominance,* which can be used for validating any type of scenario, are presented in Cody, Woelfel, and Jordan (1983). Scales for measuring the situation variables of *personal benefits, resistance to persuasion, rights to make a request,* and the *relational consequences* of trying to gain compliance are also presented in Cody et al., and can be used to study the contextual determinants of requesting behavior and those of replies to requests.

Evidence that the rule has force. We have already dealt with the use of such manifestations of force as repair or sanction in our discussion of ways in which knowledge of a rule can be demonstrated. Clearly, one does not initiate repair if she is unaware that a rule has been broken, and similarly with the application of sanctions. However, it doesn't work the other way around; that is, knowledge of a rule is not sufficient to guarantee that its breach will be regarded as a cause for concern. The presence of repair or sanction is testimony to the fact that a rule has force. There are a number of ways in which a researcher could provide a convincing demonstration that a proposed rule has force, many of which have already been mentioned in other contexts. Searching conversational records for evidence of discontinuities or repair in the event of breach is one such method. An alternative would be to determine whether or not a significant proportion of the members of a particular language community would endorse propositions like "In context C, the action *a* is frequently prohibited," or "If I didn't do *a* in context C, people would think ill of me," or "In context C, *a* is just not done." Working from the other direction, one could inquire "In what contexts would people regard you as odd or ignorant if you did *a*?" (Adler, 1978). Another method, used by Planalp and Tracy (1980), Pearce and Conklin (1979), and Rosenstein and McLaughlin (1983), is to present subjects with examples of the phenomenon of interest showing conformity (or nonconformity, or partial conformity) to the rule and have them rate the author of the action as to competence, social skill, the appropriateness of his actions, and so on. Generally, it seems that the researcher will not uncover much evidence that rule-conforming behavior is *rewarded*, unless one is willing to regard the absence of notice or the lack of sanctions as rewarding. Asking subjects to recall occasions on which they broke some conversational rule, and the reaction of their listeners, if there had been any reaction, would result in a disproportionate number of recollections of instances in which the breach was treated as a serious error, and is not a recommended technique for establishing the force of a rule, although it is a fruitful method for collecting examples of repair.

The force of a constitutive rule lies in the fact that if it is not followed the speaker may fail to be understood. Jackson (1982, p. 14) has suggested that a claim to have discovered a constitutive rule can be tested by showing "what happens if each clause of the rule is subtracted." A demonstration of force in this sense could be accomplished by showing that an alternative formulation of an act to that called for by the rule would result in a breakdown in coherence; that is, that the act would be treated by its hearers as something other than what it was intended to be. Suppose we were interested in studying indirect requests, and we wanted to show that some rule for "how-to-do-an-indirect-request," such as Labov and Fanshel's (1977), had force. We could systematically alter each of the proposed preconditions and ask subjects to form an appropriate response to the resulting version. For example, we could manipulate the sincerity condition, or we could alter one of the postulates about the significance of a *question* regarding the hearer's ability to perform the action to one which states that an *assertion* about the hearer's ability to perform the action is heard as a request. We could then present the amended version (from "Can you loan me your pencil" to "You can loan me your pencil") and see if it makes a significant difference in response to the question, "What would you (the subject) say next?" That is, does the amendment result in a significant decline in the likelihood that the utterance will be treated as a request? If so, and this can be established for all the preconditions, then the amended rule clearly has force.

ISSUES RELATED TO EXPLANATORY ADEQUACY

Arguments Against Rules as Explanatory Constructs

Lindsay (1977, p. 162) has taken the position that rules are not very useful as explanatory constructs, for three reasons: (1) it is not always clear *whose* rules constitute the standard; (2) behavioral regularities in communication can be explained without recourse to rules; (3) "it is unclear what sanctions are applied when people use language irregularly." Lindsay's first point seems to speak to the fact that there may be innumerable rules, each subscribed to by a different set of persons, which cover the same behaviors in the identical contexts, yet rules theorists have not provided us with any coherent accounts as to why persons choose to follow one rule rather than another. For example, the college seniors today who must face the rigors of job interviewing with campus recruiters report that they have been advised by acquaintances in the business world to "dress for the positions you aspire to"; consequently, many of them come to feel they must attire themselves for the recruitment interview in custom-tailored suits and exorbitantly expensive watches and shoes, even though their last "position" may have been a summer stint at the car wash, and their business dress a pair of shorts. On the other hand, they are advised by their parents to "be themselves." What are the dimensions along which such decisions are made? And is it the task of the student of interaction to answer such questions? While Lindsay's point is a sore one for many rules theorists, it may be addressed to issues which are beyond the scope of the conversational analyst, for it invokes questions of reference group identification, source credibility, and other more "macro" factors than the analyst of talk is ordinarily interested in. What often happens in conversation, however, is that persons respond to contradictory injunctions in an integrative fashion, as for example in their replies to compliments, in which they try to honor simultaneously the systematic preference for agreement and the requirement that self-praise be avoided (Pomerantz, 1978). The conversational analyst is at least obligated to deal with the *methods* by which such competing injunctions can be seen to be resolved in the discourse, and to point out the characteristics of the population from which samples were drawn, at least in some rudimentary way, so that the factors that might influence members to favor one rule over another will be laid bare.

Lindsay's point that "irregular" language use does not lead in a straightforward manner to the consistent application of sanctions is a point that is very well taken. As was mentioned in the first chapter, people often adopt the *et cetera* perspective (Cicourel, 1973) and rather than mark, repair, or punish a breach, wait to see if subsequent developments in the conversation will resolve the matter. Indeed, if the consistent presence of sanctions following a violation were the only source of evidence available for inferring the operation of a rule, then we would be unlikely to make very much progress in that direction. For example, Mura's (1983) data suggest that many impending violations may be "licensed" before they occur.

Shimanoff (1980, pp. 97-99) has suggested a number of other reasons why sanctions might not be imposed: (1) the rule may not be very "intense," that is, very salient in the particular situation in which a breach occurred; (2) there may not be a great deal of consensus about the rule; (3) the deviation may be within the tolerance limits of the violator's interlocutors; (4) the imposition of the sanctions may be uncomfortable or face-threatening for the one who imposes them; (5) interlocutors may have overlooked the breach either inadvertently or deliberately; and (6) the violation may be recognized as a case of rule-exploitation, that is, a case of conversational implicature. Although Lindsay is correct in his assertaion that the violation-sanction relationship is ambiguous, there appears to be no serious obstacle to the analyst's offering orderly and systematic accounts of why sanctions were or were not imposed in particular cases.

Lindsay's claim that rules are "redundant," that is, that what they explain can be accounted for by other mechanisms (1977, p. 162), is his most serious charge. As has been brought up in other sections of the text, to be completely thorough the researcher needs to consider if there are any alternative plausible explanations for the regularities she has observed. Butterworth (1978, p. 318) argues that investigators must take into account alternative theories which focus on the same conversational behaviors. For example, a pause could derive from two distinct production mechanisms, one neurophysiological, having to do with the difficulty of decision, and the other communicative, as one might pause for dramatic effect (Butterworth, 1978, p. 318).

Butterworth's basic concern is that the complexity of conversational interaction not be underestimated:

> It should go without saying a conversation is an intricate phenomenon in which cognitive and neuromuscular skills are put at the disposal of a range of personal and social purposes, and the whole embedded in interlocking systems of social and linguistic conventions [1978, p. 318].

As an example, suppose one were to try and account for the determinants, in multiparty conversation, of floor-yielding in instances of simultaneous starts. What factors can be invoked to account for why one person continues to talk while the other one stops, even though both claimed the turn at the same time? The answer might lie in some sort of rule that relates the right to this particular slot to turn-incumbency, such that the person who had the floor prior to the last transition-relevance place is allowed to continue to hold the floor subsequent to it, unless neither had the floor prior to the immediately previous TRP, in which case no rule would apply, but rather such factors as which of the two had secured the gaze of the hearers, or which of the two had the greater vocal intensity, or both, would determine who would continue talking and who would desist.

There are many conversational phenomena that may be susceptible of explanation at multiple levels. Before committing himself wholeheartedly to a rule or convention as the mechanism responsible for producing the phenomenon in which he is interested, the researcher should ask himself the following question: Is this conversational behavior "preferred" in this context because its alternatives place greater demands on the information processing capacities of its recipients? It is possible that in the case of such conversational phenomena as the dispreferred status of interruption, the systemic preference for acceptances in replies to first pair parts, the greater ascribed "competence" of unambiguous topic shift devices, and the myriad instances in which conversationalists erect "signposts" for one another so that they will know how to proceed, all may be fundamentally explainable in terms of cognitive processes. In any event, several plausible explanations for a given bit of conversational behavior should be examined for "fit"; to do so can only serve to strengthen the credibility of any ultimate claim that a rule is the operative underlying mechanism.

The Superiority of Theories to "Stories"

Grimshaw (1974) has outlined the steps in analysis that lead to the ultimate recovery of structure in discourse and the reconstruction of rule-sets that account for that structure. At the first stage, which he terms "fine-grained anecdotal description," the conversational phenomena of interest are identified, and "once pattern and variation begin to emerge, taxonomies seem naturally to follow" (Grimshaw, 1974, p. 422). In subsequent steps, coding systems are developed, a grammar is written, and the grammar is taken back to the natural world of conversation to see if it can account for what is found there. Unfortunately, most research on conversation structure seems to be firmly rooted in the first stage, that of anecdotal description. The field is littered with taxonomies of every conceivable kind of device, many of which overlap so considerably that it is clear that few of us are reading each other's material. A perfect case in point has to do with the simple utterance "Uh huh" and its equivalents, which have been treated as *passing moves* by Clark and Haviland (1977), *minimal responses* by Fishman (1978) and by Zimmerman and West (1975), and as *passive strategies for being civilly egocentric* by Derber (1979), as well as *back-channel* or *listener responses* by Duncan (1972) and Rosenfeld and Hancks (1980) and others. The most notable thing about this body of literature, outside of the fact that few if any of the authors seem to reference each other, is that the phenomenon keeps being "rediscovered," but little has accumulated in the way of a body of solid, non-anecdotal evidence that the simple "Uh huh" is actively and intentionally used to discourage interaction or at least to avoid taking a turn, although both of these claims have been made for it. The only really replicated finding about "Uh huh" has been that, at least some of the time, there are fewer so-called speaker state signals emitted during its utterance than during longer utterances (although the reduction in speaker-state cues has also been found for mirror responses, repetitions, and so on). It has also been found that "Uh huh" tends to precede lapses or topic shifts, particularly when men say it to women, but it appears that "Uh huh" is less a cause of topic failure than it is a symptom of it.

The point is that there is a limit to the amount of descriptive work that a discipline can absorb, and the field of conversational research is already top-heavy with taxonomies, or, as Butterworth puts its, with "stories" (1978, p. 321):

> An investigator may refrain from rigorous quantification of the data, from the construction of formal models, from strict testing of theories against facts. Instead, he will adopt a research strategy in which he contents himself with telling a 'story', arguing perhaps that a more 'scientific' version will follow in due course, and that in any case stories are necessary precursors of formal models and rigorous quantification.

Butterworth argues that stories are less responsible scientifically than theories, that they are less replicable, less specific, less coherent, and have less coverage; that is, they fail to "exhaust the domain" in the way that a good theory does (1978, p. 376). Furthermore, theories are subject to revision in the event of a disconfirming case, while it is not clear what happens to stories. Theories also make clear which if any of their principles are presuppositions, and which classes of phenomena are not covered. For any description or taxonomic work, Butterworth suggest that there are two critical questions to ask before accepting its claims: (1) what were the methods and procedures used to arrive at the conclusions reached by the author(s)?; and (2) how can the author's claims be verified (more to the point, how can they be falsified—how can we recognize a counterexample?.

Jackson (1982) has proposed a defense for a method called "analytic induction," which some might regard as a method of stories, although Jackson and others regard it as rigorous. Analytic induction is characteristic of the approach to conversation of Schegloff et al., and others, in which examples are collected, the examples are used to construct a claim, the claim is tested to see if it can account for all the examples, and counterexamples are then sought (Jackson, 1982, p. 1). Under this method a claim can qualify as such only if it is possible to falsify it. Here is one point of departure from the Butterworth notion of a story. Take for example Schiffrin's (1980) work on "meta-talk" in conversation. The bulk of what Schiffrin reported could be summarized by saying that "there is a set of devices which parties to talk use to bracket discourse." According to Jackson, qualifying as a claim requires that the statement "commit the speaker to defending the existence of some state of affairs" (1982, p. 9), and that that commitment demands that the statement be falsifiable. Clearly, a thesis like Schiffrin's cannot be falsified, and so even though the research seems to fit the analytic induction mode, in fact, it does not because it fails to make a commitment to a claim.

Where the method of analytic induction does appear to conform more to the "story" than the "theory" model is that its methods are not ordinarily explicit, and consequently they are not replicable. There is usually not an adequate basis for accepting a claim, because not only are we usually not apprised of the dimensions of the search for examples and counterexamples, and not only are we frequently asked to accept made-up examples as evidence, but only rarely are we provided with an actual breakdown of the number of conforming and nonconforming cases in the corpus of conversations that serve as the data base. This latter problem could be dealt with were adherents of the method to follow the injunction to be *complete*, which we shall address shortly, but we still may be left with the problem of a complete account of data set whose parameters are unknown and which we could not hope to replicate were we to want to conduct our own investigation of the item of interest.

Again, it cannot be overemphasized that the credibility of any claim to have a model of a significant aspect of conversational structure lies first with the adequacy of the data base, and the ability of the researcher to provide both an explicit account of her methods of collecting evidence and a convincing argument that the examples in the data base are as representative as possible of the domain of contexts to which she wishes to generalize.

When Rules Fail:
Accounting for Nonconformity

One of the most interesting features of Jackson's (1982) account of the method of analytic induction is its insistence on *completeness:* "a proposed rule which allows for coherent, unremarkable deviations is a failure, and a single genuine counterexample is enough to require its revision" (p. 11). Given what we noted earlier about the numerous and varied reasons why a rule-violation might go unremarked or unsanctioned, the first assertion, that an unmarked breach means the rule is a failure, seems a little strict. Few of us, for example, correct our friends and acquaintances when they say things like "Hopefully, I can be there," "Between you and I," or "That one has less calories," but our failure to do so doesn't require us to toss our grammars and dictionaries out the window. Suppose that we have found strong empirical evidence of a regular pattern of co-occurence of some context and the behavior called for in that context by a proposed rule. Suppose further, however, that in about 10% of the cases the behavior required by the rule is not present. Do we have to discard the rule?

Let us consider the case in which we undertake a serious attempt to determine if there is a rule prohibiting interruption. Suppose that in a large corpus of dyadic conversations we looked at each "interact," that is, each pair of adjacent turns, to see if the B turn interrupted the A turn, using a definition in which forced discontinuity of the A turn was used to distinguish interruption from simple overlap. Suppose further that in our corpus of 1000 examples we found only 10 instances of interruption. How may we account for these deviations in a manner consistent with our claim that a rule prohibiting interruption is operative in the population from which the examples were drawn? Fuller (1969) has suggested a number of circumstances under which behavior may fail to conform to a rule. First, some individuals may not have knowledge of the rule. For example, the author of one of the interruptions might be from Antigua, where the norm of "contrapuntal noise" (Reisman, 1974) makes it not only acceptable, but even a good idea to start talking once someone else does. It may also be that the rule is not very specific. For example, some people may think that it is acceptable to interrupt as long as what you say seems to be supportive of the other person, or if there's something that just can't wait. Interruptions may occur because the rule prohibiting them is superseded by other rules. As was brought out in Chapter 3, a person might interrupt to keep a partner from telling things he oughtn't (violating the Morality maxim); to repair a violation of the Quality maxim (for example, one's interlocutor may be exaggerating); or to repair an apparent breach of the Relevance maxim before total confusion sets in. One might violate the injunction against interruption because she believes that it doesn't apply in this particular case; for example, that whenever one is talking with a friend or relative, interruptions will be tolerated. If the rule is regarded as tentative, one might violate it just to see what happens; thus, for example, an interruption might be undertaken as a test of power—to see whether or not one could override the other and get away with it. Finally, the rule would be more likely to be violated if the perpetrator believed that there would be no penalty imposed in the event of a breach. Interruptions often go unmarked since to comment upon them is usually interpreted as a sign that one is being overly defensive, resulting in the violator's feeling that he can interrupt with impunity, and even increase his advantage should the victim protest. If the investigator is alert to these possibilities *before* data is collected, then procedures for assessing each plausible source of breach can be built into her research design.

DIRECTIONS FOR FUTURE RESEARCH

Perhaps at some point in the six previous chapters the reader has been struck by the fact that the bulk of the work on conversational organization derives from one of just three theoretical postures: the claim of Austin (1962) and later Searle (1975) that the happy performance of a speech act results from the satisfaction of a set of preconditions, such as that the speaker is sincere, that she wants the hearer to recognize her intent in speaking, and so on; the proposal by Grice (1975) and later Bach and Harnish (1979), Edmondson (1981a) and others of a set of *maxims* or assumptions about conversational organization that hearers know that speakers may exploit for various communicative purposes; and the proposal by Schegloff (1972) that the principle of *conditional relevance* underlies the local or turn-by-turn organization of speech acts. What is remarkable is not that these theoretical positions have found so many adherents, but rather that they have found so few skeptics; that is to say, the majority of the work stimulated by these landmark studies has been of the "spin-off" variety. Thus, for example, we have Quality, Quantity, Relevance, and Manner hedges (Brown & Levinson, 1978), and Quality, Quantity, Relevance, and Manner "licenses" (Mura, 1983), and so on. While speech act theory is being put to interesting uses by cognitive scientists interested in computer modeling of conversation, in terms of its applications to problems in conversations between real people, speech act theory seems to have become stuck in a rut, with researchers showing lots of interest in indirect requests, and very little interest in anything else.

Little if any of the work deriving from speech act theory or from the Gricean maxims framework has been of the nature of a test of the original claims. It would seem to be an obvious thing to do, for example, to see if indeed there are any real differences in the way *conventionally indirect speech* and *conversational implicatures* are encoded, understood, and treated in conversation. Similarly, few investigators have shown any interest in finding out if breaches of conversational maxims are indeed literally processed as "error" before giving rise in implicature. If, indeed, the use of such devices as the Quality hedge, or the Quantity license, or the Cognitive disclaimer, constitutes a significant conversational event, why is there no evidence to indicate that they occur with any frequency, or that they do the job that their discoverers claim that they do?

Similar problems arise when we examine the literature on adjacency pairs and other realizations of the "conditional relevance" notion. Not only have there been no serious efforts to account for *why* some acts set up expectations that other particular acts will follow, but hard evidence that adjacency-pair organization is pervasive is simply not there. The extensive attention devoted to the adjacency pair notion has tended to restrict analyses of conversational coherence to local, utterance-to-utterance relationships to the exclusion of more global relations between utterances and the context sets in which they are embedded. Further, the emphasis on adjacency-pair organization has tended to focus researchers' attentions only on the functional organization of conversational interaction, such that study of propositional macrostructures and topic have been relatively neglected.

It is hoped that future research on conversational organization will reflect one or more of the following priorities: (1) greater attention to the role of propositional macrostructures in accounting for conversational coherence. For example, can we find evidence for the

collaborative organization of macrorules such as construction, deletion, and generalization? Can such evidence be found in the discourse
itself? How well do story grammars model conversational storytelling?
(2) greater effort should be directed to uncovering the devices by
which locutions are made relevant to one another at the utterance-by-
utterance level. For example, what are the dimensions that underlie
textual sources of cohesion such as anaphora, ellipsis, and so on?
What are the factors accounting for variation in propositional
linkages such as Contrast, Parallel, Elaboration, and so forth? (3)
increased emphasis on how constraints imposed by demands for
functional relevance affect topic development, and vice versa. For
example, how does the "propositional content condition" for the
happy performance of a speech act constrain the kinds of replies one
can make to offers, requests, assertions, and so on? How does topical
organization at the global level restrict our freedom to perform
certain kinds of "underground" speech acts, such as a "brag," a
"cut" or a "pry"? (4) greater attention to the goal-directed efforts of
actors to achieve their aims through talk. For example, in what ways
can speakers compress or maneuver topical structures to accomplish
their purposes, and under what circumstances do local requirements
for relevance, as well as other higher-order rules and assumptions,
function as obstacles to goal-attainment? (5) reconsideration of the
notion of "preferredness" in terms of cognitive factors, especially
information processing time or decision difficulty. For example, are
agreements "preferred" because they are reinforcing to the speaker,
or because they don't create a need for new decisions to be made that
might require the speaker to alter her plans? Is there some other
reason why agreements are preferred? These five priorities collectively reflect a desire for increased emphasis on the role of cognitive
processes, particularly planning, in the application and exploitation
of conversational rules.

Glossary

Absolutist formulation: A statement summing up the speaker's assessment of the sense and implication of the conversation-so-far, expressed in all-or-nothing terms, which forecloses the possibility of further topical talk.

Access rituals: Sequences serving to open or close conversations.

Account sequence: A sequence, precipitated by the response to some failure event, consisting of a reproach, an account, and an evaluation of the account.

Activities of partitioning: Formulaic phrases used as guidance devices in conversation.

Adjacency pairs: Expandable pairs of adjacently placed speech acts in which the first establishes a "slot" for the performance of the second, and the second "satisfies" the demand expressed in the first.

Antecedence maxim: A maxim that the speaker is required to see to it that the "old" or given information in any utterance has a unique antecedent.

Apodosis: The "then-clause" of a rule, which indicates what behaviors are required or prohibited given the particular circumstances which the rule covers.

A posteriori presuppositions: Implicit propositions that can be derived from propositions explicit in the discourse itself.

A priori presuppositions: Implicit propositions that are believed to pertain prior to the conversation.

Argument: A discourse unit built around the expansion of an initiating speech act or proffer, and its dispreferred reply.

Back-channel utterances: Brief arguments, repetitions, or mirror responses by a listener that are believed to occur primarily during pauses in the turn of the speaker who has the floor; usually characterized by a reduced set of the normal speaker-state signals.

Bridging proposition: A supplied proposition that helps a hearer to locate an element or entity that has been ambiguously referenced.

Chained exchange: One in which all of the proffers appear to have the same ultimate goals, and whose pairs of subordinate exchanges all have the same upshot.

Closed exchange: One whose initiating move is satisfied by its reply.

Coherence: The sense in which a discourse may be said to "hang together"; the relevance of its successive utterances both to those that precede them and to the global concerns of the discourse as a whole.

Cohesion: The property of a conversation that its successive utterances can be seen to be about the same set of elements, usually evidenced through such devices as anaphora that are visible in the conversational text.

Common scheme of reference: A set of interpretive procedures or assumptions, such as that communicators have reciprocal perspectives, that language indexes larger meaning systems, that persons are consistent, that social episodes have normal forms, and so on.

Communicative illocutionary act: One in which the speaker not only intends for the hearer to recognize his attitude toward the proposition expressed in his utterance, but also to recognize that he hopes to have some effect on the hearer.

Communicative presumption: That in *saying* something, the speaker is trying to *do* something.

Condition of breach: The property of a rule, as distinct from a law, that it can be broken; that one can choose not to follow a rule.

Conditional relevance: A property of the functional organization of interaction that some speech acts appear to establish "slots" for the subsequent performance of other speech acts, such that the failure to provide the called-for speech act may be marked, repaired, or sanctioned.

Conference pass: A speech act in which the speaker shifts the burden of responding to a proffer to some third party, using the pretext of requiring another opinion.

Constitutive rules: Rules that define how social practices are constituted, or which behaviors are to "count" as particular acts.

Context set: Also described as a common ground or information structure. A stored tree of explicit propositions and presuppositions against which each successive utterance is evaluated.

Context space: A series of utterances that taken together constitute a unit or whole, such as the event-recounting portion of a narrative.

Conventional indirectness: Reference to the preconditions for the successful performance of actions to accomplish acts that might threaten face if performed more directly.

Conversation: Relatively informal social interaction in which the roles of speaker and hearer are exchanged in a nonautomatic fashion under the collaborative management of all parties.

Conversational implicature: An interpretive process that is invoked by an apparently deliberate violation of one of the conversational maxims, by a speaker who appears on all other counts to be cooperating; working out that the speaker means more than what he has literally said.

Conversational plan: A cognitive representation of a goal and a series of speech acts that can be undertaken to realize the goal.

Conversational postulates: Constitutive rules about the conventional ways of performing certain indirect speech acts.

Cooperative principle: The mutual belief of communicators that a contribution to conversation will be that which appears to be appropriate and necessary according to the common understandings of the purpose and destination of the particular exchange.

Current-speaker-selects-next technique: A name for a collection of devices for designating which party is to take the next turn in conversation.

Demand ticket: The first speech act in a summons-answer sequence.

Disclaimers: Devices to alert hearers that a forthcoming utterance by the speaker should not be regarded as grounds for viewing him as irrational, ill-informed, prejudiced, and so on.

Discourse bracket: A management speech act whose function is to set off discourse chunks that have coherent internal structures, such as stories or accounts.

Disjunct marker: A device for demonstrating that upcoming talk will appear to violate the injunction to be relevant.

Dismissal: A technique for "erasing" an attack or reproach, and/or for causing it to be withdrawn.

Et cetera procedure: An interpretive procedure that permits a listener to reserve judgment on the meaning of a problematic utterance until subsequent conversational developments have had a chance to provide clarification.

Event context space: A series of successive utterances having to do with a sequence of actions that constituted some episode.

Exchange: A minimal conversational unit consisting of an initiating move and a responding move.

Face-threatening act: A speech act that threatens the positive face of the speaker or hearer, that is, their desire to be regarded as worthy of approval; or the negative face of either party, that is their desire for autonomy and freedom from imposition.

Focus: The priority given to a discourse element; that is, the extent to which the element is of major or minor importance in a discourse segment.

Force: The property of a rule that people choose to follow it, and that failure to follow it may result in unwanted notice, repair, or sanction.

Formulation: A statement by either speaker summarizing his sense of the conversation-so-far.

Functional organization: The action structure of conversation, that is, the organization of speech acts in terms of such factors as the principle of conditional relevance.

Global topic: The overriding idea or macroproposition of a discourse.

Hesitation pause: A brief pause within the turn of a single speaker, usually associated with encoding.

Illocutionary act: What we are *doing*, as opposed to *saying*, in an utterance, particularly that which we intend for the hearer to recognize as our purpose in saying that thus-and-so.

Initiative time latency: A longer pause bounded on both sides by talk by the same speaker; regarded as the time elapsing between the intended yielding of the floor by a speaker, and her resumption of it given the failure of her partner to take the floor

Instigating: Using narrative to create conflict between one's hearers and a third party, by recounting an episode in which the third party is shown to have acted in ways inimical to the hearer's interests.

Intended perlocutionary effect: The goal an illocutionary act is designed to achieve.

Interpretive procedures: Organized knowledge bases about how to interpret contexts so that rules may be applied appropriately.

Interruption: A case of simultaneous talk in which the turn of the speaker with the prior claim to the floor is cut short of its projectable point of completion.

Issue context space: A coherent, internally consistent set of utterances devoted to setting forth the issue or point of some larger segment of discourse.

Lapse: A silence of 3.0 or more seconds occurring at a transition-relevance place, in a focused, dyadic conversation.

Licenses: Preventatives addressed to forthcoming violations of the maxims of Quantity, Quality, Relevance, or Manner.

Linguistic presumption: That persons within the same language communities can make out the sense and reference of each other's utterances, given a sufficient vocabulary and background knowledge.

Local coherence relations: Ways in which appropriate continuations of an immediately prior utterance can be made.

Local relevance: The property of an utterance that it is pertinent to, or appears occasioned by, that which immediately preceded it in the conversation, regardless of its pertinence to the global topic or purpose of the interaction.

Locution: What one *says* in an utterance, as opposed to what one does in or by it; the literal sense of an utterance.

Macroact: The global speech act that organized a conversation, possibly consisting of a main act under which are nested one or more subordinate acts, or, a series of co-equal acts whose combined impact constitutes the implicit point of the discourse.

Macroproposition: An overriding proposition that organizes conversation and accounts for its coherence.

Macrorules: Operations such as deletion and generalization which are performed on cognitive representations of the conversational structure as it develops and changes over the course of an interaction.

Macrostructure: A cognitive representation of the topical and/or functional structure of discourse, usually hierarchical in nature, containing both explicit and implied propositions and their attendant meanings as speech acts.

Management acts: Speech acts that parties use to instruct one another in where they have been, conversationally, and where they are going.

Manner maxim: A maxim that one ought to refrain from being excessively obscure, ambiguous, verbose, or unorganized in her speech.

Marked repeat: A explicit device for marking the relevance of an upcoming topic to the previous talk.

Maxims: Widely held assumptions that it is the expected behavior of conversationalists to provide accurate, economical, clear, polite, ethical, and supportive contributions to spoken interaction.

Morality maxim: A maxim that one ought not to say that which she was told in confidence, nor should she ask for privileged information to be divulged; further, that one ought not to do for the hearer what he is uninterested in having done for him.

"No later" constraint: The requirement that an interruption be placed at a point at which it is still possible to demonstrate that the interrupting speaker already knows or has grasped the upshot of the interrupted speaker's utterance.

"No Sooner" constraint: The requirement that an interruption not be initiated until the interrupting speaker has heard enough to be able to make her contribution relevant.

O.K. pass: Brief listener response thought to signal that one is declining to take a turn, also called a minimal response.

Opportunistic planning: Taking advantage of current developments in an action sequence to adjust or restructure plans for achieving some particular goal; being reminded of a possible way to proceed by current conversational events.

Overlap: An instance of simultaneous talk occurring near a transition-relevance place, in which there is no externally prompted discontinuity in the turn of the speaker with the prior claim to the floor.

Performatives: Verbs that when uttered are claimed to constitute the performance of some act.

Perlocutionary effect: The effect that a speech has on the hearer.

Phonemic clause: A unit of speech with only one primary stress, which terminates in either a rising or falling intonation contour.

Politeness maxim: A maxim that one ought not to say that which is offensive, vulgar, or rude.

Pragmatic connectives: Words like or, but, and, if, and so on which signal the illocutionary force of an impending utterance.

Pragmatic topic: The speaker's ultimate goal; the conventional perlocutionary effect of the speaker's global act.

Preconditions: One of the clauses of a constitutive rule: a requirement for the successful performance of a speech act.

Preference for agreement: A systematic tendency for disagreeable or potentially troublesome replies to initiating moves to be structurally delayed in conversation.

Preference for self-repair: The systematic tendency for other-initiated and other-accomplished corrections of violations of grammatical, syntactic, and/or conversational rules to be structurally delayed in conversation relative to self-initiated and/or self-accomplished repair.

Presupposition: A proposition that is not expressed but which by virtue of its being understood and accepted by conversational parties supplies cohesion to the successive turns at talk.

Preventatives: Devices used to obtain permission for the speaker to violate conversational rules.

Principle of charity: A principle that the behavior of the speaker should be construed so as to credit her with as few violations as possible of conversational maxims.

Processing pass: A speech act in which one speaker transfers the burden of responding to some sort of proffer to a third party.

Proffer: The initiating move in an exchange.

Property of alteration: The property of rules that they can be canceled, changed, or replaced.

Propositional approach: An approach to conversational coherence whose adherents regard conversation as being about an overriding idea or macroproposition.

Propositional organization: The topical structure of conversation; the organization of expressed ideas and presuppositions.

Prospectiveness: Degree of sequential implicativeness of a speech act; the extent to which a preceding act narrows the range of acts that could be performed as a coherent next turn.

Protasis: The "if-clause" of a rule, which specifies the circumstances under which the rule applies.

Quality maxim: A maxim that one only say that which he knows to be true, and/or for which he possesses sufficient evidence.

Quantity maxim: The maxim that one's contribution to conversation be neither too brief nor too lengthy, but rather what is required.

Reciprocal exchange: One in which the outcome of a second exchange reverses the benefits and costs to speaker and hearer of an immediately prior exchange.

Recycling: Opening sequences that have been done over because of mistaken identities or failures of recognition.

Referent approach: An approach to conversational cohesion based upon the examination of devices by which successive utterances in a discourse can be seen to be about the same referents or entities.

Regulative rules: Rules that prescribe what should or should not be done given a particular set of circumstances or sequence of acts.

Relevance maxim: A maxim that a conversational contribution appear to pertain to the current context in terms of topical and/or functional structure.

Remedial legislation: Activity undertaken to establish new rules or new understandings about rules that will govern subsequent interactions, given that the old ones have failed.

Repetition pass: A mirror response thought to signify that the opportunity to take the floor is being declined.

Rule: A proposition that models our understandings of the situated evaluation of social behavior, and the ways in which social interaction should be constituted and carried out.

Rule-according behavior: Behavior that results from an actor's automatic conformity to a rule that she knows, but makes no particular point of following.

Rule-breaking behavior: Behavior in which the actor deliberately fails to conform to the rule.

Rule-following behavior: Behavior that results from the conscious design of an actor to conform to the rule.

Rule-fulfilling behavior: Behavior that happens to conform to the rule, even though the actor is unaware that there is a rule.

Rule-ignorant behavior: Behavior that fails to conform to the rule because the actor is unaware of the rule.

Rule-violating behavior: Behavior in which the actor inadvertently or accidentally fails to conform to the rule.

Satisfy: The responding move in an exchange, which fulfills the purpose for which the exchange was initiated; the second move in a closed exchange.

Sequence: A series of three or more speech acts, which constitutes a self-contained discourse unit with a coherent internal structure. In some sequences, each act in the sequence may be functionally dependent or conditionally relevant upon the act that precedes it.

Sequential implicativeness: The property of reducing the number of possible strategies for making a coherent next contribution.

Side sequence: A sequence, consisting minimally of three acts—a request for repair, a remedy, and an acknowledgement—in which parties detour from topical talk to rectify or clarify some tangential issue raised by that talk.

Significance statement: A proposition that establishes the point of a narrative for the hearer, especially in terms of the implications of the narrative for subsequent talk.

Sociocentric sequence: A brief nonreferential expression occurring just slightly after a transition-relevance place, usually interpreted as a turn-yielding signal.

Speech act: What one *does* in saying that thus and so.

Story grammar: A set of rules for describing the structural regularities of texts corresponding to a particular kind of canonical structure, involving minimally an episode and the setting in which it occurs.

Story sequencing device: A device for displaying the relevance of one's own story to a previous recounting.

Storytelling: A coherent conversational unit consisting of a preface sequence, a telling sequence in which some event is recounted, minimally an episode and its setting, and a listener response sequence.

Substantive speech acts: The functional or pragmatic content of conversation; the assertions and agreements, the questions and answers that make up its substance.

Summons-answer sequence: A three-party sequence in which A summons B, B answers the summons, and A discloses the reason(s) for having issued the summons in the first place.

Switching pause: A silence bounded on either side by talk by different speakers.

Tangential talk: Talk that is directed not to the underlying issue or point of some narrative or stretch of talk, but that appears to be locally relevant because it exploits a topical pathway from some minor element or character in the narrative.

TCU-reserving devices: Devices for claiming a block of speaking time, that is, more than one turn-constructional unit at a time.

Top-down planning: Mapping out a strategy or action sequence that when carried out will lead to the realization of a particular goal or goals; for instance, making a list of questions before telephoning the doctor.

Topic-initiating sequences: Sequences that serve to open sections of topical talk.

Transitional-relevance place: A possible place for an exchange of the speaker-hearer role, usually coinciding with a point of grammatical completeness, in the presence of turn-yielding cues such as falling or rising intonation and cessation of gesture.

Transparent question: Also known as an indirect answer or indirect response. An obvious closed-ended question used to implicate the answer to another obvious, closed-ended question.

Turn: A structural slot, within which a speaker has the right to one turn-constructional unit, renewable with the consent of the other parties.

Turn-constructional unit: A basic unit of conversation, such as an independent clause, which is allotted to speakers one at a time, with option for renewal.

Utterance: A spoken proposition: a unit of speech corresponding to a single sentence or independent clause.

References

ADLER, K. On the falsification of rules theories. *The Quarterly Journal of Speech*, 1978, 64, 427-438.

ALBERT, S., & KESSLER, S. Ending social encounters. *Journal of Experimental Social Psychology*, 1978, 14, 541-553.

ARGYLE, M., LALLJEE, M., & COOK, M. The effects of visibility on interaction in a dyad. *Human Relations*, 1968, 21, 3-17.

ARKOWITZ, H., LICHENSTEIN, E., McGOVERN, K., & HINES, P. The behavioral assessment of social competence in males. *Behavior Therapy*, 1975, 6, 3-13.

AULD, F., Jr., & WHITE, A. M. Rules for dividing interviews into sentences. *The Journal of Psychology*, 1956, 42, 273-281.

AUNE, B. *Knowledge, mind, and nature.* New York: Random House, 1967.

AUSTIN, J. L. *How to do things with words.* Oxford: Oxford University Press, 1962.

BACH, K., & HARNISH, R. M. *Linguistic communication and speech acts.* Cambridge, MA: The MIT Press, 1979.

BALL, P. Listeners' responses to filled pauses in relation to floor apportionment. *British Journal of Social and Clinical Psychology*, 1975, 14, 423-424.

BEACH, W. A., & JAPP, P. Storifying as time-traveling: The knowledgeable use of temporally structured discourse. In R. Bostrom (Ed.), *Communication Yearbook 7.* New Brunswick, NJ: Transaction, 1983.

BEATTIE, G. W. Floor apportionment and gaze in conversational dyads. *British Journal of Clinical Psychology*, 1978, 17, 7-15.

BEATTIE, G. W. Contextual constraints on the floor apportionment function of gaze in dyadic conversation. *British Journal of Clinical and Social Psychology*, 1979, 18, 391-392.

BEAUGRANDE, R. de. Text, discourse, and process: Towards a multidisciplinary science of texts. In R. O. Freedle (Ed.), *Advances in discourse processes*, Vol. IV. Norwood, NJ: Ablex Publishing, 1980.

BELL, R. A., ZAHN, C. J., & HOPPER, R. Disclaiming: A test of two competing views. *Communication Quarterly*, in press.

BENOIT, P. *Structural coherence production in the conversations of preschool children.* Paper presented at the meeting of the Speech Communication Association, New York, November, 1980.

BERGER, C. R. The covering law perspective as a theoretical basis for the study of human communication. *Communication Quarterly*, 1977, 25, 7-18.

BERNSTEIN, B. Social class, linguistic codes, and grammatical elements. *Language and Speech,* 1962, 5, 221-240.

BENNETT, A. Interruptions and the interpretation of conversation. *Discourse Processes,* 1981, 4, 171-188.

BIGLAN, A., GLASER, S. R., & DOW, M. G. Conversational skills training for social anxiety: An evaluation of its validity. Unpublished manuscript, University of Oregon, 1980. Cited in M. G. Dow, S. R. Glaser, & A. Biglan, *The relevance of specific conversational behaviors to ratings of social skills: A review of experimental analysis.* Paper presented at the meeting of the Speech Communication Association, New York, November 1980.

BIZANZ, G. L. Knowledge of persuasion and story comprehension: Developmental changes in expectations. *Discourse Processes,* 1982, 5, 245-277.

BLAU, P. M. *Exchange and power in social life.* New York: John Wiley, 1964.

BLEIBERG, S., & CHURCHILL, L. Notes on confrontation in conversation. *Journal of Psycholinguistic Research,* 1975, 4, 273-279.

BLUMSTEIN, P. The honoring of accounts. *American Sociological Review,* 1974, 39, 551-566.

BOOMER, D. S. Hesitation and grammatical encoding. *Language and Speech,* 1965, 8, 148-158.

BOWERS, J. W. Dows a duck have antlers? Some pragmatics of "transparent questions." *Communication Monographs,* 1982, 42, 63-69.

BOWERS, J. W., ELLIOT, N. D., & DESMOND, R. J. Exploiting pragmatic rules: devious messages. *Human Communication Research,* 1977, 3, 235-242.

BRADAC, J. J., HOSMAN, L. A., & TARDY, C. H. Reciprocal disclosures and language intensity: Attributional consequences. *Communication Monographs,* 1978, 45, 1-17.

BRADLEY, P. H. The folk-linguistics of women's speech: An empirical examination. *Communication Monographs,* 1981, 48, 73-90.

BROWN, P., & LEVINSON, S. Universals in language usage: Politeness phenomena. In E. Goody (Ed.), *Questions and politeness: Strategies in social interaction.* Cambridge: Cambridge University Press, 1978.

BRITTAN, A. *Meanings and situations.* London: Routledge & Kegan Paul, 1973.

BUTTERWORTH, B. Maxims for studying conversation. *Semiotica,* 1978, 24, 317-339.

CANARY, D. J., RATLEDGE, N. T., & SIEBOLD, D. R. *Argument and group decision-making: Development of a coding scheme.* Paper presented at the meeting of the Speech Communication Association, Louisville, November, 1982.

CANTOR, N., MISCHEL, W., & SCHWARTZ, J. C. A prototype analysis of psychological situations. *Cognitive Psychology,* 1982, 14, 45-77.

CAPPELLA, J. N. Mutual influence in expressive behavior: Adult-adult and infant-adult dyadic interaction. *Psychological Bulletin,* 1981, 89, 101-132.

CAPPELLA, J., & GREENE, J. R. There ought to be a law against rules: Shimnoff's approach to then. *The Quarterly Journal of Speech,* 1982, 68, 431-434.

CAPPELLA, J., & PLANALP, S. Talk and silence sequences in informal conversations III: Interspeaker influence. *Human Communication Research,* 1981, 7, 117-132.

CHAIKIN, A. L., & DERLEGA, V. J. *Self-disclosure.* Morristown, NJ: General Learning Press, 1974.

CHERRY, L., & LEWIS, M. Mothers and two year olds: A study of sex differentiated aspects of verbal interaction. *Development Psychology,* 1976, 12, 278-282.

CHOMSKY, N. *Aspects of the theory of syntax.* Cambridge: MA: MIT Press, 1965.

CICOUREL, A. V. *Cognitive sociology: Language and meaning in social interaction.* London: Cox and Wyman, 1973.

CLARK, H. H., & FRENCH, J. W. Telephone goodbyes. *Language in Society,* 1981, 10, 1-19.

CLARK, H. H., & LUCY, P. Understanding what is meant from what is said: A study in conversationally conveyed requests. *Journal of Verbal Learning and Verbal Behavior,* 1975, 14, 56-72.

CLARK, H. H., & HAVILAND, S. E. Comprehension and the given-new contract. In R. O. Freedle (Ed.), *Discourse production and comprehension.* Norwood, NJ: Ablex Publishing, 1977.

CODY, M. J. A typology of disengagement strategies and an examination of the role intimacy, reactions to inequity and relational problems play in strategy selection. *Communication Monographs,* 1982, 49, 148-170.

CODY, M. J., ERICKSON, K. V., & SCHMIDT, W. *Conversation and humor: A look into the utility of some joke prefacing devices.* Paper presented at the meeting of the Speech Communication Association, Washington, November, 1983.

CODY, M. J., & McLAUGHLIN, M. L. Perceptions of compliance-gaining situations: A dimensional analysis. *Communication Monographs,* 1980, 47, 132-148.

CODY, M. J., McLAUGHLIN, M. L., & SCHNEIDER, M. J. The impact of relational consequences and intimacy on the selection of interpersonal persuasion tactics: A reanalysis. *Communication Quarterly,* 1981, 29, 91-106.

CODY, M. J., O'HAIR, H. D., & SCHNEIDER, M. J. *The impact of intimacy, rights to resist, Machiavellianism, and psychological gender on compliance-resisting strategies: How pervasive are response effects in communication surveys?* Paper presented at the meeting of the International Communication Association, Boston, May, 1982.

CODY, M. J., WOELFEL, M. L., & JORDAN, W. J. Dimensions of compliance-gaining stiuations. *Human Communication Research,* 1983, 9, 99-113.

COHEN, P. R., & PERRAULT, C. R. A plan-based theory of speech acts. *Cognitive Science,* 1979, 3, 213-230.

COLLETT, P. The rules of conduct. In P. Collett (Ed.), *Social rules and social behavior.* Totowa, NJ: Rowman and Littlefield, 1977.

COOK, M., & LALLJEE, M. G. Verbal substitutes for vocal signals in interaction. *Semiotica,* 1972, 6, 212-221.

COZBY, P. G. Self-disclosure, reciprocity, and liking. *Sociometry,* 1972, 35, 151-160.

CRAWFORD, J. R. Utterance rules, turn-taking, and attitudes in enquiry openers. *IRAL,* 1977, 15, 279-298.

CREIDER, C. A. Thematisation in Luo. In P. Werth (Ed.), *Conversation and discourse: Structure and interpretation.* New York: St. Martin's, 1981.

CRONEN, V. E., & DAVIS, L. K. Alternative approaches for the communication theorist: Problems in the laws-rules-systems trichotomy. *Human Communication Research,* 1978, 4, 120-128.

CROSBY, F., & NYQUIST, L. The female register: An empirical study of Lakoff's hypothesis. *Language in Society,* 1978, 6, 313-322.

CROTHERS, E. J. Inference and coherence. *Discourse Processes,* 1978, 1, 51-71.

DAVIS, J. D. Self-disclosure in an acquaintance exercise: Responsibility for level of intimacy. *Journal of Personality and Social Psychology,* 1976, 33, 787-792.

DELIA, J. G. Alternative perspectives for the study of human communication: Critique and response. *Communication Quarterly,* 1977, 25, 46-62.

DERBER, C. *The pursuit of attention: Power and individualism in everyday life.* Boston: G. K. Hall, 1979.

DIJK, T. A. van. *Macrostructures: An interdisciplinary study of global structures in discourse, interaction, and cognition.* Hillsdale, NJ: Lawrence Erlbaum Associates, 1980.

DIJK, T. A. van. *Studies in the pragmatics of discourse.* The Hague: Mouton, 1981.

DITTMAN, A. T., & LLEWELLYN, L. G. The phonemic clause as a unit of speech decoding. *Journal of Personality and Social Psychology,* 1967, 6, 341-349.

DITTMAN, A. T., & LLEWELLYN, L. G. Relationship between vocalization and head nods as listener responses. *Journal of Personality and Social Psychology,* 1968, 9, 78-84.

DONOHUE, W. A. Development of a model of rule use in negotiation interaction. *Communication Monographs,* 1981, 48, 106-120.

DOW, M. G., GLASER, S. R., & BIGLAN, A. *The relevance of specific conversational behaviors to ratings of social skill: A review and experimental analysis.* Paper presented at the meeting of the Speech Communication Association, New York, November, 1980.

DUCK, S. Interpersonal communication in developing acquaintance. In G. R. Miller (Ed.), *Explorations in interpersonal communication.* Beverly Hills, CA: Sage, 1976.

DUNCAN, S., Jr. Some signals and rules for taking speaking turns in conversations. *Journal of Personality and Social Psychology,* 1972, 23, 283-292.

DUNCAN, S., Jr. Toward a grammar for dyadic conversation. *Semiotica,* 1973, 9, 29-46.

DUNCAN, S., Jr., & FISKE, D. W. *Face-to-face interaction: Research, methods, and theory.* New York: John Wiley, 1977.

DUNCAN, S., & NIEDEREHE, G. On signalling that it's your turn to speak. *Journal of Experimental Social Psychology,* 1974, 10, 234-247.

DUVAL, S., & WICKLUND, R. *A theory of objective self-awareness.* New York: Academic Press, 1972.

EDELSKY, C. Who's got the floor? *Language in Society,* 1981, 10, 383-421.

EDER, D. The impact of management and turn-allocation activities on student performance. *Discourse Processes,* 1982, 5, 147-160.

EDMONDSON, W. J. Illocutionary verbs, illocutionary acts, and conversational behavior. In H. Eikmeyer & H. Reiser (Eds.), *Words, worlds, and contexts.* Berlin and New York: Walter de Gruyter, 1981. (a)

EDMONDSON, W. J. *Spoken discourse: A model for analysis.* London: Longman, 1981. (b)

EDMONDSON, W. J. On saying you're sorry. In F. Coulmas (Ed.), *Conversational routine: Explorations in standardized communication situations and prepatterned speech.* New York: The Hague, 1981. (c)

ELLIS, D. G., HAMILTON, M., & AHO, L. Some issues in conversation coherence. *Human Communication Research,* 1983, 9, 267-282.

ERICKSON, F., & SCHULTZ, J. When is a context? Some issues and methods in the analysis of social competence. *Institute for Comparative Human Development,* 1977, 1, 5-10.

ERVIN-TRIPP, S. On sociolinguistic rules: Alternation and co-occurrence. In J. J. Gumperz & D. Hymes (Eds.), *Directions in sociolinguistics: The ethnography of communication.* New York: Holt, Rinehart & Winston, 1972.

FELDSTEIN, S., & WELKOWITZ, J. A chronography of conversation: In defense of an objective approach. In A. W. Siegman & S. Feldstein (Eds.), *Nonverbal behavior and communication.* Hillsdale, NJ: Erlbaum, 1978.

FENIGSTEIN, A., SCHEIER, M. F., & BUSS, A. H. Public and private self consciousness: Assessment and theory. *Journal of Consulting and Clinical Psychology,* 1975, 43, 522-527.

FERGUSON, C. A. The structure and use of politeness formulas. *Language in Society,* 1976, 5, 137-151.

FERGUSON, N. H. Simultaneous speech, interruptions, and dominance. *British Journal of Social and Clinical Psychology,* 1977, 16, 295-302.

FERRARA, A. An extended theory of speech acts: Appropriateness conditions for subordinate acts in sequences. *Journal of Pragmatics,* 1980, 4, 233-252. (a)

FERRARA, A. Appropriateness conditions for entire sequences of speech acts. *Journal of Pragmatics,* 1980, 4, 321-340. (b)

FINE, J., & BARTOLUCCI, G. Cohesion and retrieval categories in normal and disturbed communication: A methodological note. *Discourse Processes,* 1981, 4, 267-270.

FIRTH, J. R. *The tongues of men and speech.* London: Oxford University Press, 1964.

FISHMAN, P. M. Interaction: The work women do. *Social Problems,* 1978, 25, 397-406.

FORGAS, J. P. The perception of social episodes: Categorical and dimensional representations of two different social milieus. *Journal of Personality and Social Psychology,* 1976, 34, 199-209.

FOSTER, S. Learning to develop a topic. *Papers and Reports on Child Language Development,* 1982, 21, 63-70.

FOSTER, S., & SABSAY, S. *What's a topic?* Unpublished manuscript, University of Southern California, 1982.

FRASER, B. Hedged performatives. In P. Cole & J. L. Morgan (Eds.), *Syntax and semantics, Vol. 3: Speech acts.* New York: Academic Press, 1975.

FRASER, B. On apologizing. In F. Coulmas (Ed.), *Conversational routine: Explorations in standardized communication situations and prepatterned speech.* The Hague: Mouton, 1981.

FREDERIKSEN, J. R. Understanding anaphora: Rules used by readers in assigning pronomial referents. *Discourse Processes,* 1981, 4, 323-347.

FREDERIKSEN, N. Toward a taxonomy of situations. *American Psychologist,* 1972, 27, 114-123.

FRENCH, J.R.P., & RAVEN, B. The bases of social power. In D. Cartwright & A. Zander (Eds.), *Group dynamics* (2nd ed.). New York: Harper & Row, 1960.

FRENTZ, T. S. & FARRELL, T. B. Language-action: A paradigm for communication. *The Quarterly Journal of Speech,* 1976, 62, 333-349.

FULLER, L. L. *The morality of law* (Rev. ed.). New Haven: Yale University Press, 1969.

GAINES, R. N. Doing by saying: Toward a theory of perlocution. *The Quarterly Journal of Speech,* 1979, 65, 121-136.

GANZ, J. S. *Rules: A systematic study.* The Hague: Mouton, 1971.

GARFINKEL, H., & SACKS, H. On formal structures of practical actions. In J. C. McKinney & E. A. Tirayakian (Eds.), *Theoretical sociology.* New York: Appleton-Century-Crofts, 1970.

GARVEY, C. The contingent query: A dependent action in conversation. In M. Lewis & L. A. Rosenblum (Eds.), *Interaction, conversation, and the development of language.* New York: John Wiley, 1977.

GARVEY, C., & BERNINGER, G. Timing and turn taking in children's conversation. *Discourse Processes,* 1981, 4, 27-57.

GARVEY, C., & HOGAN, R. Social speech and social interaction: Egocentrism revisited. *Child Development,* 1973, 44, 562-568.

GAZDAR, G. *Pragmatics: Implicature, presupposition, and logical form.* New York: Academic Press, 1979.

GAZDAR, G. Speech act assignment. In A. K. Joshi, B. L. Webber, & I. A. Sag (Eds.), *Elements of discourse understanding.* Cambridge: Cambridge University Press, 1981.

GENEST, M., & TURK, D. C. Think-aloud approaches to cognitive assessment. In T. V. Merluzzi, C. R. Glass, & M. Genest (Eds.), *Cognitive Assessment.* New York: Guilford Press, 1981.

GIBBS, R. W. Your wish is my command: Convention and context in interpreting indirect requests. *Journal of Verbal Learning and Verbal Behavior,* 1981, 20, 431-444.

GILES, H. New directions in accommodation theory. *York Papers in Linguistics,* 1980, 9, 105-136.

GILES, H., & POWESLAND, P. F. *Speech style and social evaluation.* London: Academic Press, 1975.

GILES, H., TAYLOR, D. M., & BOURHIS, R. V. Towards a theory of interpersonal accommodation through language: Some Canadian data. *Language in Society,* 1973, 2, 161-179.

GOFFMAN, E. *Relations in public.* Harmondsworth: Penguin, 1971.

GOFFMAN, E. Replies and responses. *Language in Society,* 1976, 5, 257-313.

GOLDMAN, S. R. Knowledge systems for realistic goals. *Disclosure Processes,* 1982, 5, 279-303.

GOLDMAN-EISLER, F. *Psychologinguistics: Experiments in spontaneous speech.* New York: Academic Press, 1968.

GOODWIN, C. *Conversational organization: Interaction between speakers and hearers.* New York: Academic Press, 1981.

GOODWIN, M. H. "Instigating": Storytelling as social process. *American Ethnologist,* 1982, 9, 799-819.

GORDON, D., & LAKOFF, G. Conversational postulates. In P. Cole & J. L. Morgan (Eds.), *Syntax and semantics, Vol. 3: Speech Acts.* New York: Academic Press, 1975.

GOTTLEIB, G. *The logic of choice: An investigation of the concepts of rule and rationality.* New York: MacMillan, 1968.

GOTTMAN, J. H., MARKMAN, H., & NOTARIUS, C. The topography of marital conflict: A sequential analysis of verbal and nonverbal behavior. *Journal of Marriage and the Family,* 1977, 39, 461-477.

GOULDNER, A. W. The norm of reciprocity: A preliminary statement. *American Sociological Review,* 1960, 25, 161-179.

GRICE, H. P. Logic and conversation. In P. Cole & J. Morgan (Eds.), *Syntax and Semantics, Vol. 3: Speech Acts.* New York: Academic Press, 1975.

GRIEF, E. G., & GLEASON, J. B. Hi, thanks, and goodbye: More routine information. *Language in Society,* 1980, 9, 159-166.

GRIMSHAW, A. D. Data and data use in an analysis of communicative events. In R. Bauman & J. Sherzer (Eds.), *Explorations in the ethnography of speaking.* London: Cambridge University Press, 1974.

GRIMSHAW, A. D. Instrumentality selection in naturally-occurring conversation: A research agenda. In P. Werth (Ed.), *Conversation and discourse: Structure and interpretation.* New York: St. Martin's Press, 1981.

GUMPERZ, J. Language, communication, and public negotiation. In P. R. Sanday (Ed.), *Anthropology and the public interest.* New York: Academic Press, 1976.

HADLEY, T. R., & JACOB, T. Relationships among measures of family power. *Journal of Personality and Social Psychology,* 1973, 27, 6-12.

HALLIDAY, M.A.K., & HASAN, R. *Cohesion in English.* London: Longman, 1976.

HARRÉ, R. The ethogenic approach: Theory and practice. In L. Berkowitz (Ed.), *Advances in experimental social psychology, X.* New York: Academic Press, 1977.

HARRÉ, R. Some remarks on 'rule' as a scientific concept. In T. Mischel (Ed.), *Understanding other persons.* Totowa, NJ: Rowman & Littlefield, 1974.

HARRÉ, R. *Social being: A theory for social psychology.* Totowa, NJ: Rowman & Littlefield, 1979.

HARRÉ, R., & SECORD, P. F. *The explanation of social behaviour.* Oxford: Basil Blackwell, 1972.

HAWES, L. C. Alternative theoretical bases: Toward a presuppositional critique. *Communication Quarterly,* 1977, 25, 63-68.

HAYES-ROTH, B., & HAYES-ROTH, F. A cognitive model of planning. *Cognitive Science,* 1979, 3, 275-310.

HEESCHEN, V., SCHIEFENHOVEL, W., & EIBL-EIBESFELDT, I. Requesting, giving, and taking. The relationship between verbal and nonverbal behavior in the speech community of the Eipo, Irian Jaya (West New Guinea). In M. R. Key (Ed.), *The relationship of verbal and nonverbal communication.* The Hague, Mouton, 1980.

HERINGER, J. T. Some grammatical correlates of felicity conditions and presuppositions. *Ohio State University Working Papers in Linguistics,* 1972, 11, 1-110. Cited in S. Sabsay and S. Foster, *Cohesion in discourse.* Unpublished manuscript, University of California, Los Angeles, 1982.

HERITAGE, J. C., & WATSON, D. R. Formulations as conversational objectives. In G. Psathas (Ed.), *Everyday language: Studies in ethnomethodology.* New York: Irvington, 1979.

HEWES, D., & PLANALP, S. There is nothing as useful as a good theory...The influence of social knowledge on interpersonal communication. In M. E. Roloff &

C. R. Berger (Eds.), *Social cognition and communication.* Beverly Hills, CA: Sage, 1982.

HEWITT, J. P., & STOKES, R. Disclaimers. *American Sociological Review,* 1975, 40, 1-11.

HOBBS, J. R. *Why is discourse coherent?* Technical note 176. Menlo Park, CA: SRI International, Nov. 30, 1978.

HOBBS, J. R. Coherence and coreference. *Cognitive Science,* 1979, 3, 67-90.

HOBBS, J. R., & AGAR, M. H. *Planning and local coherence in the formal analysis of ethnographic interviews.* Unpublished manuscript, SRI International, Menlo Park, Ca., 1981.

HOBBS, J. R., & EVANS, D. A. Conversation as planned behavior. *Cognitive Science,* 1980, 4, 349-377.

HOBBS, J. R., & ROBINSON, J. R. Why ask? *Discourse Processes,* 1979, 2, 311-318.

HOFFMAN, S. F. *Interruptions: Structure and tactics in dyadic conversations.* Paper presented at the meeting of the International Communication Association, Acapulco, May, 1980.

HOPPER, R. The taken-for-granted. *Human Communication Research,* 1981, 7, 195-211.

HOUSE, J., & KASPER, G. Politeness markers in English and German. In F. Coulmas (Ed.), *Conversational routine: Explorations in standardized communication situations and prepatterned speech.* The Hague: Mouton, 1981.

JACKSON, S. *Building a case for claims about discourse structure.* Paper presented at the Michigan State University Summer Conference on Language and Discourse Processes, East Lansing, MI, August, 1982.

JACKSON, S., & JACOBS, S. Speech act structure in conversation: Rational aspects of conversational coherence. In R. T. Craig & K. Tracy (Eds.), *Conversational coherence: Studies in form and strategy.* Beverly Hills, CA: Sage, 1983.

JACKSON, S., & JACOBS, S. Structure of conversational argument: Pragmatic bases for the enthymeme. *The Quarterly Journal of Speech,* 1980, 66, 251-265.

JACKSON, S., & JACOBS, S. The collective production of proposals in conversational argument and persuasion: A study of disagreement regulation. *Journal of the American Forensic Association,* 1981, 18, 77-90.

JACOBS, S., & JACKSON, S. *Collaborative aspects of argument production.* Paper presented at the meeting of the Speech Communication Association, San Antonio, November, 1979.

JACOBS, S., & JACKSON, S. *Strategy and structure in conversational influence.* Paper presented at the meeting of the Speech Communication Association, New York, November, 1980.

JACOBS, S., & JACKSON, S. Conversational argument: A discourse analytic approach. In J. R. Cox & C. A. Willard (Eds.), *Recent advances in argumentation theory and research.* Carbondale and Edwardsville, IL: Southern Illinois University Press, forthcoming.

JAFFE, J., & FELDSTEIN, S. *Rhythms of dialogue.* New York: Academic Press, 1970.

JEFFERSON, G. Side sequences. In D. Sudnow (Ed.), *Studies in social interaction.* New York: Free Press, 1972.

JEFFERSON, G. A case of precision timing in ordinary conversation: Overlapped tag-positioned address terms in closing sequences. *Semiotica,* 1973, 9, 47-96.

JEFFERSON, G. Sequential aspects of storytelling in conversation. In J. Schenkein (Ed.), *Studies in the organization of conversational interaction.* New York: Academic Press, 1978.

JEFFERSON, G., & SCHENKEIN, J. Some sequential negotiations in conversation: Unexpanded and expanded versions of projected action sequences. In J. Schenkein (Ed.), *Studies in the organization of conversational interaction.* New York: Academic Press, 1978.

KARTTUNEN, L. Presupposition and linguistic context. In A. Rogers, B. Wall, & J. P. Murphy (Eds.), *Proceedings of the Texas conference on performatives, presuppositions, and implicatures.* Center for Applied Linguistics: Arlington, VA, 1977.

KARTTUNEN, L., & PETERS, S. Conversational implicature. In C-K Oh & D. A. Dineen (Eds.), *Syntax and semantics, 3: Presupposition.* New York: Academic Press, 1979.

KEENAN, E. O., & SCHIEFFELIN, B. B. Topic as a discourse notion: A study of topic in the conversation of children and adults. In C. N. Li (Ed.), *Subject and topic.* New York: Academic Press, 1976.

KELLER, E. Gambits: conversational strategy signals. In F. Coulmas (Ed.), *Conversational routine: Explorations in standardized communication situations and prepatterned speech.* The Hague: Mouton, 1981.

KEMPER, S., & THISSEN, D. Memory for the dimensions of requests. *Journal of Verbal Learning and Verbal Behavior,* 1981, 20, 552-563.

KENDON, A. Some functions of gaze-direction in social conversation. *Acta Psychologica,* 1967, 26, 22-63.

KENDON, A. Gesticulation and speech: Two aspects of the process of utterance. In M. R. Key (Ed.), *The relationship of verbal and nonverbal communication.* The Hague: Mouton, 1980.

KNAPP, M. L., HART, R. P., FRIEDERICH, G. W., & SHULMAN, G. M. The rhetoric of goodbye: Verbal and nonverbal correlates of human leave-taking. *Speech Monographs,* 1973, 40, 182-198. Reprinted in B. W. Morse & L. A. Phelps (Eds.), *Interpersonal communication: A relational perspective.* Minneapolis: Burgess, 1980.

KNAPP, M. L., HOPPER, R., & BELL, R. A. *Compliments.* Paper presented at the meeting of the International Communication Association, Dallas, May, 1983.

KRIVONOS, P. D., & KNAPP, M. L. Initiating communication: What do you say when you say hello? *Central States Speech Journal,* 1975, 26, 115-125.

LABOV, W. Rules for ritual insults. In D. Sudnow (Ed.), *Studies in social interaction.* New York: Free Press, 1972.

LABOV, W., & FANSHEL, D. *Therapeutic discourse: Psychotherapy as conversation.* New York: Academic Press, 1977.

LAKOFF, R. *Language and woman's place.* New York: Harper & Row, 1975.

LANGER, E. J. Rethinking the role of thought in social interaction. In J. H. Harvey, W. Ickes, & R. F. Kidd (Eds.), *New directions in attribution research,* Vol. 2. Hillsdale, NJ: Erlbaum, 1978.

LANGER, E. J., & WEINMAN, C. When thinking disrupts intellectual performance: Mindfulness on an overlearned task. *Personality and Social Psychology Bulletin,* 1981, 7, 240-243.

LARSEN, R. S., MARTIN, H. J., & GILES, H. Anticipated social cost and interpersonal accommodation. *Human Communication Research,* 1977, 4, 303-308.

LAVER, J.D.M.H. Linguistic routines and politeness in greeting and parting. In F. Coulmas (Ed.), *Conversational routine: Explorations in standardized communication situations and prepatterned speech.* The Hague: Mouton, 1981.

LEIGHTON, L. L., STOLLACK, C. E., & FERGUSSON, L. R. Patterns of communication in normal and clinic families. *Journal of Consulting and Clinical Psychology,* 1971, 17, 252-256.

LEVINSON, S. C. Some pre-observations on the modelling of dialogue. *Discourse Processes,* 1981, 4, 93-116.

LIEBERMAN, P. *Intonation, perception, and language.* Cambridge: MIT Press, 1967.

LINDSAY, R. Rules as a bridge between speech and action. In P. Collett (Ed.), *Social rules and social behavior.* Totowa, NJ: Rowman & Littlefield, 1977.

LOUDEN, A. *"Telling more than we can know": What do we know? Verbal reports in communication research.* Unpublished manuscript, University of Southern California, 1983.

MAGNUSSON, D., & EKEHAMMAR, B. An analysis of situational dimensions: A replication. *Multivariate Behavioral Research,* 1973, 8, 331-339.

MANDLER, J. M. Some uses and abuses of a story grammar. *Discourse Processes,* 1982, 5, 305-318.

MANDLER, J. M., & JOHNSON, N. S. Remembrance of things parsed: Story structure and recall. *Cognitive Psychology,* 1977, 9, 111-151.

MANES, J., & WOLFSON, N. The compliment formula. In F. Coulmas (Ed.), *Conversational routine: Explorations in standardized communication situations and prepatterned speech.* The Hague: Mouton, 1981.

MARWELL, G., & SCHMIDT, D. R. Dimensions of compliance-gaining behavior: An empirical analysis. *Sociometry,* 1967, 30, 350-364.

MATARAZZO, J. D., & WEINS, A. N. Interviewer influence on the duration of interviewee silence. *Journal of Experimental Research in Personality,* 1967, 2, 56-69.

McCARTNEY, K. A., & NELSON, K. Children's use of scripts in story recall. *Discourse Processes,* 1981, 4, 59-70.

McCAWLEY, J. D. Presupposition and discourse structure. In C-K Oh and D. A. Dineen (Eds.), *Syntax and semantics, 2: Presupposition.* New York: Academic Press, 1979.

McCLURE, C., MASON, J., & BARNITZ, J. An exploratory study of story structure and age effects on children's ability to sequence stories. *Discourse Processes,* 1979, 2, 213-249.

McLAUGHLIN, M. L., & CODY, M. J. Awkward silences: Behavioral antecedents and consequences of the conversational lapse. *Human Communication Research,* 1982, 8, 299-316.

McLAUGHLIN, M. L., & CODY, M. J. Account sequences. In J. Coppella & R. Street (Eds.), *Sequential social interaction: A functional approach.* London: Edward Arnold, forthcoming.

McLAUGHLIN, M. L., CODY, M. J., & O'HAIR, H. D. The management of failure events: Some contextual determinants of accounting behavior. *Human Communication Research,* 1983, 9, 208-224.

McLAUGHLIN, M. L., CODY, M. J., & ROBEY, C. S. Situational influences on the selection of strategies to resist compliance-gaining attempts. *Human Communication Research,* 1980, 7, 14-36.

McLAUGHLIN, M. L., CODY, M. J., & ROSENSTEIN, N. E. Account sequences in conversation between strangers. *Communication Monographs,* 1983, 50, 102-125.

McLAUGHLIN, M. L., CODY, M. J., KANE, M. L., & ROBEY, C. S. Sex differences in story receipt and story sequencing behaviors in dyadic conversations. *Human Communication Research,* 1981, 7, 99-116.

McMILLAN, J. R., CLIFTON, A. K., MCGRATH, D., & GALE, W. S. Women's language: Uncertainty or interpersonal sensitivity and emotionality? *Sex Roles,* 1977, 3, 545-559.

MEICHENBAUM, D., & CAMERON, R. Issues in cognitive assessment: An overview. In R. M. Merluzzi, C. R. Glass, & M. Genest (Eds.), *Cognitive Assessment.* New York: Guilford Press, 1981.

MELTZER, L., MORRIS, W., & HAYES, D. Interruption outcomes and vocal amplitude: Explorations in social psychophysics. *Journal of Personality and Social Psychology,* 1971, 18, 392-402.

MERRITT, M. Repeats and reformulations in primary classrooms as windows of the nature of talk engagement. *Discourse Processes,* 1982, 5, 127-145.

MILLER, G. A. Review of J. H. Greenberg (Ed.), *Universals of Language. Contemporary Psychology,* 1963, 8, 417-418.

MILLER, G. R., BOSTER, F., ROLOFF, M. E., & SEIBOLD, D. R. Compliance-gaining message strategies; A typology and some findings concerning effects of situational differences. *Communication Monographs,* 1977, 44, 37-51.

MILLER, G. R., & BERGER, C. R. On keeping the faith in matters scientific. *Western Journal of Speech Communication,* 1978, 42, 44-57.

MISHLER, E. G., & WAXLER, N. E. *Interaction in families: An experimental study of family process and schizophrenia.* New York: John Wiley, 1968.

MORRIS, G. H., & HOPPER, R. Remediation and legislation in everyday talk: How communicators achieve consensus. *The Quarterly Journal of Speech,* 1980, 66, 266-274.

MURA, S. S. Licensing violations: An investigation of legitimate violations of Grice's conversational maxims. In R. T. Craig & K. Tracy (Eds.), *Conversational coherence: Studies of form and strategy.* Beverly Hills, CA: Sage, 1983.

NEWMAN, H. Perceptions of silence in conversation. Doctoral dissertation, City University of New York, 1978. *Dissertation Abstracts International,* 1978, 39, 3-B, 1,546.

NISBETT, R., & ROSS, L. *Human inference: Strategies and shortcomings of social judgment.* Englewood Cliffs, NJ: Prentice-Hall, 1980.

NISBETT, R., & WILSON, T. Telling more than we can know: Verbal reports on mental processes. *Psychological Review,* 1977, 84, 231-259.

NOFSINGER, R. E. The demand ticket: A conversational device for getting the floor. *Speech Monographs,* 1975, 42, 1-9.

NOFSINGER, R. E. Answering questions indirectly. *Human Communication Research,* 1976, 2, 171-181.

NORWINE, A. C., & MURPHY, O. J. Characteristic time intervals in telephone conversation. *Bell System Technical Journal,* 1938, 17, 281-291. Cited in C. Garvey and G. Berninger, Timing and turn-taking in children's conversation. *Discourse Processes,* 1981, 4, 27-57.

OCHS, E. Planned and unplanned discourse. In T. Givon (Ed.), *Syntax and semantics, 12: Discourse and syntax.* New York: Academic Press, 1979.

O'KEEFE, D. J. Logical empiricism and the study of human communication. *Speech Monographs,* 1975, 42, 169-183.

OMANSON, R. C. An analysis of narratives: Identifying central, supportive, and distracting content. *Discourse Processes,* 1982, 5, 195-224.

OMANSON, R. C., & MALAMUT, S. R. *The effects of supportive and distracting content on the recall of central content.* Paper presented at the meeting of the Psychonomic Society, St. Louis, 1980. Cited in R. C. Omanson, An analysis of narratives: Identifying central, supportive, and distracting content. *Discourse Processes,* 1982, 5, 195-224.

OWEN, M. Conversational units and the use of 'well . . . .' In P. Werth (Ed.), *Conversation and discourse: Structure and interpretation.* New York: St. Martin's, 1981.

PEARCE, W. B. The coordinated management of meaning: A rules:based theory of interpersonal communication. In G. R. Miller (Ed.), *Explorations in interpersonal communication.* Beverly Hills, CA: Sage, 1976.

PEARCE, W. B., & CONKLIN, F. A model of hierarchical meaning in coherent conversation and a study of 'indirect responses.' *Communication Monographs,* 1979, 46, 75-87.

PHILIPS, S. U. Warm Springs 'Indian time:' How the regulation of participation affects of the progression of events. In R. Bauman & J. Sherzer (Eds.), *Explorations in the ethnography of speaking.* Cambridge: Cambridge University Press, 1974.

PHILIPS, S. Some sources of cultural variability in the regulation of talk. *Language in Society,* 1976, 5, 81-95.

PHILIPS, G. M. Science and the study of human communication: An inquiry from the other side of the two cultures. *Human Communication Research,* 1981, 7, 361-370.

PIKE, K. L. *The intonation of American English.* Ann Arbor: University of Michigan Press, 1945.

PLANALP, S., & TRACY, K. Not to change the topic but . . . : A cognitive approach to the study of conversation. In D. Nimmo (Ed.), *Communication Yearbook 4.* New Brunswick, NJ: Transaction, 1980.

POMERANTZ, A. Compliment responses: Notes on the co-operations of multiple constraints. In J. Schenkein (Ed.), *Studies in the organization of conversational interaction.* New York: Academic Press, 1978.

PRICE, R. H. The taxonomic classification of behavior and situations and the problem of behavior-environment congruence. *Human Relations,* 1974, 27, 567-585.

REARDON, K. K. Conversational deviance: A structural model. *Human Communication Research,,* 1982, 9, 59-74.

REHBEIN, J. Announcing—on formulating plans. In F. Coulmas (Ed.), *Conversational routine: Explorations in standardized communication situations and prepatterned speech.* The Hague: Mouton, 1981.

REICHMAN, R. Conversational coherency. *Cognitive Science,* 1978, 2, 283-327.

REINHART, T. Pragmatics and linguistics: An analysis of sentence topics. *Philosophica,* 1981, 27, 53-94.

REISMAN, K. Contrapuntal conversations in an Antiguan village. In R. Bauman & J. Sherzer (Eds.), *Explorations in the ethnography of speaking.* Cambridge: Cambridge University Press, 1974.

REMLER, J. E. *Some repairs on the notion of repairs in the interests of relevance.* Papers from the Regional Meetings, Chicago Linguistic Society, 1978, 14, 391-402.

ROCHESTER, S. R., & MARTIN, J. R. The art of referring: The speaker's use of noun phrases to instruct the listener. In R. O. Freedle (Ed.), *Discourse production and comprehension.* Norwood, NJ: Ablex Publishing, 1977.

ROGERS, W. T., & JONES, S. E. Effects of dominance tendencies on floor holding and interruption behavior in dyadic interaction. *Human Communication Research,* 1975, 1, 123-132.

ROSENFELD, H. M., & HANCKS, M. The nonverbal context of listener responses. In M. R. Key (Ed.), *The relationship of verbal and nonverbal communication.* The Hague: Mouton, 1980.

ROSENSTEIN, N. E. *Perceptions of interruption appropriateness as a function of temporal placement.* Unpublished Master's thesis, Texas Tech University, 1982.

ROSENSTEIN, N. E., & McLAUGHLIN, M. L. *Characterization of interruption as a function of temporal placement.* Paper presented at the meeting of the Speech Communication Association, Washington, November, 1983.

RUBIN, Z. Disclosing oneself to a stranger: Reciprocity and its limits. *Journal of Experimental Social Psychology,* 1975, 11, 233-260.

RUMELHART, D. E. Notes on a schema for stories. In D. G. Bobrow & A. Collins (Eds.), *Representation and understanding: Studies in cognitive science.* New York: Academic Press, 1975.

RUMELHART, D. E. Understanding and summarizing brief stories. In D. LaBerge & J. Samuels (Eds.), *Basic processes in reading: Perception and comprehension.* Hillsdale, NJ: Erlbaum, 1977.

RYAVE, A. L. On the achievement of a series of stories. In J. Schenkein (Ed.), *Studies in the organization of conversational interaction.* New York: Academic Press, 1978.

SABSAY, S., & FOSTER, S. *Cohesion in discourse.* Unpublished manuscript, University of California, Los Angeles, 1982.

SACKS, H. On the analyzability of stories by children. In J. Gumprez & D. Hymes (Eds.), *Directions in sociolinguistics: The ethnography of communication.* New York: Holt, Rinehart & Winston, 1972.

SACKS, H. *Lecture notes.* Summer Institute of Linguistics, Ann Arbor, Michigan, 1973. Cited in P. Brown and S. Levinson, Universals in language usage: Politeness phenomena. In E. Goody (Ed.), *Questions and politeness: Strategies in social interaction.* Cambridge: Cambridge University Press, 1978.

SACKS, H. An analysis of the course of a joke's telling in conversation. In R. Bauman & J. Sherzer (Eds.), *Explorations in the ethnography of speaking.* Cambridge: Cambridge University Press, 1974.

SACKS, H., SCHEGLOFF, E. A., & JEFFERSON, G. A simplest systematics for the organization of turn taking for conversation. In J. Schenkein (Ed.), *Studies in the organization of conversational interaction.* New York: Academic Press, 1978.

SADOCK, J. M. *Towards a linguistic theory of speech acts.* New York: Academic Press, 1974.

SCHANK, R. G. Rules and topics in conversation. *Cognitive Science,* 1977, 1, 421-444.

SCHEGLOFF, E. Sequencing in conversational openings. *American Anthropologist,* 1968, 70, 1075-1095.

SCHEGLOFF, E. A. Notes on a conversational practice: Formulating place. In D. Sudnow (Ed.), *Studies in social interaction.* New York: Free Press, 1972.

SCHEGLOFF, E. A. On some questions and ambiguities in conversation. In W. Dressler (Ed.), *Current trends in textlinguistics.* Berlin: de Gruyter, 1977. Cited in W. J. Edmondson, *Spoken discourses: A model for analysis.* London: Longman, 1981.

SCHEGLOFF, E. A. The relevance of repair to syntax-for-conversation. In T. Givón (Ed.), *Syntax and semantics, 12: Discourse and syntax.* New York: Academic Press, 1979.

SCHLEGLOFF, E. A. *Recycled turn beginnings.* Public lecture, Summer Linguistics Institute, LSA, Ann Arbor, Michigan, 1973. Cited in A. Bennett, Interruptions and the interpretation of conversation. *Discourse Processes,* 1981, 4, 171-188.

SCHEGLOFF, E. A., JEFFERSON, G., & SACKS, H. The preference for self-correction in the organization of repair in conversation. *Language,* 1977, 53, 361-382.

SCHEGLOFF, E. A., & SACKS, H. Opening up closings. *Semiotica,* 1973, 8, 289-327.

SCHIFFRIN, D. Opening encounters. *American Sociological Review,* 1977, 42, 679-691.

SCHIFFRIN, D. Meta-talk: Organizational and evaluative brackets in discourse. *Sociological Inquiry,* 1980, 50, 199-236.

SCHLENKER, B. R., & DARBY, B. W. The use of apologies in social predicaments. *Social Psychology Quarterly,* 1981, 44, 271-278.

SCHONBACH, P. A category system for account phases. *European Journal of Social Psychology,* 1980, 10, 195-200.

SCHUTZ, A. *Collected papers II: Studies in social theory.* (A. Broderson, Ed.). The Hague: Nijhoff, 1964. Cited in A. V. Cicourel, *Cognitive sociology: Language and meaning in social interaction.* London: Cox and Wyman, 1973.

SCHWARTZ, B. *An investigation into topic change in unplanned discourse.* Unpublished manuscript, University of Southern California, 1982. Cited in S. Foster and S. Sabsay, *What's a topic?* Unpublished manuscript, University of Southern California, 1982.

SCOTT, L. M. *Formulation sequences in marital conversation: Strategies for interactive interpretive alignment.* Paper presented at the meeting of the International Communication Association, Dallas, May 1983.

SCOTT, M. B., & LYMAN, S. M. Accounts. *American Sociological Review,* 1968, 33, 46-62.

SEARLE, J. *Speech acts.* Cambridge: Cambridge University Press, 1969.

SEARLE, J. Indirect speech acts. In P. Cole & J. L. Morgan (Eds.), *Syntax and semantics, 3: Speech acts.* New York: Academic Press, 1975.

SEIBOLD, D. R., McPHEE, R. D., POOLE, M. S., TANITA, N. E., & CANARY, D. J. Arguments, group influence, and decision outcomes. In G. Ziegelmueller & J. Rhodes (Eds.), *Dimensions of arguments: Proceedings of the second summer conference on argumentation.* Annandale, VA: Speech Communication Association, 1981.

SHIMANOFF, S. Investigating politeness. In E. O. Keenan & T. Bennett (Eds.), *Discourse across time and space.* Los Angeles: University of Southern California, 1977.

SHIMANOFF, S. *Communication rules: Theory and research.* Beverly Hills, CA: Sage, 1980.

SIGMAN, S. J. On communication rules from a social perspective. *Human Communication Research,* 1980, 7, 37-51.

SINCLAIR, J. MCH., & COULTHARD, R. M. *Towards an analysis of discourse.* London: Oxford University Press, 1975.

SPELKE, E., HIRST, W., & NESSER, U. Skills of divided attention. *Cognition,* 1976, 4, 215-230.

STEIN, N. L. What's in a story: Interpreting the interpretations of story grammar. *Discourse Processes,* 1982, 5, 319-335.

STEIN, N. L., & GLENN, C. G. An analysis of story comprehension in elementary school children. In R. O. Freedle (Ed.), *New directions in discourse processing,* Vol. 2. Norwood, NJ: Ablex Publishing, 1979.

STILES, W. B. *Manual for a taxonomy of verbal response modes.* Chapel Hill: University of North Carolina Press, 1978.

STOKES, R., & HEWITT, J. P. Aligning actions. *American Sociological Review,* 1976, 41, 838-849.

STRAWSON, P. F. Identifying reference and truth values. In D. Steinberg & L. Jakobovits (Eds.), *Semantics.* London: Cambridge University Press, 1979.

SUDMAN, S., & BRADBURN, N. M. *Response effects in surveys: A review and synthesis.* Chicago: Aldine, 1974.

SYKES, G. M., & MATZA, D. Techniques of neutralization. *American Sociological Review,* 1957, 26, 664-670.

TANNEN, D. Indirectness in discourse: Ethnicity as conversation style. *Discourse Processes,* 1981, 4, 221-238.

TAYLOR, C. *The explanation of behavior.* London: Routledge & Kegan Paul, 1964.

TOULMIN, S. E. Rules and their relevance for understanding human behavior. In T. Mischel (Ed.), *Understanding other persons.* Totowa, NJ: Rowman & Littlefield, 1974.

TRACY, K. On getting the point: Distinguishing "issues" from "events," an aspect of conversational coherence. In M. Burgoon (Ed.), *Communication Yearbook 5.* New Brunswick, NJ: Transaction, 1982.

TRAGER, G. L., & SMITH, H. L., Jr. *An outline of English structure.* (Studies in Linguistics: Occasional papers, 3). Norman, OK: Battenburg Press, 1951.

TURNER, R. H. Role taking: Process versus conformity. In A. Rose (Ed.), *Human behavior and social processes.* Boston: Houghton Mifflin, 1962.

VUCINICH, S. Elements of cohesion between turns in ordinary conversation. *Semiotica,* 1977, 20, 229-257.

WAGNER, J. Strategies of dismissal: Ways and means of avoiding personal abuse. *Human Relations,* 1980, 33, 603-622.

WAISMANN, F. Verifiability. In A. Flew (Ed.), *Essays on logic and language.* New York: Philosophical Library, 1951.

WEAVER, P. A., & DICKINSON, D. K. Scratching below the surface structure: Exploring the usefulness of story grammars. *Discourse Processes,* 1982, 5, 225-243.

WEIMANN, J. M. Explication and test of a model of communicative competence. *Human Communication Research,* 1977, 3, 195-213.

WEIMANN, J. M. Effects of laboratory videotaping procedures on selected conversation behaviors. *Human Communication Research,* 1981, 7, 302-311.

WEINER, S. L., & GOODENOUGH, D. R. A move toward a psychology of conversation. In R. O. Freedle (Ed.), *Discourse production and comprehension.* Norwood, NJ: Ablex Publishing, 1977.

WELLS, G., MACLURE, M., & MONTGOMERY, M. Some strategies for sustaining conversation. In P. Werth (Ed.), *Conversation and discourse: Structure and interpretation.* New York: St. Martin's, 1981.

WERTH, P. The concept of 'relevance' in conversational analysis. In P. Werth (Ed.), *Conversation and discourse: Structure and interpretation.* New York: St. Martin's, 1981.

WHITE, P. Theoretic note: Limitations on verbal reports of internal events: A refutation of Nisbett and Wilson and Bem. *Psychological Review,* 1980, 87, 105-112.

WILLIS, F. N., & WILLIAMS, S. J. Simultaneous talking in conversation and sex of speakers. *Perceptual and Motor Skills,* 1976, 43, 1067-1070.

WILSON, D. & SPERBER, D. On Grice's theory of conversation. In P. Werth (Ed.), *Conversation and discourse: Structure and interpretation.* New York: St. Martin's, 1981.

WINOGRAD, T. A framework for understanding discourse. In M. A. Just & P. A. Carpenter (Eds.), *Cognitive processes in comprehension.* Hillsdale, NJ: Erlbaum, 1977.

WISH, M., D'ANDRADE, R. G. & GOODNOW, J. E., II. Dimensions of interpersonal communication: Correspondences between structures for speech acts and bipolar scales. *Journal of Personality and Social Psychology,* 1980, 39, 848-860.

WISH, M., DEUTSCH, M., & KAPLAN, S. Perceived dimensions of interpersonal relations. *Journal of Personality and Social Psychology,* 1976, 33, 409-420.

WOOTTON, A. *Dilemmas of discourse: Controversies about the sociological interpretation of language.* London: George Allen & Unwin, 1975.

WORTHY, M. GARY, A. L., & KAHN, G. M. Self-disclosure as an exchange process. *Journal of Personality and Social Psychology,* 1969, 13, 59-63.

WRIGHT, G. H. von. *Norm and action.* London: Routledge & Kegan Paul, 1963.

WRIGHT, G. H. von. *Explanation and understanding.* Ithaca: Cornell University Press, 1971.

YNGVE, V. H. On getting a word in edgewise. In M. A. Campbell et al. (Eds.), *Papers from the sixth regional meeting, Chicago Linguistics Society.* Chicago: University of Chicago Linguistics Department, 1970.

ZAHN, C. J. *A reexamination of conversational repair.* Paper presented at the meeting of the Speech communication Association, Washington, November, 1983.

ZIMMERMAN, D. H., & WEST. C. Sex roles, interruptions, and silences in conversation. In B. Thorne & N. Henley (Eds.), *Language and sex: Difference and dominance.* Rowley, MA: Newbury House, 1975.

About the Author

Margaret L. McLaughlin is Associate Professor in the Department of Communication Arts and Sciences at the University of Southern California. She received her Ph.D. in speech (minors in communication and psychology) from the University of Illinois in 1972. Recent publications have appeared in *Human Communication Research* and *Communication Monographs;* in addition, Professor McLaughlin will be the editor of *Communication Yearbooks 9* and *10.* She was recognized for outstanding papers in the Interpersonal and Small Group Division of the Speech Communication Association in 1977, 1980, 1981, and 1982. Her research interests include interpersonal communication, conversational analysis, and communication and the sexes.